WILDLY DIFFERENT

Manchester University Press

WILDLY DIFFERENT

How five women reclaimed nature
in a man's world

SARAH LONSDALE

MANCHESTER UNIVERSITY PRESS

Published by Manchester University Press
Oxford Road, Manchester, M13 9PL

www.manchesteruniversitypress.co.uk

British Library Cataloguing-in-Publication Data
A catalogue record for this book is available from the British Library

ISBN   978 1 5261 6869 6   hardback

First published 2025

EU authorised representative for GPSR:
Easy Access System Europe, Mustamäe tee 50, 10621 Tallinn, Estonia
gpsr.requests@easproject.com

Typeset
by New Best-set Typesetters Ltd

For my son, Tom, and my daughter, Olivia, with all my love

Contents

Prologue: on the back of a polar bear

One of my earliest memories is of sitting close to my mother in a pool of light, beyond which lurked the usual nighttime terrors of childhood: trolls, alligators and dragons with amber eyes. It was in that bright circle that my mother read to me: stories of handsome princes and beautiful princesses, brave woodsmen and hungry wolves. I listened, rapt, heart bumping, eyes wide as saucers. One story thrilled me more than any other, and I asked my mother to read it over and over again. It wasn't until years later that I realised why this tale captivated me so.

The Nordic 'East of the Sun and West of the Moon' follows many a traditional plot of a brave protagonist who ventures into the wild on an epic quest. The landscape beyond the village boundary is mighty with dark forests and knife-edged mountains and is inhabited by magical creatures, mostly dangerous, a few good and resourceful. The protagonist is a girl, not one trapped in a castle awaiting her saviour, but one who leaves her home, on the back of a polar bear, to save her family from hunger and rescue a prince. The girl repeats the powerful words 'I am not afraid' as she and the bear range desolate ridges, enlisting the help of wise witches and the north wind. When, a few years later, I clung face down in a blizzard to the bruised and socketed rhyolite of the Crib Goch arête in Snowdonia, I became that girl, holding tight to the back of a great bear as the north wind roared and the east wind flung hailstones in my face. 'I am not afraid', I shouted (although I was terrified).

As I grew older, I read about King Arthur and his knights, and the 20 years' warring, love making and journeying of Ulysses/Odysseus. Later I encountered the epic of *Gilgamesh* and the stories of the *Kalevala* and *Mahabharata*: fantastic, eye-popping fables involving giants, shipwrecks, shape-shifting monsters and talking trees. Each story told me about brave male heroes and their journeying. They were usually, but not always, elite; chiefs, huntsmen, herders, knights, sailors, warriors or kings. They set out into the wild, Gawain from his Lord's castle, Odysseus from his island palace, Mwindo of the Zairean epic from his fortified village, Tubondo, and Gilgamesh from his walled city, the ancient Mesopotamian Uruk, 'three square-miles' of fired bricks, to embark on self-making quests. But it seemed that wherever I looked and whatever I read, the landscape in myth and folktale, that wild country beyond the farm, garden, orchard, smallholding and sheepfold, was curiously devoid of women.

Yes, there were plenty of supernatural, magical or monstrous women: goddesses, nymphs, sirens, witches, fairy queens, who entrapped unsuspecting heroes or dabbled spitefully in the affairs of mortals just for fun. But of ordinary flesh-and-blood human women, there were only those who had in some way transgressed or otherwise broken the accepted social order of things, who lived in the wild, beyond the realm of human statute. For these women the wild was not a site of heroic myth making but of punishment, banishment, amidst mud, hunger and other privations. A taboo against women and girls having the desire to venture beyond the hearth and home has thus been woven, with words as powerful as magic spells, since the first stories were ever recorded.

But women have always lived in and travelled through the wild, from our hunter-gather days onwards; women have feared its monsters and enjoyed its beauties, as men have. We just need to look a bit more carefully for evidence, from prehistoric big game hunters' grave goods to private diaries, as we find little trace in histories, published memoirs or archaeological research. One recent study of the popular mountaineering memoir genre concludes that 94 per cent of all published climbing memoirs are male authored, and we know that he who gets to tell his story controls the narrative.

What follows here are the stories of five women across the last more than one hundred years who, in the face of insults, disapproval and even imprisonment and physical violence, challenged for the right to explore, enjoy, conserve, investigate and, ultimately, protect an increasingly fragile wild. They didn't ride on the back of a giant polar bear, but their achievements are nonetheless epic.

Dramatis personae

Mina Hubbard

Born Mina Benson into a family of Irish immigrants in rural Ontario in 1870, Mina worked as a schoolteacher before training as a nurse in New York. There she fell in love with one of her patients, Leonidas Hubbard, who was suffering from typhoid. They married in January 1901, but in October 1903 Leonidas died of starvation while trying to find the headwaters of the Naskaupi River in northern Labrador. In the face of widespread criticism, Mina set out on her own expedition in early summer 1905 to finish Leonidas's work, which included mapping the Naskaupi and George rivers up to Ungava Bay and witnessing the great summer caribou migration.

Evelyn Cheesman

Born in 1881, the middle of five precocious children, Evelyn's idyllic childhood in Victorian Kent inspired in her a love of the outdoors, particularly its insects. After being appointed curator of insects at the Zoological Society of London, she won a place on a research expedition to the South Pacific to find exhibits for London Zoo. On her return in 1925 she left the Zoo and became an unpaid volunteer for the British Museum's natural history section. Growing respect for her research ensured she won grants for further travels, and between the 1920s and 1950s she travelled across the islands of the south Pacific, including Vanuatu and Papua New Guinea, in her quest to unravel an entomological mystery she was pursuing.

Dorothy Pilley

Dorothy was born in 1894, the eldest of four children, to a strictly traditional father. While on holiday in Snowdonia in 1915, she fell passionately in love with the mountains. But living in a time that limited women's opportunities, she had to fight her father, and social strictures, to be able to climb on an equal footing with men. She completed several first ascents, in the Alps, Snowdonia and the Rockies. Her diaries and published writing sought to express how the female body and mind respond to the challenges of high-altitude mountaineering.

Ethel Haythornthwaite

Ethel was born Ethel Mary Bassett Ward just outside Sheffield in 1894. She married Henry Gallimore in 1916, during the First World War, but became a widow a year later. She became dangerously ill and only survived through walking out on the moors and tops of the Peak District, often trespassing across forbidden moorland. After she recovered, she devoted her life to saving the Peaks that had saved her, and in 1924 formed a small local countryside protection committee that would become the Sheffield and Peak District branch of the then-named Council for the Protection of Rural England (CPRE).

Wangari Maathai

Born in rural Kenya in 1940, Wangari, a brilliant and hardworking student, won a place to study in the United States in the 1960s as part of the 'Kennedy Air Lifts'. On her return to independent Kenya she campaigned for academic women's equality and learned of the struggles of rural women in an environment now seriously degraded by tree felling and resource extraction. She founded the Green Belt Movement, planting more than 30 million trees. Her campaigns for women's rights and democratic accountability brought her into direct confrontation with President Daniel arap Moi many times, and she was arrested, imprisoned and suffered physical abuse on a number of occasions.

Introduction: it is a quiet place, cold and beautiful

In the story of *Gilgamesh*, often called the first story ever written down, the only human woman found in the wild is the courtesan Shamhat, 'the luscious'. She is instructed by men to leave the city of Uruk and go into the wilderness, to 'civilise' the wild man Enkidu through a two-week-long marathon of sexual intercourse. Her body is used to transform the wild to the urban, so Enkidu and King Gilgamesh may embark upon their heroic adventures together. After she has fulfilled her purpose, Shamhat returns to the sacred temple within the city, behind those thick brick walls. Described as a 'harlot' or 'prostitute', Shamhat is a social transgressor, tempting noble men from their wives' beds, and symbolises the threat to the traditional family unit in Mesopotamian society.

In the Middle English romance *Lybeaus Desconsus*, the unmarried mother of Sir Gawain's illegitimate son raises the 'Fair Unknown' in the Welsh borderlands, far beyond the walls of Camelot. She lives a miserable life 'under the forest-side', and when her son is joyfully reunited with his noble father, she disappears from the narrative, back to her shame in the mud and brambles. The wife who flees her failed marriage in the Finnish epic the *Kalevala* is abandoned even by her own family and condemned to be an 'outcast on the wanderer's road', living 'in the ragged border regions, the benighted northern marches'. There is a fascinating scene in the third book of the Indian story cycle the *Mahabharata* when the audience realises that Rsyasrnga, the young and naive man brought up in the wild, has never seen a woman in all his life (his mother was a doe impregnated by an ascetic, or holy man). He describes to his father the 'man' he has just seen (another courtesan sent by a king to 'civilise' him): 'And he had two round globes below his throat, hairless and charming. And he was slender-waisted in the region of his navel.' It's a confusing moment for young Rsyasrnga. He is, naturally, seduced by this strange man and thus 'tamed', brought to the king in his city where he marries not the courtesan but the king's virginal daughter, who has been sequestered all her life behind the harem walls.

There are so many other stories, too numerous to count, in written and oral traditions across the world, embedding messages to boys and girls, men and women, about who gets to go into the wild and who should stay at home. The most extreme case is possibly that of Polyphonte of Greek myth. As a young and marriageable woman, she committed the unpardonable sin of rejecting the correct gender role assigned to her: to marry and bear children. Instead she went off to the forest to follow Artemis, the virgin goddess of the hunt. Her punishment for this transgression is severe and out of all proportion, one might think today, to her sin. The goddess Aphrodite provokes in her an insatiable lust for a bear, with whom she conceives two ferocious humanoid cubs. Artemis then punishes her for this lust by turning the wild animals of the forest against her. Eventually Polyphonte is transformed by Zeus into a *strix*, a malevolent owl-like bird that feeds on human flesh. Thus, a panoply of gods from Olympus wreaks devastating revenge on a girl who simply refuses marriage and motherhood and wants instead to hunt in the forest like a man. If we read myths and folktales as both reflecting social attitudes and as having an implicit teaching role, then young girls hearing the story of Polyphonte would surely be terrified of stepping out of line. It's a powerful, controlling message delivered at a time of extreme rates of infant, and maternal, mortality. For the tribe or city state to survive, fertile women had to produce many babies in the hope that a few would reach adulthood to become the warriors, huntsmen and smithy operatives of the future, as well as the begetters of more infants.

Histories of slavery in ancient times point to women as being the first subjects of enslavement, taken for forced labour, rape and forced procreation, far from their destroyed homeland and what might be left of their family. While young men were killed, young women were abducted during raiding parties against neighbouring regions, or bought from slave traders, their primary role to provide infants. And how do you keep a foreign slave from running away? You make her fearful, pregnant and probably barefoot too. You warn her that the life of a slave and mother is better than being torn apart by wild beasts in the mountains between her new and old homes.

At a time when humans were transitioning from nomadic herders and hunters into settled city dwellers, ideas of property and land ownership were becoming established. In patrilineal societies, as most early civilisations were, men needed to know that the sons they were feeding and passing their land

and status to, often won at enormous cost, were their own flesh and blood. As the ancient Greek poet Hesiod wrote, in a successful society, 'the woolly sheep are heavy with fleeces, *the women bear children resembling their fathers*'. In the days before DNA testing and equality in gender relations, the only real way of knowing whether your children were your own was to keep their mothers locked up or closely surveilled. Powerful traditions underline these commandments that women must stay at home while men can travel. This practice of 'purdah' still exists today, in parts of what is known as the 'patriarchal belt', encompassing Afghanistan, Bangladesh, Pakistan, parts of India, China, Turkey, Iran and north Africa. In Morocco, until very recently, the daughters, wives, sisters and other female relatives of wealthy, propertied men were kept behind the harem walls, 'the geometric line organizing my powerlessness', as one woman born into a Moroccan harem in 1940 described it. In Bangladesh, extreme forms of female subordination result in even the women in poor agricultural communities being kept inside the familial compound; their unpaid work revolves around home-based duties such as rice processing, poultry raising, kitchen gardening and food preparation. A family's status is undermined if its women are found to be working in the fields. In Mesoamerican tradition, when babies were born, a boy's umbilical cord was taken far from the home and buried on a battlefield; a girl's cord was buried under the hearth, denoting that this was her place and she must never leave it. In some cultures, even keeping guarded harems wasn't considered a powerful enough control of women, so in southern China, for hundreds of years, girls' and women's feet and toes were repeatedly broken and tightly bound so walking any distance was excruciatingly painful. The result? They were submissive, faithful and practically immobile.

Early medical superstition and religion held that women's bodies, with their natural processes of bleeding, childbirth and lactating, were both uncontrollable and frightening; while this creative and chaotic power was necessary to the survival of the tribe, in many cultures the response was to police women's bodies. They were secluded in unhygienic menstruation huts, they were banned from public places, including the first Olympic Games, and from various sacred sites around the world, from Mount Athos in Greece to Mount Omine in Japan. Women were banned from Japan's Mount Fuji until 1912, as the mountain's sacred cave-wombs, or *tanai*, were considered so holy that, ironically, only men were allowed near them. Add to all this a tradition of storytelling that essentially forbids women from leaving the home, village or city wall, and half your population is as afraid and domesticated as the homestead's sheep and goats. These stories and myths go back thousands of years; the *Gilgamesh* epic dates from the third millennium BCE. Something that goes way down deep into the human psyche, beyond ancient Greece, beyond Mesopotamia, tells that while men can leave the city and go off into the wild, hunting, warring or questing, women must stay behind those kiln-fired brick walls. And even though these tales were first told thousands of years ago, their power persists. Western backpacking guides written as recently as the 1970s and 1980s attempt to reassure women who are attracted to wilderness exploration that they will not undergo some supernatural transformation if they put on walking boots or don't wash their hair for a few days. 'By going outdoors will I lose my femininity, will I become like a man?' poses one such guide. And, in an instant, we are back in time, listening to stories of those transgressive females who broke the social compact, who did wander into the forest and who magically transformed into monstrous, cursed creatures.

Where did it all begin? The origins of patriarchy are hotly contested, as are the origins of men's at times obsessive control of women's bodies and their mobility. But where, and when, too, did the idea of 'the wild' emerge? The 'wild' can only exist when there is its opposite: the city, the built-on, the farmed, the fenced, the tamed. Nearly 60 per cent of the world's population may now live in cities, some so vast they would take literally days to cross on foot, but we are essentially creatures of the wild. Our ancestors lived among the beasts of the forest and savannah; for millennia we hunted and gathered, fishing in the rivers, collecting shell-fish by the shore; early hominins living in the forest of East Africa are now thought to be responsible for the first mammalian extinction, that of the enormous and meaty bear-otter, whose main fault was that it ate the same kind of plants and animals as this clever, upright creature that was able to wield tools.

During the early millennia of human existence men and women faced and lived off the land together. Archaeological evidence shows that in subsistence societies, before the development of bow-and-arrow technology, women hunted big game alongside men. To take down a large beast like a mammoth took the whole tribe using *atlatls*, or spear throwers. Only very small children and the very old did not take part. Graves of female big game hunters have been found in north and south America, their bones surrounded by a toolkit including *atlatls*, stone projectiles, a stone knife and tools for extracting bone marrow, which would have been done at the site of the kill. At first, male archaeologists couldn't believe that women hunted big game and categorised the hunting kits as merely ornamental, until mounting evidence forced a change of mind.

The conclusion is that in these societies, labour was relatively undifferentiated. *Atlatl* use was easy to learn, although not very accurate; juveniles between the ages of six and 12 could throw spears, making them useful members of a hunting party where strength in numbers was vital. Palaeontologists suggest that the first real division of labour occurred with the technological development that moved hunting from spear throwing to the bow and arrow, a development that took place in different time frames, but in all cultures, all around the world. While the bow was far more accurate, and faster, it required more strength, body height and more learned skill to master. By the time teenage boys and girls might be tall enough, and strong enough, to master the bow, young girls had already reached puberty and might well be pregnant or have babies to feed and thus, the theory goes, the gendered division of labour began when humans abandoned spear-throwing for bow-and-arrow technology.

Contemporary hunter-gatherer societies that still live and hunt with bows and arrows in what is left of the wild on earth show this division of labour. Both men and women of the Agta people of the Philippines hunt game, but women hunt smaller animals and are mainly responsible for planting and tending their forest gardens. In Venezuela, Hiwi men are often away for days, travelling by canoe, searching for game, while women travel only short distances on foot to dig roots and collect honey. In Tanzania, Hadza men hunt big game and only collect plants for themselves, while women collect berries, nuts and fruit for the village and their children. In every culture examined, while some women do hunt for small game, only men hunt big game, the hunt taking them away from the family unit or settlement, sometimes for several days. Women's activities keep them closer to the village or settlement.

Men take greater risks by travelling further afield, but their rewards are also great: the most successful men who bring back rich supplies of meat and fat have the most wives and the most children. It seems that the real changes in our attitudes to women and the wild happened when early nomadic societies began to settle and build cities, and when powerful men – great warriors or hunters – began to accumulate property and to wield dominion over their people. It was about control, in exchange for so-called protection, and not just control of women but of all subjugated groups: enslaved and indentured men for their labour; women for their labour and their bodies. When societies' boundaries became delineated by walls, ditches, dykes or fences, then wild nature, and also the people who lived there – brigands, raiders, fallen women or witches – became something to be feared.

5

There is of course much variation to this general idea, both through time and through geography and economy. Pre-industrial rural European households had much more fluid gender roles, especially when war or disease took their toll, and much of the outdoor labour, including ploughing and harvesting, was done in common by the whole community. Women, however, always did more home-centred work than the men. Contemporary agrarian societies, which still live on the margins of the wild and regularly clear and leave to renew patches of forest, have perforce far less strictly delineated roles. In modern-day Cambodian forest farming villages, although it is the men who travel furthest in the densest part of the forest, women go, always in groups, into the 'small' or partly cleared forest to gather fruit and vegetables. Sometimes the whole family goes together deep into the trees. One female Cambodian forest farmer conveys something of the pleasure these journeys bring her:

> We are very happy when we go into the deep forest: women with the *kapha* [basket], men with the long knife, the dogs, the children … I also like to go collecting vegetables in the small forest because it *is a quiet place, cold and beautiful, and cuts down stress*. We go together with friends, we gather the products and when we have collected enough we relax and chat, then we go back to the village and cook. (Emphasis added)

Similarly, in modern-day pastoral societies roles are much more fluid, particularly when, as increasingly happens, men leave their families to go looking for work in the city. But in traditional households the women's work centres around milking, poultry rearing, childcare, food processing and caring for the young animals kept close to the house while the men take the animals out of the *boma* (enclosure) and onto the wild grasslands beyond.

But what is the wild? How can we define it and what does it mean?

Throughout human history we have looked upon mountain ranges, vast green jungles, endless deserts, wide blue oceans and tried to comprehend them. Recent evidence shows that prehistoric humans ascended peaks of up to 20,000 feet (6,700 metres), far above the liveable hunting or wood- and fuel-gathering regions. The highest peaks where evidence of prehistoric mountaineering has been found, in the Himalayas, the Andes, the Kaghan district in Pakistan and in Japan, all have remains of altars or other religious edifices at the top. From the very earliest religions, the wild was the home or earthly resting place of the gods. Buddha is said to have planted his first footprint on the mountain Sri Pada, in Sri Lanka. Confucius climbed Tai Shan in China to gain an idea of humanity's insignificance. The Kikuyu believe their God *Ngai* lives on Mount Kenya and rests in the sacred fig trees in the forests around it. Mohammed received his first revelation from the Angel Gabriel in the remote Hira Cave on *Jebel-an-Nur* ('The Mountain of Light') just outside Mecca; Zoroaster worked out his philosophy in the rugged heights of ancient Persia. In the Old Testament of the Bible, Abraham, Moses and Elijah all found moments of revelation or triumph on mountaintops. Recorded in the *Mahabharata*, with stories dating back thousands of years, Indian ascetics journeyed into the wild, far from temptation, so as to find spiritual fulfilment. In the New Testament both John the Baptist and Jesus were tested in the wilderness, working out their relationship with God while standing up to the trials of a country offering little, except locusts and honey, for physical sustenance.

There has always been a spiritual side to our connection with nature, one that still exists today, even though we are now responsible for its demise. But these examples show that that sublime awe, fear and spiritual connectedness was, for millennia, only enjoyed by an exclusive, privileged group: able-bodied men and leaders of men, priests, shaman and latterly western and still mostly male explorers and mountaineers. For most 'ordinary' mortals, the wild, even if it is just beyond the bamboo-fenced compound or ring of tents, has been a dangerous place, inhabited by wild animals, fierce strangers and supernatural beings, where food and shelter are hard sought and won.

When the Canadian Mina Hubbard journeyed through northern Labrador in 1905, as we shall shortly see, it was strange country to her, but she was aware she was travelling through First Nation homeland. When she met a group of Innu women and children (their husbands were away trading furs), they were terrified of her, shouting at her to go away and believing she was a supernatural being come to do harm. But the wild is much more than our imagined home of monsters, wider than the socially constructed space of rules about who can go where, and with whom; the wild is living nature at its most unfettered and dynamic. It's the last remaining place where the laws and qualities of nature are so robust: hillsides so steep, jungles so dense, seas so vast, deserts so dry, and most animal and plant life within them so utterly insouciant of man, the great narcissist, that human laws become meaningless. There is no point in contemplating constitutional democracy while you are fighting to breathe on the top of a mountain; little value in asserting human boundaries when you are trapped in a giant spider's web in the penumbra of the Colombian rainforest, as was the entomologist Evelyn Cheesman, whom we shall shortly meet. And although she was physically trapped, she had also found an exhilarating freedom far from the world of men who told her she shouldn't study science. Thus, the wild also represents freedom, if you are brave enough to take it, from human rules, many, as we know, drawn up through prejudice, fear or folly.

And while the act of journeying into the wild, whether to invade other countries, to hunt big game, to write romantic poetry, to map 'new' worlds or to commune with god, is an implicitly masculine act, often with domination at its heart, nature has always been seen as a female. We have already noted the womb-like caves of the Japanese mountains, and 'mother' or female earth, Gaia, underpinned many cultures and religions. From India's holy river Ganges to the Paps of Jura in Scotland, landscape features are mostly, although not always, described as female. One of the most arresting imaginings of how nature came from a female body is recorded from Mesoamerican myth, written down in 1543. According to the myth, the earth was created when the goddess Tlaltecuhtli was tempted down from the heavens, in human form, by another, male god:

> And before she came down, there was already water upon which she walked, but nobody knew who created it … and they squeezed her so hard she split in the middle, and from the back half they made the earth; and they took the other half to the sky, which caused the other gods to be very ashamed … And to compensate [for it], they made trees, flowers and grass from her hair; from her skin small herbs and tiny flowers; from her eyes, wells and springs and small caves; from her mouth, rivers and small caverns; from her nose, valleys and mountains.

There is both beauty and extreme male violence and control in these images, as well as an understanding that gorgeous nature, her abundance of flowers, herbs and trees, is made from the broken body of a woman. There is in much nature writing, or writing about nature, a sense of dominating or taming a wild female landscape. In the poem 'Kubla Khan', Coleridge's 'deep romantic chasm' slanting through a 'cedarn cover', ejecting bursts of sacred fluid, leaves little for the brain to figure out. The travel writer Bill Aitken's description of climbing Nanda Devi, the 'bliss-giving goddess', reaches Mills and Boon levels of sticky groping: 'Nanda Devi tops the scene at 25,645 ft serenely aloof and set back apparently from the company of her courtiers. It took me twenty years to prise out the secret of her innermost lair and those who see only the outer majesty of the mountain would find it hard to apprehend the magic of her inner fastness.' Studies of nineteenth- and early twentieth-century Finnish literature about the country's icy 'north' portrays the wilderness as a stage 'on which the attainment of masculinity is transformed into a romantic story:

like a woman, it fulfils a man's needs'. This state of mind is perfectly summed up in the iconic sculpture by Louis-Ernest Barrias, 'Nature Unveiling herself to Science' (*La Nature se dévoilant devant la Science*), commissioned for a new medical school in Bordeaux, France, in 1899. Now on display at the Musée d'Orsay in Paris, the sculpture is of a young girl slowly lifting her clothing to reveal her downturned face and upturned bare breasts. Carved from pure white marble, decorated with precious stones, the image is charged with teasing eroticism, evoking Salome's Dance of the Seven Veils. The message couldn't be clearer: nature is woman, lovely, primitive and created for the male gaze.

Exploration of the wild, whether individually and on foot as a poet or thinker or at the head of vast invading armies, is heroic and epic, rooted in the western myth of mobility which implies men gain status by rejecting settlement and family values, but which condemns women for the same. Here is the 'grandfather' of contemporary white north American wilderness living, Henry David Thoreau, who figures the modern wilderness walker as a modern-day 'knight errant', traversing the wild, writing in 1862:

> If you are ready to leave father and mother, and brother and sister, and wife and child and friends, and never see them again, if you have paid your debts and made your will and settled all your affairs, and are a free man, then you are ready for a walk.

God forbid if, as a woman living at the same time, you tried the same thing. Here is the then council member and later President of the Royal Geographical Society of Britain, the explorer and aristocrat George Curzon, wading in on the debate as to whether the Society should accept women fellows in 1893: 'We contest *in toto* the general capability of women to contribute to scientific knowledge … their sex and their training render them equally unfitted for exploration.' The late nineteenth-century European man was at his highpoint – of imperial voyaging and appropriation, of gender superiority – having successfully persuaded 'the fairer sex' that she should live forever in the separate, domestic sphere, metaphorically no different from the walled palaces of *Gilgamesh*'s Uruk. Thus bolstered and enriched, he set forth to far-off lands, rendering in his matchless classically educated prose his complete mastery of the world seen from a hilltop or promontory. Richard Burton's 'first' view of Lake Tanginika, described in 1860, is the classic 'Monarch-of-all-I-survey' genre: his imperial eye takes in everything, the distant cloud-topped mountains, the gentle lapping shores of the foreground, the villages and fishermen beneath him, finding them magnificent but also wanting:

0.1 Nature Unveiling herself to Science, by Louis-Ernest Barrias, 1899

[A]s the eye dilates, it falls upon a cluster of outlying islets, speckling a sea horizon. Villages, cultivated lands, the frequent canoes of the fishermen on the waters, and on the nearer approach the murmurs of the waves breaking upon the shore, give a something of variety, of movement, of life to the landscape which, like all the fairest prospects of these regions, wants but a little of the neatness and finish of art – mosques and kiosks, palaces and villas, gardens and orchards – contrasting with the profuse lavishness and magnificence of nature and diversifying the unbroken *coup d'oeil* of excessive vegetation to rival, if not to excel, the most admired scenery of the classic regions.

The description is picturesque, to be sure, but utterly superficial, his eyes roving over a surface that reflects back what he wants to see. The people, in their canoes and villages, are not real; it's as if they are in a painting and are just another part of the scenery, undifferentiated from the waves of the lake or the islands in it. In that moment of non-connection, we see more of him, writing himself into history, than of what is actually there.

By the late nineteenth century, some women, at first usually either aristocratic or fabulously wealthy or very well connected, were beginning to contest the idea that wild nature was just the arena of men. Henriette d'Angeville, an elite French woman, and, before her, Marie Paradis, a Swiss maid, had reached the top of Mont Blanc in the Alps (although Marie Paradis admitted she had been carried the last few hundred feet). Mary Kingsley's *Travels in West Africa* (1897) caused a sensation, partly because the way she presented herself, from below, sloshing through leech-infested mangrove swamps, was so very different from accounts written by David Livingstone, Richard Burton and others. But also because there was so little of this kind of exploration narrative written by a woman. Kingsley's swampy fumbling may suggest a deeper connection with wild nature but her writing still reflects a colonial mindset, particularly in relation to the people she met. Later, as the twentieth century dawned, more women, less well connected, less well off, less able-bodied, asserted their right to be in the wild, to enjoy its beauty, to write about the feelings it provokes, to discover its fabulous plant and animal life and, latterly, to help protect it from our species's depredations.

This book is about five of these women, whose lives spanned the last 150 years, and who, each in her own way, challenged centuries of myth, superstition and tradition for her place in nature. They lived in North America, Europe and Africa, and their work and actions covered most of the globe. They are not representative – no five individuals possibly could be – but in their stories we might see how five different women negotiated the part they wanted to play in humanity's relationship with our wild, wide world. The first three women, Mina Hubbard, a Canadian, and Evelyn Cheesman and Dorothy Pilley, both British, represent the worlds of exploration, scientific discovery and mountaineering. All three faced enormous, sometimes life-threatening, challenges in the wild places they travelled through, but none was more difficult than the prejudices they faced from the men who controlled access to these worlds. They in turn challenged established thought: Mina Hubbard saw in the northern Labrador landscape, in the fishing traps, the portage routes, the tree blazings and tent rings, evidence everywhere that while this country may be claimed by white men as 'empty' frontier, it was homeland to the First Nation Innu. Evelyn Cheesman, through her insect-collecting, worked out, in the days before plate tectonics, that some of the islands in the south Pacific must have moved, as if afloat, through vast spaces of the ocean. Dorothy Pilley, in both her personal and mountaineering life, confounded ideas of female stereotypes as she completed and then wrote about one of the most difficult Alpine climbs of the twentieth century. Her writing seeks connection with the natural world in a very different way from the 'conquering hero' style of contemporary mountaineering literature: time and again she is swallowed by a crevasse or loses her way in a blizzard; at times the snow, the hillsides of dazzling gentians are so perfect that she dares not even tread upon them.

As the century wore on, evidence of our destruction of the wild became increasingly apparent. Today, there is no part of the world that humans have not touched, both physically with our hands and feet but also via our rapacious exploitation. The Great Pacific Garbage Patch, the microplastics at the bottom of the deepest oceans, the bleached coral reefs, the melting permafrost: all is evidence that not only is the wild in retreat but what is left of it is severely damaged, maybe beyond repair. The last two women, Ethel Haythornthwaite, British, and Wangari Maathai, Kenyan, became involved in the urgent work of conservation and rewilding. Haythornthwaite, by turning grief and love into organised action, ensured that the Peak District became the first National Park, securing protection for her beloved moorlands as well as access for the people of Manchester, Sheffield and beyond to land previously the jealously guarded preserve of grouse-shooting dukes. Maathai suffered imprisonment, threats and physical violence to begin a movement that would see more than 30 million trees planted in Kenya and the recovery of some of its looted forests so wildlife can now return. In 2004 she won the Nobel Peace Prize, but her greater achievements are the millions of copses, thickets and patches of new forest which have secured water supplies, and the return of wildlife, including the African Crowned Eagle and the Colobus monkey, to the once-dying Karura Forest at the edge of Nairobi.

To draw together the threads of these women's stories, I have read their memoirs, published articles, private diaries and letters, and interviewed living friends and relatives. I have pored over tiny, migraine-inducing journal scrawls in dimly lit libraries and tracked down to an obscure storeroom the poison-tipped spear that Evelyn Cheesman sent to King George V from Vanuatu. Where possible I have travelled to the sites of their journeyings: I have roamed Ethel Haythornthwaite's Peak District, climbed Tryfan in Snowdonia, one of Dorothy Pilley's first climbs and where, after she died, her ashes were scattered, visited the Alps, and wandered in Evelyn Cheesman's childhood garden and paddled in the stream where she first gathered snails and frogspawn. Where travel was not possible, I have read geographies, guidebooks and botanical sources.

This book is divided into three parts. Part I: Saplings sets out these women's motivations and tries to understand their personalities as they made their way through their early years and encountered their first obstacles. Part II: Trees takes us through their greatest achievements, often completed at enormous personal cost, and Part III: Forest concludes their lives and considers their legacies. Throughout this book we will see the many ways in which women challenged for their right to be 'Wildly Different'.

For those interested in my sources, there is a notes and references section, and bibliography, at the back.

Part I

SAPLINGS

Mina: northern Labrador, 1905

'Mrs Hubbard's strange visit'

The soft ground was cut with scribbles of caribou trails weaving between bone-white islands of moss. The cloudberry bushes, only recently released from the winter snow and soon to be covered again, were blossoming and fruiting just as fast as they could in this brief, thawed window. Mina crammed the berries into her mouth: yellow, sharp and not quite ripe, like the hard green apples she had eaten on the farm as a child. Enough to satisfy the urge to pick and eat, but a safe enough quantity to avoid indigestion.

She was standing at the watershed, the 'height of land' in northern Labrador, a range of barren sandy ridges carved out by glacial meltwater and fast, wide rivers. The lake to the south formed the headwaters of the great Naskaupi River, up which she and her guides had toiled for nearly two months and 300 miles; to the north the headwaters of the George River (*Metsheshu Shipu*) flowed in the opposite direction. From here the land fell away all around her. South and east, down the Naskaupi's winding rapids, gorges and valleys lay the Atlantic Ocean; to her north and ahead of her were nearly 300 more miles of walking and canoeing to Ungava Bay. This was a liminal place: from which rivers flowed north and south; between water and ice, short summer and long winter, homeland and borderland, deep in the wild of western imaginings. 'Far from the world', she wrote in her diary entry that evening, 10 August 1905: 'I wish I need never go back.' Everything charmed her: the booming of the romancing loons calling to each other across the shining water; the scented pink bells of the *Linnaea borealis* (arctic honeysuckle); the surface light and the dark depths of the lakes. It was 'all so grand and beautiful', 'the air full of fragrance'. Again and again her diary records tranquil delight, wonder and the excitement of seeing, hearing, smelling and tasting new things: catching and gutting *namaycush*, learning Cree, tracking a bear, even eating caribou innards when food became scarce.

She should have been terrified. Already in the sharp mornings the water was frozen inside drinking cups and ice pans were forming on the lakes. She was running low on sugar and flour; the bacon she had brought with her was on the turn and she was at the furthest point from the trading posts and trappers' tilts that might provide food and shelter. Warnings of death were all around her: she had passed several Innu graves, including those of children, fenced around with palings, beads, bones and other offerings hanging from the wooden crosses. One of her guides had nearly drowned when a canoe capsized in a rapid; they had seen bears and once heard a wolf cry out from a high ridge. But much more than this was the whole reason for her being 1,500 miles from her suburban home in upstate New York. Two years earlier her husband, Leonidas, had died near here, alone, 'busted', as he wrote in his last journal entry, from almost continuous diarrhoea, exhaustion and starvation. His expedition to trace the source of the Naskaupi, where she was now standing, had made her a widow at 33 and after just two years of marriage. From a hill not far from where she now stood, she saw the maze of swamps and lakes her husband had reached, 'weak and starving but with unbroken spirit and unafraid', just days before his death. There, realising to continue onwards would mean all three men in his party would certainly perish, he turned around to try to get back to the North West River trading post before winter set in. He died just a few miles short of supplies that might have saved him.

Mina's desire to stay in this place where, like a fairy queen, she slept each midsummer-bright night on a scented bed of spruce and balsam fir, 'softer than a mattress and as fragrant as a thousand Christmas trees', was born of complex and contradictory emotions. Several entries in her journal muse on the meaning of time and how she wished it would stop, even 'just for a minute or so', leaving her suspended in this quiet space. Not for her the triumphant and trumpeted return to 'civilisation', bearing news of 'the wild' as Leonidas and other adventurers had dreamed of. Here she was at peace, for the first time since news of Leonidas's death had been confirmed to her by telegram in January 1904.

While she certainly did not seek out death, her journal conveys the idea that here, far from family and friends, she could feel Leonidas's spirit with her in the still mornings and around the smoky camp fires. Maybe she wouldn't mind so much if she didn't return. 'This work keeps me from feeling utterly desperate', she wrote. 'Wonder what I shall do when this is done.' She did not, as many had assumed, have any intention of visiting the place Leonidas had breathed his last, on the banks of the Susan River. While her stated reason for going was to finish her husband's work in creating an accurate map of the Naskaupi, her journal reveals a voyage of self-discovery, of finding an inner strength to sustain her for the rest of her life. In her transformed persona she left her role of homely wife and sad widow and sought to confront the monsters of the wild: hunger, cold, exhaustion, despair, and avenge her 'Laddie', as she called him.

In October 1903, Leonidas Hubbard had died, aged just 31, in his attempt to explore and map the Naskaupi River, one of the last great wilderness challenges in north America. The tragedy was not only a sad loss of a young man's life, but needless; a mix of poor planning, over-optimism and arrogance. In a country that celebrated its rugged 'frontiersman' qualities, Hubbard's shocking 'lonely death' was front page news of several New York newspapers and leisure magazines. It even made it across the Atlantic to the British newspapers, with the *Manchester Evening News* reporting 'No Tidings' of the Hubbard expedition: 'It is believed that all members of the party perished.'

When his death was confirmed in early 1904, much was made of his lack of preparation for a journey through a land where even First Nation Innu suffered hunger and sometimes died of starvation during the long winters. In northern Labrador the ground is still frozen in June; ice forms on lakes in August and winter storms can arrive as early as September. Innu folktales have recurring themes of food scarcity and starvation: wicked women hoard and hide bear meat or cook caribou so badly it is inedible; they use the promise of eggs or partridge to lure the unsuspecting to their doom; good people share what little they have. Despite the challenges, many scoffed at the Hubbard party's lack of 'woodcraft'. After all, they were passing through a veritable larder of 'porcupines, woodchucks, hares, red squirrel, lemming and ... so many small rodents that one is not likely to go hungry unless he is squeamish', one contributor to a New York outdoors magazine wrote.

Although Leonidas was an enthusiastic outdoorsman and travel writer for an adventure journal, his preparations for the 600-mile journey failed to respect the climate and landscape. As a boy growing up on a farm in Michigan, he had dreamed of a great pioneer adventure, 'dressed in skins, paddling bark canoes' like some latter-day Davy Crockett. Had not his ancestors hacked a living out of the Michigan forest, hunting deer and wild turkeys; had not American engineering flung railroads across the vastness of the land? His forebears had been among the very earliest Europeans to arrive in the 'New

World': two of them had become the fifth ever Christian couple to marry in New Amsterdam (now New York) in 1640. But by the turn of the twentieth century very little of the great American 'wilderness' was left to survey. Only pockets of the far north still remained to be mapped for the American Geographical Society. Until the fieldwork was written up and the maps produced and approved, the region remained officially 'unexplored', despite the fact that both Innu and illiterate trappers regularly plied the waterways of northern Labrador and knew each rapid, lake and waterfall.

Trappers and Innu moved in ceaseless motion between coast and interior. The Innu, following the caribou migration in the summer and hunting seals across the ice in winter, navigated by landmarks: stone cairns, tree blazings and following well-trodden portage routes used for centuries to bypass rapids and waterfalls. Latterly, now powerful brokers in the lucrative fur trade, the Innu men's migration patterns also took in the Hudson's Bay trading posts on the coast. Leonidas Hubbard was burdened by memories and legends from his forebears, who saw the land as unclaimed and empty, a great bounty to be explored for personal heroism and for exploitation of its vast resources. His dream was to explore 'a region where no footsteps would be found'.

Even by 1903 this dream was naïve. Archaeologists had already found evidence of hundreds of years of Innu occupation in northern Labrador, particularly at the coast: stone tent rings, burial cairns, fox-traps, fishing weirs, hearths and food stores, 'in the most desolate and inhospitable terrain'. Nevertheless Hubbard, like so many explorers and adventurers viewed 'the wild' as his personal struggle, and thus, in his mind, he created obstacles, risk and opposition. Hubbard's diary of his tragic encounter with the wild is full of negative language. Even at the outset when he and his two companions, fellow New York professional Dillon Wallace and their part-Cree guide, George Elson, set off from North West River trading post with a canoe full of supplies, it is a 'nasty place'. The point from which they depart on 8 July 1903 is 'desolate'; the settlement where trappers and indigenous families live is 'dirty'. In describing the women, 'like furies – ragged, haggard, brown', he associated his journey with epic myth.

It must be like this, an almost insuperable challenge which only the truly rugged American male, the legendary frontiersman, can overcome. Even after turning back that September, lost in the shining ribbons of lakes and streams of the central plateau and already suffering from exposure, he saw the journey as material for a 'bully story' for *Outing* magazine. Just days before his death, he was imagining the great adventure story he would write about his battle to overcome mortality in the wilderness. Although he recorded in his diary his observations of countless indigenous camping sites and canoe portage routes, he maintained the fiction that he was the first to set foot in this land. His final comfort, too, was thinking of Mina waiting for him at home. Underlining his tragic delusion, he thought of how on his return, he and his wife in future would only go on short, safe camping trips, none 'too hard for Mina to share'. Part of his construction of himself as the rugged pioneer hero was his woman at home, cooking a fine meal, delicate and unadventurous. Venturing into the Labrador interior was still 'a man's game', he told his travelling companion and biographer Dillon Wallace, who barely survived the expedition himself. Hubbard had died a 'man's death', Wallace wrote, the snow raging around his tent, the last of the boiled caribou bones by his side, swallowed up in the wild.

Meanwhile Mina, two years later, had already gone further than he and although mice had eaten through her shirt, hat and bag, and the infamous Labrador flies had bitten her exposed flesh to a swollen, blood-sticky mess, her spirits were high. She floated, temporarily immobile, 'at home in the lovely amplitude of time' at her journey's farthest point from western civilisation. 'In a way that I could hardly describe or understand', she later wrote, 'it was comforting.'

She may have been at peace, but her presence in the peninsula was hugely contested and problematic, both to the men who guided her, and to 'society' back in New York. Northern exploration was still overshadowed by the disappearance of the 1845 Franklin Expedition to find the North West Passage, and subsequent rescue attempts through the latter part of the nineteenth century. Arctic and sub-Arctic exploration was the latest way colonial explorers could achieve mythical status, fraught as it was with obvious danger; but this was exclusively a man's world, with names such as Captain Sir William Parry, Captain Sir James Clark Ross and Captain William Alexander Baillie Hamilton, as well as Robert Peary and Fridtjof Nansen, associated with the idea of man versus nature in its most extreme form. Mina's four male guides expended vast amounts of energy keeping her on the portage path and in the camps they struck. Whenever she wandered off, to look at a rapid, to follow a bear trail or climb a hill to take readings, they ran after her, or shouted at her to return. Exasperatedly she wrote in her diary: 'They will scarcely let me out of their sight. Wish I didn't have to be watched so close.'

In turn they were exasperated with her: they had never met a woman, they said, who didn't do what she was told. Their concern for her safety was born of genuine care, for she had built a good rapport with her guides, but also of assumptions, until she proved otherwise, about her abilities to survive in the wild. During the early weeks of the expedition, George Elson constantly admonished her not to go near the rapids, in case she became dizzy and fell into the river, and she hated this image they had of her of some fainting hothouse flower. The truth was that her guides were terrified of returning to the trading post without her. All four guides were either mixed race, or, in the case of Job Chapies, First Nation Cree, and so occupied a lowly place in the dominant white society. Losing a white woman in the wilderness would have meant an end to their reputations and careers as guides in the burgeoning exploration industry. George Elson had already been indirectly criticised for Leonidas Hubbard's death, with some commentators questioning his hunting skills. After one incident, when for a few hours Mina did disappear from view, they became frantic. George Elson in anguish asked her when he found her: 'And what would we do if you got lost and fell in the rapid. Just think what could we do. Why I could never go back again.' Elson saw 'back' as the white society where he now needed to make his life and career. His vision of the wilderness, like Mina's, is of a different place from 'back'. Yet at its borders the structures of white culture exerted their influence, dictating his behaviour as well as Mina's. He must protect her; she must agree to be protected.

In those rare moments Mina did break free from her guides' watchful eyes, she experienced a glorious sense of freedom, tinged with the thrill of transgression. On one of these occasions, in a symbolic move, she removed her veiled helmet that protected her from the biting flies, using only a piece of spruce brush to wave across her face, 'because I was seeing things I wanted to very much'. Finally free, she can fully see. 'I could feel my ears and neck wet and sticky with blood, for some of the bites bleed a good deal. Still, what did flies matter where you were free.' In her diary that night she wrote: 'I felt a good deal as I used to when a child and started out to do something I knew I ought not to … How delighted I was to be allowed just once to go someplace and do something alone.'

While her guides had understandable reasons to restrain her freedom, back in New York others simply displayed prejudice. The mystified newspapers, searching for the 'why', portrayed her as a grief-stricken widow who had taken leave of her senses. On its front page the *New York Tribune* described her journey as 'Mrs Hubbard's strange visit' and decided it was 'sentimentally inspired'. The *New York World*, seeking to explain such an outlandish action, opined: 'We

1.1 Mina on the Labrador trail, summer 1905

cannot blame her, for wishing to investigate, in her grief'. A deranged widow was one sort of public nuisance. A woman *speaking* about her plans – Mina had given an interview to a newspaper reporter when she arrived in St John's on her way to Labrador – was intolerable.

One of her severest critics was Leonidas's old boss, Caspar Whitney, the editor of *Outing* magazine. In a thundering editorial, published just as Mina was reaching the middle part of her journey, Whitney wrote it distressed him 'to feel the necessity of publicly noticing the public utterances of the widow of a man whose memory is so dear to me'. In his editorial, he accuses 'the widow' of sullying Leonidas's companion Dillon Wallace's name, by implying he didn't do all he could to save her husband's life. 'In common decency, if not in common gratitude', Whitney wrote, 'the widow ... should be the last person on earth to say an unkind word against him.' In other words, Mina should shut up, be grateful, stay at home. For that summer, Dillon Wallace was also on the Ungava Peninsula, also completing his dead friend's work. Who would succeed? Who would make it back first? And so the newspapers created a delicious rivalry, stoked by Whitney, giving a name to Mina's journey: not only was she a woman driven half-mad by grief, she was ungrateful and 'cruel', making 'false accusations' against a decent man and furiously bent on bitter revenge.

Apple orchards and meeting Leonidas

Mina Benson was born on a farm of mixed arable and apple orchards in southern Ontario, Canada, in April 1870. Her father, James Benson, had crossed the Atlantic, aged 20, with six brothers and sisters in 1846, fleeing the Irish potato famine. In 1847 the eldest brother, John, and three others purchased Lot 29, 600 acres on the fertile land at Bewdley, between Rice Lake and Lake Ontario, today still a patchwork of fields, with scrubby woodland along the creek bottoms. Existing place names – 'Little Germany', 'Campbell Croft' and 'Pengelly Landing' – are echoes of the time when settlers fleeing Irish famine, the Scottish Highland clearances, persecution or simply seeking a better life, arrived from all corners of Europe. The brothers named the track around which they settled the Cavan Road in memory of their Irish provenance and for years its intersection with County Road 9 was known as Bensons' Corner. Other, scarcer names – Paudash Island, Muskrat Island, Hiawatha – echo a time even further back, when First Nation Americans, the Wendat,

Iroquois and Mississaugas, lived here and, having cleared the forest, established parklands for deer or vast fields of maize, until gradually, after a series of land surrenders in the eighteenth and nineteenth centuries, they retreated to reserves. The Europeans, ignoring native maize production, switched to wheat, barley and orchard fruit farming.

James Benson married another immigrant, Jane Wood, who had arrived aged six in the previous decade to him, from Yorkshire. They lived with their eight children (four died in infancy) in a single-storey timber-framed house near James's older brother, John. The families were non-conformist: James was a strict Methodist and John even stricter Plymouth Brethren. While her father had received a poor education in Ireland, Mina and her siblings went to school until at least 14, and Mina, bright and hard working, stayed at school until she was 16. Little is known of her early life, but it was simple, religious and sparse. Her father by now had become 'respectable', a justice of the peace in Bewdley and trustee of the Plainville Bible Christian Church.

She was a small woman – around five foot tall – with dark brown hair and eyes. One newspaper reporter described her as 'delicate', but from childhood she had enjoyed the outdoor life. A relative of Mina's remembers Mina in old age being able to name all of the 27 varieties of apple that grew on the farm, and, younger, skipping across logs floating down Cold Creek to her uncle's sawmill at Bensons' Corner. On leaving school Mina spent the next ten years as a county primary school teacher, still living at home until, at the age of 26, she went to New York to train as a nurse in Brooklyn. After qualifying she was transferred to the S. R. Smith Infirmary on Staten Island, a gothic, turreted structure, now demolished. In May 1900 she was assigned a patient with raging typhoid fever, a young journalist by the name of Leonidas Hubbard Junior.

It was a long and touch-and-go convalescence in the days before antibiotics. Untreated typhoid can leave permanent damage to the digestive system, heart and kidneys, and it is quite possible that three years later, under the strain of his journeying through Labrador, surviving on boiled up caribou bones and the occasional partridge, with very little carbohydrate, his system simply gave out. The intestines, in particular, can be permanently damaged by typhoid, and it is interesting to note that Hubbard was reporting bouts of diarrhoea just a few days into the expedition. In the infirmary quarantine ward, nurse and patient fell in love. Within a year they were married. They immediately embarked on a five-month honeymoon, trekking and camping through the mountains of Virginia and North Carolina right down to Mississippi. After Hubbard was promoted to assistant editor of *Outing*, they moved to a pretty, shingle-roofed house with a veranda in Friend Street, Congers, New York State, which still stands today. From here, they set off on their excursions, which Leonidas would write up for *Outing*, sometimes mentioning 'Madam', his unnamed companion: 'Madam and I had canoed before and were rather well acquainted ... in the centre, on a tent and tarpaulin, sat Madam.'

Something of Mina's spirit is revealed in these articles. With Hubbard, 'Madam' wades streams, fights through underbrush and climbs mountain ridges on hands and knees. She caught a ten-pound pike on Jackfish Lake, just north of Lake Superior. When their guide told them that 'Madam' could not go to Jackfish Lake because 'No white woman has ever seen this lake', it made her even more determined to go: 'This latter remark', wrote Hubbard, 'was a spark in powder ... If no white woman had been there, she was going.' While Hubbard described Mina's outdoor endurance in his articles, his imaginary view of her in the wild was more fantasy. Just before leaving on his fateful journey into Labrador, Leonidas gifted her *Little Rivers* by Henry Van Dyke, a romantic account of the outdoor life the author spent with his wife in rural Canada. Van Dyke calls his wife 'My Lady Grey Gown', who leaves no footprints as she walks and likens her to a mythical dryad, a silver birch or a forest spirit sleeping on balsam fir boughs 'a foot deep'.

Mina and Leonidas's last journey together was in the summer of 1903 when Mina accompanied her husband, Dillon Wallace and George Elson as far as Battle Harbor, on the Labrador coast just south of their starting point at Lake Melville and North West River. With them on the last part of the journey was the travel writer and explorer William Cabot, who observed with interest the small group, three of whom were about to set off into the Labrador wilderness and one of whom would never return. Cabot noted that Leonidas and Mina were inseparable, sleeping in their own tent away from the rest of the party, and that while Leonidas was excited, jolly, cheerful, Mina was 'pale' and 'weak' with a look of despondency on her face – she had always suffered severe seasickness but Cabot thought he saw something else. She had, after all, been Leonidas's nurse and knew of his physical limitations: 'The voyage in the small uneasy steamer had left her weak and the desolation of the place, doubly forbidding in the gloomy northeaster, confirmed her depression at the parting with her husband. If this was the nearer Labrador, what would it be a thousand miles further north? It is certain that at the parting she expected never to see her husband's face again.'

The watershed

And now it was Mina, without Leonidas, with her mouse-eaten hat and bite-swollen features, very far from the romantic image of the Lady Grey Gown. On the night of 10 August 1905, having reached the mid-point of the journey, Mina, dressed in her best Sunday blouse, made a fine rice pudding for herself and her four travelling companions. George Elson, Job Chapies, Gilbert Blake and Joe Iserhoff had dreamed of this meal for days. Mina also wore her red tuque, the long woollen bonnet worn by French Canadian settlers, and the little party danced and sang for joy in the long light of the summer's evening. Afterwards she sat in her tent and wrote her diary, happy to have come so far with relatively little incident.

Mina's diary was born of loss. A young widow of modest means, her future was one sad question mark. Yet although born of loss, the diary's, and journey's, theme is reconciliation. She heard deer calling to each other across the bog and imagined it was Leonidas's voice congratulating her on having got this far. She also wrote that this day had interested her 'in a way I did not suppose I should ever be interested again'. The 'ever … again' implies the possibility of a new beginning for her, that life without Leonidas could go on. Her response to the wilderness is the complete opposite of Leonidas's: where he found nastiness and adversity, she finds deep connection with the natural world. When the canoes seemed to lose themselves down between the big grey waves of Lake Michikamau, she wasn't afraid; instead, the 'sense of littleness grew upon me' and made her able to appreciate the magic of being 'deep in the wilderness' all the more. She surrenders to it. There is a sense that she is re-writing Leonidas's experience of the wilderness and thereby finds redemption for the both of them.

She is also deliberately marking her difference from previous European explorers of the Canadian bush, who depicted it as an empty land. In this entry – one of the longest and certainly the most significant in the journey, marking its halfway point, she wrote that she saw tree blazings, fresh tree cuttings, an Innu landing stage, well-worn portage routes and the remains of a fire with goose bones attached to a wooden pole, offerings to the spirits of the forest. She then noted that the party had seen a crow, the renowned Innu symbol for wisdom and luck, for the first time on the whole trip. Mina is here consciously and serenely receptive to this wilderness, not only to its natural beauty and grandeur but also to its being someone else's home. She planted no flag, although she did scratch her name on a rock and leave it in a tree

1.2 Mina stepping into her canoe, Labrador, summer 1905

part-way through her journey: a modest gesture and very much paying tribute to Innu customs. She had no interest in inscribing her unique singularity into the history of exploration: many people had been here before her.

So how had she got here? Throughout this long and arduous journey she faced all manner of privations and challenges, being unable to wash for days on end, having to eat bush meat and body parts that she was unaccustomed to, walking for hundreds of miles, her face bitten to shreds. The expense of the journey was significant: not only was she paying the wages of her four guides but she had bought huge quantities of provisions for the party to survive, anxious, no doubt, to avoid her husband's fate. These included two 19-foot canoes, two balloon silk tents, one stove, 392 pounds of flour, 12 pounds of tea, 12 pounds of chocolate and 200 pounds of bacon, plus two kodak cameras, a compass in a brass case, a sextant and artificial horizon, a barometer, a thermometer and, as luxuries, a small feather pillow and a hot water bottle. In all, the equipment weighed 1,000 pounds. All this represented a considerable financial outlay and made a significant dent in her husband's $15,000 estate. One newspaper estimated the total cost of her trip would be $2,500.

The previous autumn, Dillon Wallace, who was writing what would be a sensational adventure story of his and Leonidas's journey, returned to Mina Leonidas's expedition diary. In it Leonidas noted meticulous daily measurements of latitude and longitude of the wrong river, the Susan, but also something of his state of mind and his almost constant yearning for Mina and home – even on 15 July, the day after leaving North West River, he recorded wanting to 'see my girl for a while'. In the only interview she gave before leaving Halifax, Mina told the reporter of the *New York World* that the thought that she could go to Labrador to complete her husband's work dawned in January 1905. The desire to do so occurred to her well before this but she dismissed it as impossible: 'I … wished time after time that I were a man, so that I could take up this work', she said. It then, suddenly and miraculously, occurred to her that she could, she told the journalist. She would later elaborate on this pivotal moment in an article she wrote for the *Englishwoman's Review*: 'I suppose no one will ever quite know with what a sickening sense of limitation I longed to be a man so that I could go away and do the work to which my husband had given his life.'

The moment of realisation is an almost religious revelation, as if Leonidas is instructing her from beyond the grave: 'it came like a sudden illumination of darkness and it meant, "Go to Labrador"'. The first thing she did on making her decision was to hire George Elson, the man who had gone to Labrador with her husband, to be her guide. She had spent several weeks with him on the journey from New York to Battle in the summer of 1903, in the wheezy little steamer *Sylvia*, and her own acquaintance with him, plus her realisation that it was Elson, and not Wallace, who had been the real hero of the 1903 expedition, helped her make this astute choice.

It's not surprising she wished she were a man. Had she been a man the newspapers and outdoors establishment would not have tied themselves in knots over her motivations. Her stated reasons were simple and straightforward. She went to finish her husband's work, and because, as a young widow with a reasonable legacy, she could. Far better than mourning and mouldering in her widow's weeds, wondering what to do with the rest of her life. And so, on 16 June 1905 – three crucial weeks earlier than her husband had done in 1903 – she departed Halifax, Nova Scotia, on the *Harlaw*, which was also carrying 55 lumbermen on their way to cut down trees to provide paper pulp to feed Canada's newsprint industry. The wooded shores of Newfoundland were in their 'spring green', and as the ship sailed further north, the green gave way to 'much snow' and icebergs floated past. She imagined them as ghost ships, one a 'three-master', as they made their stately way south and to oblivion. On the five-day journey to Rigolet, on the Labrador coast, Mina practised taking readings with her sextant, reassuring herself that the 'Capt says mine is a very fine little instrument'.

It was vital – indeed the whole stated reason for Mina's journey – that she take accurate readings for distance and altitude so on her return she could complete her lasting contribution: the creation of an accurate map of the Naskaupi and George rivers. This had been Leonidas's primary goal. The most recent official map of the region, drawn by state surveyor Albert Peter (A. P.) Low and published in 1897 by the Geological Survey of Canada, had not covered the course of the Naskaupi and simply left blank space and a series of dots of conjectured water courses. What was marked was wrong. This was one of the reasons why Leonidas's trip erred in its course almost from the start. His party had missed the entrance of the Naskaupi at the head of Grand Lake and instead set off up the smaller and far more difficult Susan River, where they quickly wore themselves out in having to carry their heavy canoe across land, rather than paddling up the wider Naskaupi.

As a tribute to her husband's work it was essential that her map be technically flawless, so as to be accepted by the American Geographical Society. Mina spent hours sketching lake perimeters, climbing hills for better views and making sure her readings were as accurate as possible. The map's accuracy is a theme of the diary and many times she worries that she has not got the right measurements. Her artificial horizon relied on water, and not the more accurate mercury, and at several points along the route her measurements were lost because of moisture building up in the instrument. Her lack of confidence may be a reason why she briefly re-enrolled at high school while lodging at Williamstown, Massachusetts in the autumn of 1904, at the age of 34. Despite having received a good education and having spent ten years as a teacher herself, she felt her intellectual development lacked something. The mathematics would enable her to use the navigational instruments with confidence and complete the map her husband had begun.

While by 1905 women had begun to study geography at university, and elite women travellers had been publishing accounts of their colonial adventuring since the mid-nineteenth century, the actual basic fieldwork, taking measurements using sextants, compasses and theodolites was considered very much a man's job. In colonial-era Canada, 'surveyors marched alongside soldiers', first for reconnaissance and then for appropriation and exploitation. European rulers, often thousands of miles away from the conquered territory, would draw boundaries, dividing the spoils between each other, never intending themselves to set foot in the occupied land. Mina's diary also shows that she viewed the 'wilderness' quite differently from army surveyors or geographical society explorers. For the duration of the journey, this landscape was her home. After confirmation of Leonidas's death, she had left the veranda-wrapped house in Congers, visiting and staying with family, and then boarding with strangers who became friends, for a restless, peripatetic year and a half. What good had it done her, to be the patient little wife waiting in the kitchen for news of her husband's death, and what kind of home was it, without Leonidas? Having abandoned everything a woman was supposed to want, a neat little house and well-appointed kitchen, this long, arduous journey was about walking back into herself on her own terms.

But right now, she had 300 miles of river, rapid, portage and falls ahead to navigate and very few supplies left. Bush food had so far been plentiful, and most nights she and her companions feasted either on caribou or young goose, 'the most delicious thing I have ever tasted'. But winter was coming. The water she washed in was bone-breakingly cold. She anxiously checked her barometer every morning for signs of the storm that set in about this time two years earlier, and which led to Leonidas's death. Having marked the source of the Naskaupi, she agonised over turning back to North West River, a long, hard journey but a journey she knew, or pushing on into the unknown, possibly risking her life and that of her four companions. 'There must be a way', she wrote in her diary, 'and I guess I shall be able to find out what it is when the time comes.'

Meanwhile, the world outside continued to pour scorn on her. On 15 August, as she made those first steps beyond the headwaters of the Naskaupi, the *New*

York Times published a story on its front page titled: 'Woman Explorer Gives Up'. Apparently, according to the reporter's impeccable source, Mina had abandoned her attempt, while the heroic Dillon Wallace 'is pushing forward beyond any white man's previous track'. In that same month *Outing* claimed that 'Wallace has definitely located the Nascaupee', even though he was by now several weeks behind Mina. In the wild Mina may have been facing cold, starvation, bears and drowning but her most implacable and vicious foes were the humans back in New York, almost every man of them willing her to fail.

2

Evelyn: Gorgona, Galapagos and Tahiti, 1924–25

Glow-worms and giant spiders

The island was full of noises. And snakes. The sawing and whining of unseen insects and tree frogs, a symphony of tiny drills, counterpointed the constant drip of water permeating through layers of leaves. All was mossy fringe, tendril, spike, pod, scale. And beneath it all the shuddering boom of the Pacific waves coming to rest against the shore. Gorgona, just off the coast of Colombia, is an island rainforest: the mahogany, balsa and banyan figs as well as the orchids, epiphytes and tropical ferns in trees eight storeys tall, harbour more than 400 species of reptile, many deadly. The snakes inspired Spanish explorer Diego de Almagro in 1524 to name the uninhabited island Gorgona after the serpent-haired women of Greek myth, who could turn men to stone with one murderous look.

Evelyn Cheesman had no time to consider cartographical etymology or the monstrous-feminine of ancient poets' imaginings. She was trapped in the bonds of a giant spider's web from which no amount of chewing or tearing with her teeth and fingers could release her. The more she tugged, the more the silk, stronger in tensile strength than steel, cut into her hands. While she was too large to be considered a meal for the spider that had woven this web, the sight of a shrivelled and decidedly *post-mortem* gecko hanging from the skein in front of her was not encouraging. She had been trapped like this for over an hour, having momentarily lost concentration as she wandered through this strange country that thrilled her with its tintinnabulating life. Although it was the middle of the day and the equatorial sun was at its peak, beneath the vaulting tree canopy it was a damp, twilight world where shafts of light sieved through the greenish gloom.

This was her first trip into the wild beyond her childhood roaming in the hills and woods around her home and things had started badly when she stunned a snake and put it in her belt pocket, thinking it was dead. She had designed, and made, the heavy cotton pockets herself, for collecting specimens. She had to endure first the snake's drowsy reawakening and then its increasingly frantic wriggling for several hours until she worked out how to remove it without being bitten. She had joined this scientific expedition to the South Pacific in order to gather exotic species for the Zoological Society of London, where she was curator of the Insect House. When she had started work as a lowly keeper at the Zoo in 1917, wartime visitors seeking escape from the food shortages and relentlessly grim news were satisfied with the paltry collection of native mayflies and aquatic beetles. Now, six years after the end of the First World War, the public was demanding more to see than the bugs she had scooped out of home counties ponds and hedgerows.

She was currently trapped and in danger of being collected herself, by a giant Nephila spider, and her expedition, on a tight schedule and next bound for the Galapagos, wouldn't wait more than a few hours for her. How different her position was from that of the 'monarch-of-all-I-survey' colonial adventurer who gazed on so-called 'uncharted' lands. For Cheesman it was the swampy world under the trees where, on a level with the reptiles and insects who hid in the dark, she was more prey than predator. The party had left Dartmouth three months earlier, in April 1924, aboard the three-masted steam yacht the *St George*. Its departure was a minor news sensation, dubbed by the *Daily Mail* as a 'Second Voyage of the Beagle' after Charles Darwin's famous expedition to the Galapagos nearly a hundred years earlier. Press photographs of the departure show Evelyn, a diminutive figure, eyes cast down beneath a large felt hat standing on deck as the vessel left the quay. The *St George* had sailed uneventfully across the Atlantic, through the Panama Canal, and Gorgona was their first major stop. It had been difficult enough to persuade the Scientific Expeditionary Research Association's all-male committee that a woman entomologist should be one of the eight scientists on board, their free passage covered by the tickets of the other passengers. It would never do, so early on in the two-year journey, for the expedition's only woman scientist to have got herself trapped inside a spider's web. How ignominious her end compared with the discoveries of the great Charles Darwin.

Much of the tropical foliage from which hung the curtains of webs was strange to her, only half-remembered from books that she had studied as a child. One plant however, with elongated shining oval leaves, carpeting the steep gullies on either side, was reassuringly familiar. These Hart's Tongue Ferns, varieties of which are abundant throughout the tropics as well as more temperate climates, covered the walls of the little river valley in the back garden of her childhood home in Kent. Among those damp leaves she had first hunted for snails, water boatmen and glow-worms; first set out exploring in the deep-cut valley worn by a tiny chalk stream bubbling up from the Downs above the house, returning triumphantly with a jar of frogspawn or mayfly larva: 'carefree happy days soaking in wildlife'. On Gorgona, despite being in such a perilous position, the sight of the ferns was comforting, reminding her of her childhood home.

Lucy Evelyn Cheesman was born at Court Lodge, Westwell, on 8 October 1881, the middle of five imaginative and precocious siblings, daughter of affectionate if distracted parents who allowed their offspring to roam the little river valley behind the house alone. Very often the children's sole guardian on these forays into deep banks of mud or forests of stinging nettles, was their devoted Collie dog, Shep. The Cheesman parents, Evelyn said, were 'wrapped up in one another', and 'it was as though the responsibility of parenthood had never entered their heads'. But this parental neglect had its benefits. In notes she made, many decades later in preparation for her own obituary, she wrote: 'A happy childhood spent in the country developed in her a passionate love of natural history and a flair for handling animals.'

Kent childhood

The red-brick village of Westwell lies hidden in a crook of the Kent Downs, a small ledge of chalky ground beneath the humpbacked ridges and the vale of Ashford below, halfway between sky and sea. Court Lodge, beside the square-framed church of Saint Mary, is made up of four farm workers' cottages knitted together from the ruins of a twelfth-century monastery and given a sturdy mid-Victorian façade. It's one of those houses built on layer upon previous layer: behind and beneath the Georgian and Victorian makeovers lie medieval passages supported by thousand-year-old oak beams hardened to the strength of iron over the centuries. Deep down in the cellars the cold stones suck the warmth from the damp air; upstairs, the uneven floors make for games of marble racing. The children's former nursery, on the first floor, looks out onto the flint walls of the old monastery, each crevice harbouring another kind of lichen, moss and invertebrate that Evelyn would watch, and sketch, for hours.

It was in this house that Evelyn and her siblings: the older two, Edith and Robert, and the younger two, Percy and Eric, played, dreamed and imagined, their curious minds fired by the picture books of birds and animals and insects of distant lands their father gave them, and which they carefully copied, or traced the fine line drawings and woodcuts. They imagined, and then drew these fantastical, faraway places, sketching out mountain ranges, swamps and coastlines. A relative from Australia sent them animal skins and Evelyn would watch, half fascinated, half disgusted as Robert performed amateur taxidermy on dead kangaroos and platypus, often creating monstrous misshapen hybrids. Their Bible was the three volumes of the Reverend John George Wood's *Illustrated Natural History*. Robert, who would go on to be an amateur ornithologist, received Volume II, *Birds*, Edith had Volume I, *Mammals*, and Evelyn *Reptiles, Fishes etc*, the 'etc' encompassing the entire invertebrate world that would become her life's work. Percy and Eric were at the time too young to have a book at all.

Sitting in the nursery, or lying in bed recovering from one of the severe attacks of bronchial asthma that she would endure throughout her life, reading and looking at the illustrations, Evelyn was transported. She read of the glow-worm: 'The reason of the name of this insect is obvious, namely, the glowing light, which, at a certain period of the year, emanates from its body. In a dark night these diminutive creatures shine with such brightness as to bear some resemblance to stars.' Wood continued, 'It is commonly met with under hedges and, if taken up with care, may be kept alive for many days, upon fresh tufts of grass, all which time it will continue to shine in the dark.' That June, Evelyn explored the lanes around Court Lodge with Shep and brought back 32 glow-worms, which she kept in jars in the nursery. Lying in bed at night, she watched the bright stellate lights adorn the shelves of the room, a complete and private universe of living stars. After the glow-worms came toads, cockchafer beetles that flew around the nursery like miniature bi-planes, and then the pale and stately Roman snails which, let loose inside the house, left 'wonderful silver filigree-work over carpet and furniture'. The children marvelled but the snails were thrown out.

As she grew older, the gardens metamorphosed from playground to an outdoor laboratory for entomological fieldwork. On my visit, beyond the bolted beech hedge that marks the boundary of the kempt part of the garden, it is still as wild as it was at the turn of the last century. A fast-flowing chalk stream disappears into a narrow ravine; fallen quince and elder trees form bridges across the mud; the remains of stepping stones barely surface from the brown ooze. A tiny wren watches me, a ball of feathery alertness; a heron unhurriedly lifts its weight skywards like a barrage balloon. The steep sides of the ravine are covered in mass of Hart's Tongue Ferns, snails clinging to their undersides. Above the ferns, a footpath leads out onto the Westwell Downs, sheep pasture crowned with beechwoods, where Evelyn and Shep would start their forays.

After a patchy, unambitious and mostly home-based education, it was time for Evelyn and her elder sister Edith to find what work was open to unmarried women in need of an income. While the boys of the family went to university and qualified for careers in medicine (Eric), agriculture, the army and then international scientific exploration (Robert) and the fledgling telecommunications industry (Percy), the girls' professional prospects were overlooked. A series of lonely postings as governess awaited them. Edith wanted to go to art school but instead became a governess in Surrey. Evelyn, naturally, wanted to be a vet but the Royal College of Veterinary Surgeons did not admit women until 1927. Evelyn had applied twice, once using her full name and a second time using a male pseudonym but foolishly the same surname and address so the admissions officers saw through her 'ruse' and she was rejected again. Instead, she went to look after a small boy in the Leicestershire village of Gumley, where she introduced nature rambles for Sunday school children.

At night, 'those hours that belonged to me', she explored the deep beechwoods that surrounded the village, her body pressed against the leaf mould and dog's mercury, observing the badgers, 'grey forms gliding through the shadows'. During quiet moments of leisure, she read *A Girl of the Limberlost*, a novel about a young woman growing up in the Indiana swampland at the turn of the twentieth century. Like Evelyn, Elnora, the hero of the story, is captivated by the forest creatures around her, particularly the moths. She spends hours watching, recording and collecting the gaudy, silent night-fliers. Gradually, for Evelyn as well as Elnora, the desire to work somehow with the natural world, and animals in particular, became overwhelming. Just before the First World War and now in her 30s, she applied to be a canine nurse in a large south London vets' practice. It wasn't the career of discovery and investigation that she had dreamed of, and working with dogs, however much she loved them, could never satisfy her quick, inquiring, restless mind, always seeking new stimuli.

Women and science

Evelyn's difficulties in pursuing a career in the sciences mirrored the experience of most other women of this time. Through the second half of the nineteenth century, women had begun to study at university, although, initially, they were not admitted to degrees. Bedford College, based in central London and founded in 1849, was the first institution to provide higher education for women, from the start offering classes, a guinea a time, in natural philosophy, plant biology and chemistry although initially there were no laboratories. The college began preparing women students for a London University BSc, which covered Geology, Biology (and later Botany, Chemistry and Zoology) from 1884. But the women students, as at other universities, initially had to beg or borrow laboratory space and the use of microscopes, or study, secretly, in the long summer vacation when the eminent male professors, many of whom refused to teach women science, were away.

The great leaps forward in scientific discovery and scholarship through the Victorian era, in understanding anatomy and reproduction, and Darwin's revolutionary theory of natural selection had, ironically, hindered, rather than helped, the cause of women and science. Discoveries only confirmed in the minds of learned men, that women, with their 'missing five ounces' of brain, and their reproductive organs so closely tying them to the primitive world of animal functions, couldn't possibly study a field as demanding as science. Pushing women's limited brains to intellectual leaps might actually do them untold harm, incapacitated as they were, for a quarter of every month, by menstruation.

There had been a brief period earlier, around the time of the French Revolution, when elite women had started to pursue an interest in science, and particularly in botany after Queen Charlotte, the wife of George III, began collecting, drawing and studying plants when the royal household moved to Kew Palace. She and her daughters created a dedicated 'small green room' where they withdrew from court life and the King's increasing bouts of mental illness, to 'botanise' – sort, identify and draw plants and flowers – in peace. Then, science was still the preserve of wealthy amateurs who studied in home-based laboratories, and at a time when women of the household were expected to assist husbands, fathers and brothers in all their endeavours, they became laboratory assistants to their male relatives, cleaning equipment, recording results and sorting specimens in the herbarium.

The naturalist Joseph Banks's sister Sarah Sophia had a vast natural history collection of her own, much brought back from overseas by her brother's adventuring. The mycologist Gulielma Lister began her ground-breaking work on under-studied slime moulds as assistant to her father, the naturalist Arthur Lister, cleaning samples and helping illustrate and edit his book, *Monograph of the Mycetozoa* (1894). For years, Gulielma was content to be her father's quiet helpmeet in studying the tiny, seething, bifurcating organisms that bind trees to the earth, and the earth to itself in their myriad, complex networks. After his death in 1908, she continued revising her father's work, and the new 1911 edition of his book, her name now joining her father's as author and illustrated with her own gorgeous water colours, is considered a classic work. One of the first women elected to the Linnean Society in 1904, Lister's father's name and reputation brought her openings and acceptance that other women did not enjoy.

Women also wrote extensive popular science books, aimed mostly at other women, and children. Priscilla Wakefield's *Introduction to Botany* (1796) and Jane Marcet's *Conversations on Chemists, Intended More Especially for the Female Sex* (1805) were both best sellers and were promoted as a way that women could acquire a certain amount of knowledge in order to be more interesting companions for their husbands. But while women were encouraged to draw, and write about, plants, they were still discouraged from studying botany from a scientific point of view and from venturing out beyond their gardens or the immediate countryside to collect specimens. The Swedish botanist Carl Linnaeus's breakthrough classification of plants in the mid-eighteenth century, which laid the way for botany to be studied as a scientific discipline, was based on the sex organs of plants, more particularly, the male sex organs, with plants with the highest numbers of male stamens classified as the most evolved. Not only did the Linnaean system confirm the idea that the more pronouncedly masculine a species, the more evolved it was, but the focus on sexual organs did not accord with ideas of female modesty and thus excluded women from the more intellectual aspects of botany. They could admire, observe and draw but they could not investigate, discover, analyse or theorise.

Keeper of insects

The First World War, as for so many women, opened the door for Evelyn's escape from her canine cul de sac. Thanks to her fluency in German, she was recruited to an office at the Admiralty investigating British firms trading with the enemy. It was long, absorbing and bureaucratic work that tied her to her desk, though it was alleviated by long trips into the countryside with her recently widowed mother, who had rapidly lost weight and wasn't sleeping, to try to get her to see a reason for living. Her mother had gone into steep decline, but gently coaxed into the woods and meadows around Evelyn's flat

2.1 Portrait of Evelyn Cheesman, 1924

in St Albans and, later on, in Croydon, she began to recover. They became absorbed in identifying rare species of wildflowers, both making lists, and maps, and collecting specimens.

As well as these rambles on her days off, Evelyn would also take advantage of being close to the Natural History Museum, and she would spend her lunch hours examining the cases containing fossilised remains of great leviathans, or the taxidermied skins of exotic birds and mammals, reminding her of her childhood at Westwell. She became friendly with another civil servant, Grace Lefroy, who was responsible for improving the typing and clerical skills of women like Evelyn: enthusiastic and clever volunteers but whose knowledge of how to change a typewriter ribbon was minimal. Grace Lefroy, Evelyn discovered, was also an amateur naturalist and the pair would exchange intelligence about where rare species of orchid might be found in the countryside around London. Grace's cousin was Harold Maxwell Lefroy, Professor of Economic Entomology at Imperial College and honorary Curator of Insects at London Zoo. The keeper of insects was away fighting the Germans in France and Professor Lefroy was looking for someone to take charge of the day-to-day running of the Insect House.

Lefroy was a flamboyant and often controversial scientist who rose to fame as government entomologist at the Department of Agriculture in India in the early years of the twentieth century, where he was charged with solving the Empire's various and intractable insect-related problems. The invertebrates of India, Australia, Africa and the Caribbean, unheard of in damp, cool Britain, destroyed crops, ate through wooden buildings and spread disease. Worst of all, the termites, the 'white ants' of South East Asia, threatened the very foundations of colonial bureaucracy, for they loved eating paper. White ants destroyed judicial records, promissory and currency notes, registers, indexes, dictionaries, maps and 'books wholesale' – document-keeping upon which the whole edifice of Empire was built. They ate through wood, destroying the railway infrastructure, gnawing their way through sleepers and carriages, as well as the foundations of district officers' bungalows and even ships in harbours. They also ate through the roots of important crop plants, including sugar cane, groundnuts, wheat, chilli and mangos.

Professor Lefroy became famous for developing insecticides, based on his research, published in his book *Indian Insect Pests* (1906). Not only did his preparations kill termites but also other destroyers of the Empire's sources of wealth, including the Tobacco Caterpillar and pests that threatened the Indian silk industry. Lefroy was celebrated for saving from woodworm the medieval roof of Westminster Hall, at the height of the First World War. As the Zeppelins floated overhead, he ascended the vaulted heights using ladder and rope and treated the ancient beams with a preparation of cedar wood oil, paraffin wax and solvent. He was also credited with solving the problems of pests that destroyed Australian wheat on its long journey around the world to feed an increasingly hungry and demoralised Britain. His view on insects and all wildlife was anthropocentric and imperial: that these were either problems that undermined the efficiency of Empire, trade and control, or indeed vast booty to be exploited for the British economy. Small wonder, then, that the task of cleaning out the display cases at the London Zoo Insect House, and the adjacent Small Mammal House, and feeding the grubs and larvae in the basement storerooms did not appeal to the great professor. What was needed was a keen, hardworking young woman who would happily apply herself to these menial tasks.

Evelyn leapt at the opportunity and on 4 May 1917, she started work at London Zoo on a wage of £2 a week. It was a life-changing moment: the Zoo was the place from where her 40-year period of almost continuous travel and exploration into the wild parts of the world would shortly begin. The start was inauspicious, however. The Insect House at London Zoo was, in 1917, dark and neglected, with few visitors and even fewer specimens on display, 'most of the glass-fronted cages were empty; one lonely aquatic beetle swam in the largest tank'. A combination of sugar and other foodstuff shortages, and interruption in international scientific exploration during the war years had seriously depleted the exhibits. The exotic butterflies, usually the most popular attraction, consumed sugar solution so they could not be justified at a time when people were scrabbling for every calorie they could find. Evelyn had to fill the tanks and display cases herself, and most of her Saturdays that summer were spent, with butterfly nets and buckets, catching mosquito larvae, water snails and mayfly, as she had done in her childhood around Westwell. The collection was enhanced by the donation of a nest of wood wasps from Hampshire, at the time a thrilling bonus although she had to provide the wasps not only with wood but also small grubs and larvae on which they fed. She visited the fruiterers of Covent Garden, who donated hairy arthropods, stowaways from distant lands found in their boxes of bananas. Once a new exhibit was ensconced, she would then take pen and ink and carefully draw diagrams of the creatures, again as she had done as a child, labelling their different body parts and creating informative displays for young visitors.

2.2 London Zoo Insect House, built 1913, and as it would have appeared to Evelyn. It was demolished in 1993

The Insect House had opened just four years earlier, in the autumn of 1913, heralded as one of the first in the world to use 'aquarium principle lighting', where the public corridors were darkened and the exhibits lit from within, creating a magical effect as the illuminated cases showed visitors enormous bird-eating spiders and water beetles with opalescent wing cases. Professor Lefroy had promised readers of the *Times* in 1913 that entomologists would track and bring back exotic insects from across the world to fill the aquaria, and for a few months, news of the new exhibits at the Insect House regularly made it into the pages of national newspapers. The most popular exhibits had been the peacock butterflies, which opened their dazzling wings as they rested on warm pipes. Opposite the butterflies the amber, gold and green Atlas moths, among the largest insects in the world, with a wingspan far greater than a human hand, flew among tropical foliage. In the aquaria, dragonflies with iridescent blue bodies swooped and soared. The Caird Insect House became so popular that in the Easter holiday of 1914 policemen had to control and direct the crowds as they swarmed into the darkened corridors to watch these mesmerising projections of Empire.

As war ended, Evelyn was determined to replenish the exhibits. In January 1920, Professor Lefroy left day-to-day running of the Insect House as he began developing more commercial methods of killing pests. His unconventional and rule-breaking approach to life had brought Evelyn not only her first job at the Zoo, but also membership of the Royal Entomological Society, an unusually egalitarian learned society that had admitted women from its incorporation in 1833. In 1919 she was elected a member after a vote by the fellows, having been proposed by a scientific illustrator, Hugh Main, and seconded by Professor Lefroy.

The two-guinea annual membership brought Evelyn a degree of acceptance and respectability within the entomological establishment, although she would have to fight her whole life to be taken seriously by some. Evelyn was offered the post of Curator of Insects, and her salary increased to £2 18s a week. She attended public lectures at the Royal Institution, and at Imperial, many given by Professor Lefroy, who she described as an 'erratic' but also 'unusually interesting' teacher, to build up her knowledge, learning about the woolly aphis, the blowfly and the life-cycle of the silk caterpillar. She also began tentative scientific research, successfully mating a pair of Gambian land crabs that had somehow survived the journey from Africa, having been sent to London by a local colonial officer and amateur naturalist. Her descriptions of the crabs' successful tunnelling, mating and producing of eggs, and how she kept them alive on a diet of boiled rice and raw potato, made up her first scientific paper, published in 1923.

The problem of exhibits was a serious one, however. The post-war crowds of the roaring 20s, liberated from four long years of privation, wanted more than the dull native mayfly and small brown moths. Even appeals through the new BBC radio for home counties children to bring in interesting specimens, and the exciting addition of a bird-eating spider in 1920, couldn't hide the fact that the Insect House was a big disappointment. The chance to travel and add to the Zoo's collection came in 1923 when a scientific expedition to the 'South Seas' was planned. Professor Lefroy encouraged her to apply to be the official entomologist, on behalf of the Zoological Society of London: she impressed the committee with her no-nonsense approach and precise answers to their questions, gaining her place as the only female scientist on the expedition.

Always careful and meticulous, Evelyn put the same attention to detail into her planning for the trip as she did when studying insects under a microscope. She designed her own 'bush suits': close-fitting long tunics with deep pockets made from dark green, strong, lightweight cotton. She had the sides of her shoes pierced by a cobbler before leaving England so the water could run out, and brought her own hammock in case of emergency, which was just as well as she would end up sleeping in it for a year. Her elder brother and sister, Robert and Edith, had both 'escaped' before her, to Arabia where Robert had been engaged as private secretary to the High Commissioner in newly independent Iraq since August 1920. In October 1923 he had set out on his own naturalist expedition across the Arabian Desert. Edith, now an accomplished water colourist, had gone with him in 1920 and beaten them both to a first published book: a collection of sketches simply called *Mesopotamia* and depicting desert scenes, the flora, fauna and picturesquely crumbling architecture. There was a certain amount of sibling pride that Evelyn should now match, and better, her older brother and sister who had goaded her to wade through the mud and nettles in Westwell until her legs were covered in purple welts, taunting her that she, with her asthma and slight limp, would never be as brave or adventurous as them.

The voyage Evelyn looked forward to so much revealed that men's unwritten rules controlling women's freedom and behaviour could be exercised far from England. The steamer's 'ingenious' funding, by wealthy, amateur naturalists who accompanied the scientific researchers as paying passengers, set up, immediately, a power imbalance on the *St George*. Some of the passengers had paid hundreds of pounds to be part of the expedition. Evelyn had £10 for the entire two years' predicted duration of the voyage. The funding was also through means of sponsorship by firms, many of whose names are still known today: Cadbury Brothers supplied cocoa, Bryant and May matches and other sources of fuel, and Kilner Brothers the storage jars for collecting specimens. The paying passengers also claimed access to the on-board laboratories and equipment.

The eight researchers were: archaeologist James Hornell; ornithologist Colonel Harry Kelsall; marine zoologist Dr Cyril Crossland; geologist Dr Lawrence John Chubb; geographers Major Archibald Douglas and Philip Henry Johnson; botanist Lawrence Athelstan Molesworth Riley; and Evelyn, the 'official' entomologist. Because Evelyn was the only woman in the scientific party, an advertisement seeking a woman naturalist as Evelyn's assistant was published, and this was answered by amateur dragonfly enthusiast Cynthia Longfield. In accounts of her journey, Evelyn takes great pains to emphasise that she was the trip's official entomologist. However, an amateur naturalist and entomologist, Cyril Collenette, was also on the voyage as one of the paying passengers, and this was to become a source of conflict. It was partly why, at the farthest part of the voyage, on Tahiti, Evelyn left the expedition and continued for another year to study and collect on her own. It was a brave and, for a solitary female in 1924, controversial move. Another note for her obituary records how she 'had to fight against the stifling Victorian standards of her day to be allowed to live the kind of life she wanted'. She couldn't work within the hierarchical structures men created, even on a boat in the middle of the Pacific, so she would go it alone.

When she finally wrote the full story of her first Pacific journey some 30 years later, while she warmly referred to the other scientists on the expedition, she could barely bring herself to name either Longfield or Collenette. She simply noted, possibly mischievously, that 'Miss Longfield and Mr Collenette collected ardently' and obliquely referred to difficulties she had organising her research around the demands of other people. Conflicts with Collenette occurred almost immediately, when he commandeered Longfield as his assistant. The expedition only had one large (6′ × 8′) insect-catching screen, which entomologists would use to trap insects both during the day and, using powerful lamps, at night. Collenette took control of the large insect screen, leaving Evelyn with inferior, smaller ones.

2.3 Basalt cliffs of the Marquesas, sketch by Evelyn Cheesman, 1924

This wresting of the right to study unknown species in the wild by a man was why, in July 1924, Evelyn found herself alone, off the beaten path on Gorgona and trapped in a spider's web. It was early on in the trip, and Collenette had already taken control both of the moth screen and, as he called Longfield, 'my assistant'. They would take the more productive nocturnal shift, which left the *St George* for the island at 10.00 pm, so Evelyn had to take the smaller screens on her own during the day. The results were inevitable: her collecting on Gorgona, which, because of its being unexplored and uninhabited, promised much of interest, was in fact disappointing. She did discover one new species: a type of orchid bee with gorgeous metallic green and blue colouring and lighter bronze markings, which was named in 2013 *Euglossa gorgonensis Cheesmanae*. She also made friends with the *St George*'s mast boy Frank Carels, whom she invited into the laboratory to show him the insects dazzling like jewels in her collecting jars. Ten years later and by then a Petty Officer, he wrote to her and recalled how on the expedition she had sparked a love of science in him and how the knowledge she had shown him helped him in his career. In the letter he described his admiration for how 'in the face of opposition you did show us how things could be done'.

But now here she was, alone on Gorgona in the perpetual twilight beneath the canopy, the trees, creepers and fungi around her engaged in their slow, sticky, silent symbiotic struggle. Wisps of cloud, torn remnants of the ocean's moist exhalations, clung to the treetops above, releasing droplets that trickled downwards in streams. Growing tired of fighting to escape from the spider's web, it was 'by the merest chance' that she felt, in the lining of her tunic pocket, something small and hard: her nail file, 'that economic instrument put to a thousand uses for which it was not intended', and with it she began sawing through the strands until she was free. She did not mention the incident to the other members of the trip for fear of confirming in their eyes the folly of allowing a woman on board, or of letting a woman go off into the jungle alone.

The *St George* continued its journey of discovery: on the Galapagos she collected a hitherto unnamed species of wild tomato that would become the first named species suffixed '*cheesmanae*', one of more than 200 species of insects and plants to take her name. Charles Darwin had collected a specimen on his *Beagle* voyage but it had not been good enough to be classified. Evelyn's care in picking not only the plant stem and leaves, but also the large, scented yellow flowers, ensured that the expedition's botanist, Lawrence Riley, had enough material to complete its taxonomy on his return to England. On sheer, dramatic Nuku Hiva in the Marquesas, one of the *St George*'s last stops before arrival on Tahiti, she climbed an almost vertical 2,500-foot cliff onto the central desert plateau alone, only the second person ever to do so in the memory of the islanders. For several hours she wandered in an earthly paradise: drinking water from cups she made from Arum leaves; the birds, who had never seen a creature like her, were unafraid and came close, singing, it seemed, just for her. The beauty was intoxicating; she stopped every few minutes to take it all in, enchanted. She later wrote that she felt 'at one with all nature, part of the calm landscape and the friendly birds, as if with a finger on mother earth's pulse one felt the movements of that mighty heart of hers'. She became aware of her insignificance, 'one atom … in the vast universe', but it made her strong, not lonely.

Here she had another, and this time far more serious, brush with death after mistaking the brilliant green tops of tall bamboo for grass growing on the ground – the bamboo had in fact started their journey skywards at the base of a hidden gulley some 30 to 40 feet deep, itself part of a series of tall, narrow clefts in hundreds of feet of rock that formed the outer wall of the plateau. She tumbled into the gulley and then continued to fall hundreds of feet, desperately trying to slow her descent by grasping tufts of fern as she rushed past them until one held firm and she finally stopped hurtling, 'more than three quarters over a shining wall of rock … there I sat waiting for the end, which would be a long time in coming, for I knew I should take a very long time to die, while nature would look on quite unconcerned at the pain which would sap my energy, and the gradual separation of the spirit from the body'.

With the joys of the birds and flowers of the plateau in so recent memory, she came to the realisation 'that life is very sweet and ought not to be snatched from me like this – it must not be allowed, I would not let it go'. And so, she inched backwards, testing each bracken root carefully until she found the trunk of a young guava that had somehow lodged its roots in a small fracture of rock. From here she worked out a fraught route down the cliff. It took her several hours to find a way back onto the solid earth. Once again, her fear of being labelled a liability meant she kept quiet when she finally found the *St George* and its passengers, but the incident haunted her for the rest of her life. It made her more determined to leave the fatuous Collenette, who was authoring his own account of the voyage, calling it, somewhat pompously, *Sea-girt Jungles*, and go it alone.

News of her unhappiness, and also the expedition's increasingly precarious financial situation – it was taking far longer, and costing far more, to make the journey than anticipated – reached her younger brother Percy, who wired her £100 to the bank on Tahiti. This enabled her to extract herself from the expedition and continue her studies alone. She rented an abandoned hut by the side of the ocean, far enough from the island's main settlement of Papeete to give her the peace she craved. Her inventory of furniture was modest: one deal table, 3′ × 6′; one hammock; one zinc bath, one camp chair. She kept food in a woven palm basket suspended from the ceiling and made a bookshelf out of wooden planks.

Sitting alone in the leaky two-room house gazing out at the still lagoon, so smooth that at night it reflected the blizzard of stars above her, she was finally free. Her studies were 'no longer cramped by having to adjust them to other people's arrangements'. She began to study the small, busy, solitary wasps that made their homes in the curls of the palm leaves of the roof, or drilled holes in the timber uprights of her room. She caught several of the annoying, biting but slow-flying and brilliantly orange and yellow flies that had yet to have a Latin name and would later be called *Simulium cheesmanae*. She was neither afraid, nor lonely. She was for all the world like one of those solitary wasps: small, alert, busy, industrious and completely self-sufficient. She was also aware of the myriads of life-forms all around her, from the phosphorescent toadstools glowing at night like earth-bound stars, to the millions of insects 'engaged in their small affairs with the liveliest concern, with indomitable zeal ... nobody need feel lonely, or even be alone in the tropics'. These life-forms were her diminutive companions. In this room she began her life's work on Pacific insect evolution and distribution, and the role of winds, tides and volcanic events in carrying tiny, gauzy-winged creatures about the planet.

3

Dorothy: Snowdonia, the Alps and the Rockies, 1915–25

How well the body fits the rocks

Tryfan, Wales: 3,000 feet of old and broken gritstone and rhyolite surfaces from a sea of bilberry bushes and cotton grass, like the fin of some fossilised leviathan. It has a formidable reputation, the only peak south of Scotland that is impossible to reach without putting one's hand to the rock. Its pitted surfaces hide steep gullies; crevices keep the winter's snow in old brown pools well into summer. Experienced climbers find the Snowdonia peak a challenge. Novices often turn back after losing balance on the treacherous scree that skirts its lower slopes. Over the past two centuries, it has regularly claimed climbers' lives in summer as well as winter.

For 20-year-old Dorothy Pilley, the thought of scaling the monster had kept her awake, 'sleepless with excitement', the night before, and she rose before dawn to don her knickerbockers hidden under a billowing skirt for modesty. It was spring 1915 and the bluebells and ranunculi were blazing in the Llyn Dinas valley; all she could think of were the foot- and handholds she would employ to bring her to the summit. She noticed only 'how well the body fits the rocks', and how scrambling with grit flakes under her fingernails brought her to a state of happiness she had never before experienced. An unusual attitude, perhaps, for a young woman who from childhood had been prepared for marriage and children, starching collars and making milk pudding.

You could tell by her choice of bedtime reading that Dorothy had little interest in domesticity: *The Early Mountaineers* (1899) by Francis Henry Gribble and *Rock Climbing in the Peak District* (1897) by Owen Glynne Jones were among the carefully kept lists of books ordered and read and recorded in her diary. In Gribble, she read not just about the Victorian men who leapt blue-ice crevasses to reach summits where no human foot had ever trodden, but of the early 'lady mountaineers', including Marie Paradis, the first woman to reach the top of Mont Blanc in 1808 (even though she was carried up the last few hundred feet). She also read about Henriette d'Angeville, the first woman to climb Mont Blanc unaided, in 1838, carrying with her a flask of blancmange for sustenance. Even at the age of 69, d'Angeville insisted on sleeping out on the snow above the tree line so she could watch the moon, and then sun, rise above the shredded horizon.

For Dorothy, whose earliest desires were of wanting, when looking at anything tall – a hill, a London bus or school building – 'to be up there, on it, as high as it is possible to get', these adventure stories struck a chord. Wanting more, even, than being at one with nature, Dorothy, who just a few months before had been learning how to make custard (she burnt it), in preparation for wifehood, now sought oblivion in the mountains. Her early climbing diaries record the exhilaration of being caught in 'blinding snow, rain, wind and darkness'; of being enveloped in 'grey soft mist' that renders her invisible, of embracing an oncoming storm, 'black clouds rolling up' to engulf her. Later diaries positively welcome real, physical danger, the mid-air suspension above the void, the fragile ice cornices that may or may not take her weight. For Dorothy Pilley, the mountains offered not just conventional escape to fresh air and natural beauty – all of which she appreciated deeply – but also a more profound route to freedom, a way out of a life planned for her that even at the age of 17, made her 'feel like a caged bird'.

In the Welsh hills, the sudden and unexpected 'feeling of unity' with the earth, the rocks, the black peat, hit her with all the force of a *coup de foudre*. Dorothy's schoolfriend Winifred Ellerman, who accompanied her up Tryfan that day, recorded in her memoir that Dorothy's encounter with her first serious rockface was transformational: she took to it like one possessed, as if she had been waiting her whole life for granite and height. Ellerman noted: 'I am afraid I was hauled on several occasions but Dorothy went up as if she had been used to precipices all her life … Dorothy had found her destiny and was in a state of ecstatic happiness. I was there the day it all began and have always been grateful. She widened my world.' For Dorothy, that first climb up Tryfan was a turning point: 'Something had happened that couldn't ever be reversed.'

Discovering the hills had been a happy accident. Dorothy's first close-up encounter with a mountain happened in September 1914, on her twentieth birthday, when her Aunt Clara took Dorothy and her cousin Elsie to Snowdonia for a fortnight. In her diary she records: 'The cottage has splendid views of a giant mountain with a torrential stream running down its face.' A week later, after a few tentative forays and soggy picnics, she went out late in the afternoon, alone: 'Wander about and afterwards get caught in the twilight and have to come down the bare rock in the dark.' This deliberate courting of physical danger, incomprehensible to many, was to Dorothy life-affirming. Not only life-affirming, but a rescue from the brink.

She was born on 16 September 1894, the eldest of four siblings, into a wealthy middle-class family. She had a happy early childhood in a large, comfortable home in Camberwell, south London: family costume plays, pottering with her father in the garden, listening to his lantern lectures on meteorites and fossils, and playing tricks including sewing her parents' night gowns together for April Fool's Day. As she grew older, though, she began to realise that she was doomed to a life of fighting for every ounce of freedom she could take. After she had left school in 1912, her authoritarian father had spent the next two years extinguishing her desires to forge any kind of career for herself and even, after August 1914, denied her requests to train for nursing or gardening to help in the war effort. He aspired for her, instead, the life of the middle-class housewife, confined to a well-upholstered drawing room. She suffered headaches, 'all those black creatures which haunt me with a throbbing head', fits, boils and black moods as she gradually realised that for a young woman in 1912, life would mean a continuous battle for even small freedoms. This experience, then, of the mountains, represented a small ray of light in a world she would describe as being 'stuck in a dark sub-terranean cave'.

After that first visit in 1914, Dorothy returned to Wales, this time with the whole family. The Pilley family – father John, an industrial chemist, mother Annie Maria and the children, Dorothy, Evelyn (known as Violet), John and William, usually holidayed on the south coast, or the Isle of Wight where the circus performers amused and diverted along the esplanades. But in January 1915 they had gone to north Wales, staying at Llyn Dinas near the stone village of Beddgelert, with its 'grey village street, the tawny blotches of bracken, the reeds swaying in the breeze, the smell of the moss and the peat'. This change in habits was on account of the war, when much of the Channel-facing coastline was out of bounds to civilians, and Zeppelin air raids across east and southeast England, including London, forced holidaymakers north and west. After the first attack, over Great Yarmouth on 19 January 1915, people living under the flight path of those silent whales of the sky felt exposed as never before. This was the first time the civilian population had faced attacks from the air. Street lamps were dimmed, blackout curtains were put up and people shrank as shadows passed overhead.

The change of Pilley family holiday destination was also a fashion statement. Since the turn of the century, rising incomes, better rail services and shorter working weeks had led to more opportunities for holidays away from south coast piers and boarding houses. John Pilley had acquired his wealth through his part ownership of a baby food manufacturing firm, Mellins, established to cater for a late Victorian vogue in pre-prepared infant nutrition. Prior to this he had been a lecturer at the Charterhouse School of Science and Arts and was the author of several textbooks on chemistry and hygiene. With his wealth came the late Georgian villa, stuccoed like a wedding cake, at the top of Camberwell Grove, high above the smokestacks of south London. To match the villa, a French governess, a motor car, with chauffeur, and ambitions for his children: his sons would go to university and his daughters, particularly Dorothy, his strikingly handsome eldest, would marry well. A holiday in Wales among the tweed-wearing anglers and shooters would benefit the family's status.

Wales, and particularly Snowdonia, had attracted city dwellers since the late Edwardian period. The London and North-Western Railway company, in partnership with Welsh tourist attractions, began to advertise the 'delectable' joys of fresh air, dramatic scenery and adventurous hillwalking. The LNWR boasted the 'quickest and most comfortable route between London and north Wales' in newspaper display advertisements from 1904. In 1909, an intrepid *Daily Mail* journalist braved the rugged Welsh interior on behalf of his readers, who were more used to the suburban commute to their jobs as clerks in the metropolis, declaring himself captivated by Betws-y-Coed, 'the prettiest village in the British Isles'.

Dorothy, too, was captivated. In her diary she wrote: 'A spring day suddenly awakened in January ... Feel full of life, hope and happiness.' She spent hours by a waterfall, watching the 'bubbling froth' fall, eternally, down the sheer rock, searching for the right words to express what she was seeing. Did the water lip, or lap, or foam the edges of the rock pools? Later in the spring of 1915, she returned to climb Tryfan and after her friend Winifred Ellerman departed, Dorothy stayed for several weeks on her own. It seems she had some kind of breakdown, one of several attacks of ill health, both physical and mental, that plagued her all her life. She suffered recurring pleurisy in her left lung, and a problem with her eyes throughout her school days had held her back from intensive reading and studying.

Although her writing later in life reveals a stunning ability to capture the interplay of emotion and landscape, her school reports were underwhelming.

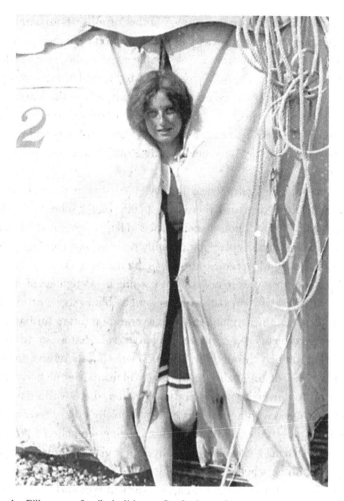

3.1 Dorothy Pilley on a family holiday to Seaford, south coast

One report, from Wentworth Hall in Mill Hill, when Dorothy was 13, notes for English: 'Has done no written work for class. Spelling evidently a great difficulty.' In History, the cryptic remark: 'Very fair considering drawbacks.' Scripture was simply 'Weak.' The only subject for which her teachers ascertained any aptitude and enthusiasm was Nature Study. One result of her poor eyesight and many, many missed school days for her 'roaring' headaches was that she failed the entrance examination to Clapham High School for Girls, which Violet passed. In the Edwardian era, the school was a beacon of girls' secondary education, part of the North London Collegiate network of girls' schools.

These schools catered for an increasing number of girls whose parents wished to see their daughters end up with a better education than their mothers, and in some cases, to attend university. Violet would go on to the academic Roedean School for her sixth form, before studying Medicine. Dorothy instead went to Queenwood Ladies College on the south coast, where she learned to play tennis and the piano and little else. The closest she got to science was the Christmas and the New Year children's lectures on astronomy and wildflowers, at the Royal Geographical Society and the Royal Institution that her father took her to.

Queenwood Ladies College, near Beachy Head, was small and unambitious. When Dorothy arrived in 1910, there were 45 girls on the school roll. Modelled on an Edwardian country house, the school had large, light-filled bay windows, cosy sitting rooms with fireplaces and highly polished parquet floors. Scented roses tumbled around pergolas and crept in through open windows. The spinster schoolmistresses were tasked with keeping the daughters of Edwardian England's middle class, dressed in ankle-length blue serge and thick white flannel blouses, healthy, virginal and able to entertain future husbands on the piano. There was plenty of hockey and tennis, and also nature study, conducted in teacher-led rambles through the South Downs, but there was no ambition for the girls, either on an intellectual or practical front. No one from Dorothy's year went on to university although the year after, there was a day's holiday when the first pupil won a place at Oxford. Dorothy's diary records that she was initially utterly miserable at the school, being wrenched from home at the age of 15, sharing a dormitory with five other girls and nursing a hopeless crush on one of the teachers whose bicycle she fixed. She spent days in the school sick room with 'racking' headaches, swollen eyes and boils. As often as she could, she was outdoors either walking in the South Downs, or working in the school's garden and, as she grew older and bolder, tackling her first climbs up the side of the school's walls.

After she left school, Dorothy wanted to train to be a gardener: her mind was already, and unknowingly, directed strongly to an outdoor life, of plants, and of earth. Her father objected, believing gardening was not a 'respectable' profession for a young lady. He also wanted to keep his eldest at home to help with the domestic chores as his wife was becoming increasingly erratic and unreliable. Annie Maria Pilley was a 'highly strung, nervous woman', who spent long periods of time away from the family home, at the theatre or on shopping trips, escaping the demands of running a household. Dorothy had to step into her mother's shoes from an early age, washing up, cooking

3.2 Dorothy Pilley climbing in her school uniform

and cleaning, as, despite the family's wealth, it seems servants rarely stayed long. There were scandals of missing maids and missing property – on one occasion the police being called in. In her diary the September after she left Queenwood she wrote, 'Rather dreading ride with Father for fear of interview about future career. It is so hard to decide definitely for the gardening with everybody against you.'

It would have been perfectly possible, in 1912, for Dorothy to take a course in horticulture. In 1903, Swanley Horticultural College in Kent had become a women-only institution partly in response to the so-called 'surplus women problem' identified in the late nineteenth century, and partly in response to agricultural depressions both in Britain and across the Empire, the solutions to which were more gardeners and horticulturalists, and, specifically, more women gardeners. This need became more acute after the outbreak of the First World War. In January 1915 Viscountess Wolseley, who ran the College for Lady Gardeners at Glynde in Sussex, issued a national appeal for young women to staff the kitchen gardens of England, offering two years' training, a 'comfortable cottage large enough for three or four ladies', who would receive in addition to 18 shillings a week, coal, milk and all the vegetables they needed. Despite both Dorothy and her best friend from school, Winifred Ellerman, begging their fathers to be able to help the war effort through gardening, both parents refused to sign the papers granting permission. It was a lifelong regret that she had not trained to be a gardener, and she knew she had been forced into professional uselessness and thus her only source of financial support would have to be a husband. At 20 years old, Dorothy faced a desiccated routine of shopping with mother, writing letters and paying chaperoned visits, sitting stiffly in hardback chairs and talking about the war. This superbly athletic, vibrant young woman, who would soon be leaping glacial crevasses in the dark and making first rope-assisted ascents of Alpine peaks, was for now caged in her parents' house in Camberwell, forced to attend cookery and laundry classes for which she was clearly unsuited, creating disasters with blancmanges and soufflés – her father guarding her virginity like a dragon its gold.

When war broke out, Dorothy was in that awkward gap between school and marriage. Not allowed to nurse or work for the Land Army, instead she volunteered to help war widows navigate the labyrinthine process of obtaining their husbands' pensions. Diary entries from this date show she was steadily becoming politicised, reading Mary Wollestonecraft, realising more and more how social structures conspired against women: 'Argument with father … women have the most unpleasant time, not men. Violet and I are agreed on the intolerableness of this attitude … enough to rouse any spirited woman. *Anyway I've had enough of it.*' She later took a paid position at the British Women's Patriotic League (BWPL). Founded in 1908, the League was a pro-imperial, pro-suffrage organisation, with several titled ladies including Lady Winifrede Cowan and Mary, Baroness Emmott on the governing committee. The League worked to instil practical and vocational skills such as first aid, financial organisation and public speaking in women of all classes, to foster self-reliance and independence. At the League Dorothy worked diligently, but without much satisfaction. She discovered, she wrote, that most lives become little more than compromise: 'mine certainly is'.

At least now she had Wales, and she got away as often as she could – four times in 1915 alone. Her younger brother John, then 16, whose diary was normally restricted to school appointments, wrote in October 1915: 'Do' has left us again. Oh what a girl! She must dislike us awfully.' After one expedition in July 1915, when a member of her party fell and was injured, the incident drew the conservative Welsh village of Beddgelert's attention to the fact that a young, unmarried woman was climbing with men who were not a brother or father. Desperate to avoid scandal, her father once again tried to squash her passion. This was a step too far: he may have succeeded in preventing her from being a gardener, Egyptologist, nurse or Land Girl, but over mountaineering, where she finally felt 'fully alive', Dorothy at last resisted.

It was a battle won, she would write later, only 'after endless fighting', something she hated but had to do. Her parents, who adored her, grudgingly accepted their daughter's passion. Her mother sewed her a green tweed skirt to be worn over matching baggy knickerbockers so at least she could 'escape condemnation' while walking through small Welsh villages on her way to her next climb. New Year's Day 1919 found her sitting on a windy Welsh ridge eating a sandwich after cutting steps in the ice to reach the top. 'This is life, adventure, joy', she wrote in her journal. In the summer of 1919, she made her mark by becoming the first woman to climb the 'Devil's Kitchen', a 300-foot-high chimney of dark, wet rock where the wind roars and groans, trapped inside the narrow rift between the slabs of Cwm Idwal in Snowdonia. Her picture appeared in the *Daily Graphic*, describing her as 'Miss D. E. Pilley, the mountaineer': not bad for being barely three seasons into her climbing career. Dreary weeks were offset by mad dashes out of Euston on a Friday night, ice axe and rucksack slung across her back, returning late on Sunday, the mud still under her fingernails. Her role at the BWPL brought a salary of £200 a year, enough for her train fares (£4 return) to Bangor, Wales, the wagon ride up from the station into the high valleys and a fortnight's rental of a farm cottage or outhouse for £1. Her father, she wrote scornfully in her diary, 'wouldn't supply a penny for any mountaineering'. In 1920, she listed the requirements for a woman climbing in Britain: 'A knickerbocker suit, lots of pockets, a hat or cap which will stay on, puttees to keep snow out, two thicknesses of stockings, woollen gloves, a sweater and a muffler for the moments of greatest cold. With such a kit, a brandy flask, map and compass added, any healthy town girl in fair condition should be able to go north during these winter months.'

Dorothy's thoughts on climbing as a pursuit for any healthy girl would not have gone down well with the elite Ladies Alpine Club (LAC), formed in 1907 and with its headquarters at the Lyceum Club in Piccadilly. The LAC was conservative, and membership was highly exclusive: its seven founder-members would assess the qualifications of candidates: the documented ascent of at least ten 10,000-foot peaks, a feat which thus demanded international travel. In 1910, the Club held an exhibition of equipment that lady Alpinists would need for their expeditions. In stark contrast to Dorothy's rudimentary list, these included a silk sleeping tent, an eider-down sleeping bag, a 'climbing costume of Scotch tweed', a Norfolk coat, lined with silk with elasticated wind-cuffs and a 'soft leather bonnet made of gazelle skin'. From its birth, the LAC always saw itself as subordinate to the men's Alpine Club, a 'child' of it, as it was described at its inception. It did not rock the boat and it accepted the men's rules: that women were not to climb using ropes, without at least one man in the party: and he, of course, must lead. Even if nominally they climbed in all-women groups, they were led by guides, and were '*never* alone with a guide; a companion of some kind, or at least a porter was *de rigueur*'. In 1874, for example, a group of five women were celebrated for being 'the first party comprised of only women to climb Mont Blanc'. However, the five women, who called themselves 'very plucky to go about without gentlemen', had several male guides with them.

The problem for women was that, according to society's rules, the shape of women's legs must not be seen: and it's hard to climb a mountain with any kind of gradient in long skirts. The writer E. H. Young, in a record of her memories of climbing in Wales before the First World War, described how 'the skirt was decently worn for as long as possible, then hidden under a rock, or carried in a neat bundle ... people on the road near Ogwen would walk backwards for quite a long way, in astonishment and mirth at the sight of my sister and me in our corduroy breeches'. While rocks and moss and streams care not who walks upon them, when mixed-sex social groups reached the wild outdoors, there were strict limits on women's presence in it and they found themselves ridiculed, and their abilities questioned. Where women and girls climbed alone, they encountered no such restrictions. The educationist Mabel Barker climbed in the Lake District as a young woman at the end of the nineteenth century. She often would not meet another soul, and deliberately tested her skills and the limits of her safety, for example walking into a bank of mist 'to see what it felt like ... wandered for a long time in a grey mysterious fairyland'. Her feelings of enjoyment stemmed from her solitary presence: 'I not only went there alone – I met nobody. The fells were empty, and they were mine.' There is no desire for domination in Barker's expression; it is more the desire of the lover for complete union and mutual possession, 'a secret intimacy with something intangible, far from the world of men', as she described it.

Ivor

In 1917, Dorothy met a climbing partner who shared her devil-may-care attitude to danger. His understanding of her love for the wild meant that in the mountains, at least, they enjoyed complete equality. The bookish, loose-limbed young man strolled among the Welsh hills in a green corduroy suit and a wool felt beret, accompanied by his spaniel, Sancho Panza. Meeting Ivor ('I. A. R.') Richards was for Dorothy like waking up from a long sleep, a complete and happy meeting of minds. 'You were the first original thinker I had met', she wrote once. 'In your conversation, I discovered, even as barely more than a school girl, the something more in life, which I had ever so vaguely suspected – a country of the mind. It gave me an immense satisfaction, soothing and terrific, like coming into a great mountain space.' Linking her feelings for Ivor with the exhilarating freedom she had first encountered walking alone in the Welsh mountains illustrates both the strength of her emotions but also the enormous difficulties she would have in contemplating marriage to him. While Ivor, love and the mountains meant freedom, marriage meant the opposite. Even in I. A. R., a self-proclaimed anarchist, Dorothy saw threats to the freedoms she had won, inch by stubborn inch, from her father.

When they met in January 1917, friends were wounded, or away fighting; the outcome of the war was hanging in the balance, rationing was about to be introduced, the winter was grim and cold and apparently endless. Ivor, a year older than Dorothy, had completed his degree at Cambridge but was unsure as to what he wanted to do with his life. He had gone up to Magdalene College to study History in 1911, but his studies had twice been severely interrupted due to successive bouts of tuberculosis, which also kept him out of the army. One of Ivor's early supervisors was the quintessential Edwardian man of letters Arthur Christopher (A. C.) Benson, later Master of Magdalene, who wrote of Ivor in his diary: 'declares himself an *Anarchist* – he says he won't take up any profession, or accept any payment by Govt. He means to till a plot of land and preach non-resistance. He's a silly boy ... found him a sincere lover of liberty, even unreasonable liberty.'

Sent to north Wales by his mother to recuperate from a third attack of TB, sometimes he left his bed, in a cottage at the top of the Nant Ffrancon pass, barefoot and clothed in nothing but a sheepskin overcoat. His slim, bespectacled figure belied enormous strength and courage as well as adventurousness, which spurred him to look for new climbs. He met Dorothy while they both, in different, mingling climbing parties, were scrambling around the slopes of Cwm Idwal. They became friends and correspondents almost immediately. Just days after both had returned, Dorothy to London, Richards to Cambridge, Ivor wrote a postcard: 'Dear Miss Pilley. Here are two diagrams of the Glyder Fach buttress, and the Idwal Slabs. I think they help you get an idea of the slabs.' The words are accompanied by Richards's spidery diagram of the rocks. A rather unusual first love letter, perhaps, but perfect for a young woman whose idea of happiness was 'To lie on the summit of Moel Hebog alone with aneroid, compass and map and successfully identify all the mountains in sight.'

During those first summers in Wales, they delighted in their shared love of the outdoors, encouraging each other up difficult and dangerous climbs, bathing in mountain tarns, finding both escape and freedom in each other's company. But always, and too soon, there was the train journey back to London and captivity, where the closest she got to nature were the fake flowers in her hat. All she wanted was to 'tramp all day among the torn ridges, to see them disappear in the sudden whiteness of the rain', and to disappear into this other dimension, become part of the landscape.

She was painfully aware of I. A. R.'s brilliance and deep, wide reading and her own lack of education. When they met, Ivor was already formulating the ideas that would make up the defining works of his career, *The Foundations of Aesthetics* (1922), *The Meaning of Meaning* (1923) and *Principles of Literary Criticism* (1924). He had studied under the Cambridge philosophers Bertrand Russell and G. E. Moore. Dorothy, on the other hand, endured dull intercourse in stifling drawing rooms, from which she politely fled. Their separate and very different activities on Armistice Day illustrate the gulf between their lives. Richards, in Cambridge, went to bed early but was woken by a riot as students ransacked a bookshop run by the philosopher C. K. Ogden, whose *Cambridge Magazine* supported pacifism. Half-awake and halfway up the stairs to the small attic room he occupied, Richards and Ogden discussed, quietly and earnestly, ideas on the limitations of language that would become Ivor's treatise

The Meaning of Meaning. Dorothy, meanwhile, in London, was typing at her desk in Victoria Street when she heard the cannon fire announcing the end of the war. She joined the crowds surging towards Buckingham Palace, whereupon, spying the Victoria Memorial, she decided to climb it, scaling cherubim and angels' harps, until she reached the head of Victoria herself. 'By this time I was exhilarated as only climbing can make me … and there, looking across the grey misty sky, the wind blew gently and the mob gathered til they were so thickly packed that only the vivid colour of the massed hats filled the valley below.' Reporting on the 'spontaneous joy' at the Palace, the *Daily Mail* described the crowds surging towards Buckingham Palace shortly after 11.00 am: 'dense masses who had swamped every tree, balustrade, or vehicle' and that 'Women' – one of them Dorothy – 'perched themselves on the Queen Victoria memorial'. As a mutual friend would later describe, their different temperaments were 'so great as to seem implausible'.

The Alps, at last

In the summer of 1920, Dorothy achieved a long-held dream: to climb in the Alps. As the train steamed through France, she stayed up all night, watching for the longed-for shapes blotting out the sky, but 'the excitement was so great that I could hardly look at what appeared between the separating cloud'. The first glacier 'held me spell-bound and somewhat aghast … These towers, split and splitting, and leaning forward one behind the other in close-packed ranks over the valley, were all the more terrifying for their beauty of clear white and palest greens and blues against the sky.' High up in overnight Alpine huts, 'thousands of feet above the rest of the world', she would eat rucksack suppers of bread, cheese, sardines and 'tea in gallons', often the only woman at that height. The conservative Alpine guides looked at her, she recorded, with contempt and suspicion. She completed several major climbs, including the Grand Dru (12,300 feet) and successfully applied for membership of the Ladies Alpine Club. From the start, though, she fought against its conservative outlook, which abided by the rule set by men: that women should not climb using ropes without at least one man in the party. At the LAC, she met Lilian Bray: another rebel and accomplished climber. Pilley, Bray and a number of other women climbers who were tired of playing second fiddle to men, began discussing starting a different kind of climbing club – one that wouldn't submit to rules set by 'those A. C. dotards', whose feet were planted in the mid-nineteenth century.

The spring of 1921 was very difficult for Dorothy, pressured by her father to find a husband and watching her younger siblings make their way in life. John was finishing his degree in Natural Sciences at Oxford; William was at Cambridge; Violet was studying to be a radiologist. Again and again, her diary records black moods, inertia and apathy. Despite her gloom, she, along with her new women rock-climbing friends, was hatching a revolutionary plot. They had run out of patience with the three great climbing clubs of the day.

The Alpine Club was rigidly men only, its members and forbidding journal stolidly of the opinion that women climbers were a wholly unwelcome addition to their mountain fastness. Formed in 1857 at the height of Victorian masculine ascendancy, the Alpine Club embodied the 'manly' virtues of physical prowess, self-reliance and dominion over nature. Virginia Woolf's father, Sir Leslie Stephen, was an early member and his attitude to women climbers was not uncommon. Meeting a woman who had successfully traversed the Jungfrau in winter, he described her as a 'queer dressed up little woman' and confessed that he hoped that she had suffered frostbite. The *Alpine Journal*, founded in 1863 and published twice-yearly, was, in the 1920s, comfortably assured of European man's dominant position in the world. Within its pages nature, like other countries and peoples, was there to be subdued. Peaks were 'attacked', 'laid siege' to, 'defeated'. While the pages of the *Alpine Journal* did include reports of women climbing, it was only when they climbed in parties with men. When, in the mid-1920s, women began pioneering 'manless climbing', the journal was either patronisingly humorous on the subject of 'lady mountaineers', or else condemnatory of 'foolish' or 'insane' women who had the audacity to climb without a male guide or leader. When it became apparent that some women were indeed 'capable', such as Gertrude Bell, the explorer and diplomat, the *Alpine Journal*'s narrative was one of a 'great' and 'rare' Englishwoman whose exceptionalism meant that few women could contemplate following in her footsteps. In a tribute paid to Bell on her death in 1926, the *Journal* described an incident in 1902 when Bell and her party had been trapped in a blizzard on the northeast face of the Finsteraarhorn, exposed and clinging to ropes for 53 hours. The team eventually retreated, but survived, according to the *Journal*, because Bell 'insisted on our eating from time to time', emphasising woman's domestic role even dangling, vertically, for more than two days on an ice-riven rockface.

The mixed-sex Fell and Rock, which Dorothy had joined in 1919, for all the jolliness and *politesse* of its members, was firmly controlled by men and still insisted on the tradition that women should not climb alone. Moreover, its members became tiresomely infatuated with the women members, particularly Dorothy, underlining for her that the men in the club could not see beyond her sex. The Ladies Alpine Club was even less satisfactory, seeming too timorous to assert women's rights, not even daring, or wanting at that time, to have a proper journal of its own wherein women could record, in public, their triumphs.

When the moment came and Dorothy and her friends formed a feminist splinter group, many LAC members joined her and the other rebels. The Pinnacle Club was the world's first feminist rock-climbing organisation, formed on 26 March 1921 and announced in the *Manchester Guardian* on 2 April. The *Guardian* welcomed the new club, asserting that 'a woman of any experience, climbing second on a rope, is usually quicker and neater than the average man in that position'. At last, women could now train to be leaders in the sport, as well as be nimble seconds. By the end of that year, the club already had 60 members.

The Pinnacle Club's founders believed that women needed to learn to become leaders in all walks of life if they were to achieve true equality. The currents of social progress were beginning to run against them. While across Europe and Russia women had made advances and changes to the law had paved the way for women to be able to work in some professions, in Italy Mussolini was gaining popularity and a dark force that would send women back into the home was gathering momentum.

In July 1921, Dorothy, Lilian Bray and another Pinnacler, Annie Wells set out for Switzerland, keeping their plans, to traverse the Mittaghorn without men, 'a dead secret'. They travelled by train, dressed in ladylike frilled skirts and bonnets, arriving with their trunks at the Alpine station of Stalden. The transport coach did not appear, however, so on the platform the women opened their suitcases, 'strewing the whole platform with clothes, which seemed to entertain the station officials'. Instead of 'frills and furbelows, out came tins of herrings in tomato sauce, worn corduroys, woolly mufflers, battered aluminium saucepans and spirit stoves, a box of Keating's (matches) and mud-stained leather gloves'. They packed everything they needed for the climb into one rucksack, which they took in turns to carry across the 20 kilometres of steady ascent to the village of Saas Fee, a walk of several hours in intense heat.

The next morning, they rose before dawn. In her diary, Dorothy wrote: 'Up 4.am, glorious morning, bright moonlight over *Fee Gletscher* (Glacier) and over summit. Breakfast 4.30, off 5.' The trio then walked for two hours to the foot of the climb, where they had a second breakfast at 7 am. Lilian Bray, the more experienced of the three, led the rope climb and just two hours later they were at the Mittaghorn ridge, 'very hot and partly thickly misty'. There followed several hours of hard climbing as they traversed from the Mittaghorn to the Egginergrat, and then on to the summit of the Egginerhorn (11,000 feet), with some 'distinctly hard' passages. 'We arrived, none of us having breathed a word of complaint in a collapsed condition. Each lay prostrate with an altitude headache and beyond the stage of polite conversation.' It was the first 'manless' ascent using ropes of an important Alpine peak. A marker, a statement of intent. By the end of the 1920s, 'those fatuous mandarins' at the Alpine Club would see women climbing all over their previous men-only territory. Naturally the women wanted to tell the world of their achievement but the Ladies Alpine Club annual report only permitted a blunt list of ascents, not the long, detailed narratives published between the sombre green pages of the *Alpine Journal*. Dorothy and Lilian tried to persuade the LAC to publish a journal or magazine so women's achievements could be celebrated and shared, but they were refused, and when they insisted on the issue being put to a vote, they were defeated. Their only option was to start up their own *Pinnacle Club Journal*, which they did, and in 1924, finally, the account of that historic climb was published.

After the Pinnaclers' success, Dorothy met up with I. A. Richards later in the summer, and together with their guide Joseph Georges, completed the ascent of the Pointe Sud des Bouquetins (12,100 feet). It was by now September and autumn had come early – the tea in their flasks froze. Afterwards Dorothy and Ivor looked across the snowy peaks to the swelling ridge of the Dent Blanche, a ferocious mountain, 14,300 feet high, whose overhanging northern ridge, like a breaking wave frozen in time, had so far repelled all attempts. The mountain, she wrote, 'seems to lean over wildly to the left as though under pressure from a great wind ... the white peak seems to soar up unsupported out of the meadows'. They promised each other that, one day, they would climb it together and for the next few years its great precipices and windswept walls dominated her thoughts and plans.

Flight to Canada

But Dorothy was now 30, and the pressure to marry was becoming unbearable. She was receiving proposals not only from I. A. Richards (four times) but also from several 'old faithfuls' who regularly asked her the question. She loved

Ivor and was happiest when out on the mountains with him, but she couldn't accept the sacrifices getting married would involve. Her great fear was that she would fade into the shadows, always playing second fiddle to Ivor's brilliant work. How could she ever be his equal, with her patchy, broken education, her professional uselessness, her lack of a university degree? He didn't really help her either, telling her his work would always be the most important thing in his life. As any man in the 1920s expected, his wife would live where he wanted to live, fit in with his plans. But she had had a lifetime, already, of fitting into others' plans and the pain of fighting with her father had exhausted her. Would she spend the rest of her life fighting Ivor? She was torn, 'broken in spirit', 'mentally deranged' and in the summer of 1925 suffered another nervous breakdown.

And so, she ran. She ran as far as she could, taking up the opportunity to travel to Canada on a fact-finding mission with Lady Cowan and the British Women's Patriotic League. In an unsent letter to Ivor, she described her decision to go to Canada as being based on distance from London but also a desire to 'disappear into the void' of the great Canadian wilderness. Like Mina Hubbard 20 years earlier, she would give herself up to the wild and let it decide what would become of her. Initially she was disappointed with what she saw of the wild in Canada, seeing even this vast land of trees and lakes and mountain ridges fading into the infinite as a place controlled by men. Steaming for days through the endless pine forests, she viewed settlers' 'little wooden cabins' from her train window without enthusiasm, imagining the women inside them struggling through winters of freezing temperatures, their freedom still curtailed by social convention, 'a living sacrifice to the future'.

In the summer of 1925, in the Glacier National Park, British Columbia, she embarked on a manic period of physical activity which culminated in a record-breaking 25 peaks, beginning with Mount Odaray (10,165 feet) at the end of July. Then Mount Victoria (11,365 feet) on 2 August, Mount Huker (11,401 feet) on 4 August, Mount Hungabee (11,447 feet) on 6 August, Mount Stephen (10,485 feet) on 8 August, right through the summer, every other day another monstrous peak, each dangling the possibility of death, finishing in September with Mount Temple (11,626 feet), Mount Field (8,645 feet) and Mount Rundle (9,828 feet). It was determined, grim climbing on 'rotten rocks', 'dark and colourless' valleys, in the face of churning clouds and freezing ice storms, pushing her body to its most extreme limits. It was joyless, too, and her notes contain none of the delighted descriptions of her Welsh or Alpine days. In another unsent letter to I. A., she recalled the Alps, 'climbing among

3.3 Dorothy Pilley at Glacier National Park, Canada

that scintillating whiteness where rainbows flash and disappear, where there are grey-blue shadows and the sound of hidden water running below … the mesmeric spell of plodding in the lantern's circle of light'. It seemed that she and Ivor could only find unity thousands of feet up on a mountain. Back at sea level and in society, beyond that magic circle of lantern light, their inequality meant that happiness was impossible. Her dream of that first ascent of the Dent Blanche by its northern ridge, with Ivor at her side, shimmered to nothing, like a desert mirage. She climbed on, alone, her physical self shrunk to insignificance on the backs of petrified beasts.

4

Ethel: the Peak District, 1924–31

'With all the strength that grief has brought, I dare'

As Dorothy Pilley was preparing to seek her freedom in Canada with ice pick and nailed boots, another young woman was carefully filling her ink pen beside a ruled, red, cloth-bound minute book, freshly purchased from Loxley Brothers stationers, Sheffield. She wrote the date – 7 May 1924 – in the margin in her looped, broad-nibbed handwriting and waited for the other members of the newly formed Sheffield Society for the Preservation of Local Scenery to arrive. Ethel Gallimore, small, 'spare and frail, like a bird', was sitting in the dining room of her parents' dark and over-decorated villa in the grand Endcliffe suburb at the western edge of Sheffield. The stone mansions: miniature country houses with lodges, stables and staff quarters, were built on a shoulder of steeply sloping hillside during Sheffield's mid-Victorian boom time which made its forge masters and steelworks owners very wealthy, very fast. Its name, Endcliffe, preserved its origins as once at the very edge of town, borderland with the wild, from the time before the houses and grand gardens were laid out on its flank.

The other members of the committee began to arrive: doctors, academics, engineers, lawyers, aldermen: the carefully chosen great and good of interwar Sheffield. They were joined by a small, pugilistic man with a walrus moustache and from a very different section of society. George Herbert Bridges (G. H. B.) Ward, leader of local socialist walking group, the Sheffield Clarion Ramblers, had just been prosecuted for trespassing on private Peak District moorland, and fined £18 and four shillings. Not the kind of person, you might think, who would be welcome inside the sober, God-fearing, well-to-do home of Ethel's parents. But Ethel, who 'inclined to the left', cared little for class or social niceties and was as happy in the company of working-class ramblers as she was with the aldermen and lofty academics of Sheffield University – maybe happier. Her parents had every desire to cosset their eldest daughter, who was recovering from a deep and dangerous bout of mental illness, which she almost hadn't survived. Ward was also an old-fashioned sexist and had little truck with women ramblers – he had banned them from the Clarion's nighttime wanderings on the moor and from leading any ramble at all. But Ethel had done a bit of trespassing herself, climbing forbidden peaks and sloming, as she called it in the Derbyshire dialect, across sanky brays in defiance of the gamekeepers' 'Keep Out' notices that everywhere defaced the wild country. She had shared poetry and songs with fellow trespassers in fugged-up smoky tea rooms across the Peak as the sleet shot arrows of ice outside. She was also determined, 'indomitable', an acquaintance described her. She gave G. H. B.'s sexism short shrift and he called her 'Dear Boss'.

After the meeting, Ethel wrote: 'No particular business was done, but a strong feeling was expressed against the proposed new motor road through the Winnats.' At this point, Ethel's ink ran out and she changed from blue to black to continue her record of the meeting, with the note that she was authorised by the committee to write to a national amenity charity about the Winnats Pass, a narrow, wind-scoured limestone gorge in the High Peak. She then wrote to the charity, the National Trust, proposing to join forces in opposing the motor road. She also wrote to the *Sheffield Daily Telegraph*, informing its readers about the new 'small, local committee' and its aims. And thus, through nib and ink and written inquiries and letters to the newspapers and carefully minuted notebooks, are wild places saved. The National Trust was established the year after Ethel's birth in 1895 to protect forever historic buildings and natural landscapes, so they could be enjoyed by everyone. Ethel's tentative approach to the Trust was the first move in the territorial defence of the countryside around Sheffield. But she had bigger, far bigger, plans than simply objecting to a new motor road. What she had in mind was the protection, and public enjoyment, of hundreds of square miles of rocky escarpment, wooded valleys, waterfalls and those forbidden high heather moorlands, the wild High Peak country, patrolled and guarded by gamekeepers and their dogs.

From this first meeting, where Ethel was elected Honorary Secretary, she would go on to attend thousands of committee meetings, as Chair, as President, as ordinary member, as Hon. Sec., in Sheffield, in London, in inns and hotels across the Peak moors; she would deliver hundreds of lantern lectures in draughty church and village halls. Over her life she would help preserve tens of thousands of acres of Peak District wilderness, from the soft contours of

Dovedale in the south to peaty precipice-rimmed Kinder Scout. From the age of 30, every day of her long life she fought to save the Peak. She fought to save it because it had saved her, from the 'hideous jangled nerves and ceaseless pain' and the 'black and starless wall' that once made her wish, before she went to sleep each night, that she would not wake in the morning. When she was not taking notes in her parents' dining room she was out on those moors, face into the wind, walking for her life: 'My God, how I do love Thy stinging sleet'.

But Ethel was not just interested in saving the wild open spaces for their own sakes or her own personal salvation. At the heart of her work was the goal to secure access to the moorland for the people of Sheffield, who lived, often suffering greatly, 'under a cloud of … smoke'. This was why G. H. B. Ward was at that first committee meeting and would be a permanent member of her committee until his death in 1957. By the early twentieth century, the railways, better bus services and increased leisure time, combined with a growing appreciation that fresh air, exercise and beautiful scenery would to some extent compensate for the arduous work at mills and factories, had created a mass working-class rambling movement. Yet the Peakland moors, a few short miles from the mills and factories of Sheffield and Manchester, were owned by the Dukes of Norfolk, Rutland and Devonshire, fenced off under successive Enclosure Acts and guarded by aggressive gamekeepers. 'Notice boards saying that Trespassers will be Prosecuted afront the walker on all sides; ancient trackways over which his ancestors passed freely before the enclosure of the moors are walled up or fenced off with barbed wire', wrote another friend of Ethel's, the photographer and access campaigner Phil Barnes. In 1924, only 12 footpaths across 215 square miles of the northern 'dark' Peak exceeded two miles in length. The great masses of Kinder and Bleaklow 'are without public access of any kind', wrote Barnes in his call to arms, *Trespassers Will be Prosecuted* (1934). Some of the most dramatic Peak scenery, including the three highest waterfalls in the district – steaming Kinder Downfall, Black Clough and Alport Clough – had no right of way giving access to them. These places were – still are – home to the grouse: solid, auburn, ground-nesting gamebirds, protected by landowners and their game-keepers until, every year from 12 August to December, they would be shot in their thousands by tweed-wearing aristocrats and industrialists. Their unfortunate habit of being faster fliers than pheasant or partridge makes them particularly attractive to men with guns who can't resist a challenge.

While a *de facto* 'Right to Roam' had been established on Lake District uplands, parts of Snowdonia and on Ilkley Moor in Yorkshire, the grouse

ROADS AND FOOTPATHS BETWEEN MANCHESTER AND SHEFFIELD

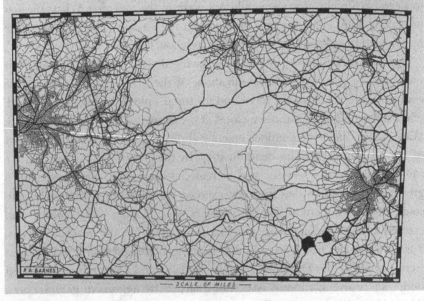

SCALE OF MILES

4.1 Map of Peak District, 1930s, to show the lack of footpaths by Phil Barnes

moors of Derbyshire remained forbidden, 'Because', wrote Barnes in 1934, 'a few score "sportsmen" spend the lovely autumn days in slaughtering as many grouse as possible'. One interwar walker wrote in *Country Life*: 'Unfortunately over certain moors (and especially in Derbyshire), access of any kind is stubbornly denied and brute force is used to turn the public off the moors. Walkers are treated, not as free Englishmen, but as escaped convicts from Dartmoor.' Class had played its part in the dukes' zealous privatisation of the uplands. While the Lake District and Snowdonia had been associated with Romantic poets and the holidaying middle classes, the Peak District is a wedge of green and brown between the two great industrial cities of Manchester and Sheffield, described in 1914 as 'noisy with the din of machinery, grimy with coal dust'. A certain amount of sympathy was extended to the dukes in wanting to keep 'hordes of Easter or Whitsuntide mill hands' off their moors, opined one early twentieth-century travel guide. The opening of the Dore and Chinley railway in 1894, now known as the Hope Valley Line, brought

4.2 Misty morning, Hope Valley

walkers right into the heart of the Peak District from Manchester at one end, and Sheffield at the other, for one shilling, 11 pence for a third-class ticket. It wasn't long before the newspapers were full of complaints about the uncouth rabbles who dropped sweet wrappers and ginger beer bottles and, *hatless*, sang popular songs as they marched along the muddy lanes between Hathersage and Grindleford, and any sympathy for the pale-faced millworkers evaporated. Which is why there was great surprise when in 1951 the Peak District, and not the Lake District or Snowdonia, became the first National Park. It came as no surprise to Ethel, or those who worked with her and knew her quietly forceful ways.

Ethel Mary Bassett Ward was born on 18 January 1894 at Grove Lodge, Millhouses, at the edge of nineteenth-century Sheffield. As a child she listened to the rooks' harsh calls, sang to the trees and danced among the wildflowers, learning more about the magic of the world, she would later write, on day trips out to the moors than she ever found in fairy books. Later these ribbons of reminiscences were what would call her back from the abyss she found herself in in her early 20s, and 'held me sane'. Hand-holds of happy memories as she climbed that black and starless wall.

Ethel's father, Thomas William ('T. W.') Ward, was the son of a forge master who worked at one of the many steelworks that made Sheffield the heart of Britain's cutlery, tool, machine and instrument-making industry. Thomas Ward started work as a coal merchant, providing the raw materials for those blazing furnaces where iron and carbon and superheated gas combined in red hot liquid to create the strongest metal known to Victorian engineers. At this time the West Riding of Yorkshire was strongly Nonconformist, and as well as being an energetic entrepreneur, T. W., like many other Sheffield industrialists, was a committed Methodist. Civic virtue, citizenship and progressive thinking were at the heart of the Methodist belief system. There were three Wesleyan ministers and several vegetarians and abstainers in the family, and as Thomas William and his brother Arthur became wealthy, they donated funds for the building of the austere Wesleyan chapels that were springing up around Sheffield.

At one of these congregations T. W. met his wife-to-be, Mary Sophie Bassett, daughter of a workman's overall manufacturer and related to the Bassetts Liquorice Allsorts business. Like fellow Victorian sweet makers Rowntree and Cadbury, the Bassetts were Nonconformist, entrepreneurial, progressive and politically liberal. Mary and T. W. were both Sunday school teachers. Churches and Sunday schools, particularly the Nonconformists, led early excursions into the hills from the smoke-blackened towns of the industrial north. Fresh air and exercise for the children of mill and steelworkers would to some extent allay the noxious effects of poverty and pollution. Some of the earliest groups affiliated to the Manchester and Sheffield Ramblers Federations were Non-conformist churches: the Trinity Wesleyan Sunday School Rambling Club and the Old Chapel Rambling Club just two among many. When they became parents, T. W. and Mary Sophie took their children along the path out of town from Hathersage, over the slabby Packhorse Bridge and into the sheep-cropped hills patrolled by lone wild crab apple trees. Ethel remembered wriggling though the sheep holes in drystone walls, and gazing up at Win Hill, to her childish eyes an unconquerable peak. Then her little legs were only strong enough to take her to the old stone horse trough at its base.

Ethel's parents eventually had five children: Thomas Leonard, the eldest, born in 1891, then Ethel, then just a year later, Gertrude, then Alan and baby Frank, born in 1899. The children were close, particularly the two girls, Eppy and Gag, as they called each other, and formed an intense, supportive bond within which they would look after each other and share in each other's campaigning throughout their lives. As the family grew, so did T. W.'s fortunes. His scrap metal business burgeoned as the demand from the steelworks increased. He began buying up and stripping decommissioned ships and selling the scrap, the steelworks' lifeblood. At its peak T. W. Ward, employing 1,235 workers, was shovelling 1,000 tons of scrap metal a day into the hungry furnaces that burned and smoked throughout Sheffield.

When Ethel was seven years old the family moved to Endcliffe Vale House, a grand, bay-fronted mid-Victorian house with stables, harness room, butler and cook's pantry, and a 22-foot-long entrance hall, the floors covered with Axminster and 'Turkey' carpets. Ethel and Gertrude, when they were older, would go riding on their ponies across the moors, taking the old packhorse track from Redmires. At 11, Ethel started attending the newly established Sheffield High School for Girls, a private girls' day school, part of a number that opened across England as Edwardian parents began to have aspirations other than marriage for their daughters. For sixth form, as befitted the clever daughter of the newly enriched middle classes, Ethel was sent to boarding school. West Heath was a small and inconspicuous girls' school in Ham Common, west London, which became briefly famous 70 years after Ethel's attendance there as having been the alma mater of Lady Diana Spencer. At West Heath she studied Drawing, Wood Carving, Domestic Economy, Literature, Natural Science and Swedish Drill, a keep fit exercise routine developed initially for new army recruits. She passed her final examinations, set by the Royal Drawing Society, and the qualification enabled her to attend Westfield College in Hampstead, established in the decade before Ethel's birth to prepare women for degrees at the University of London.

Before she went to Westfield, she, her mother and her sister Gertrude went on a trip to France, where she kept a travel journal, 'Written in a thundering hurry and in bad style' and which gives us a few glimpses into the teenage Ethel's sensibilities and interests: 'the equality of the sexes', the characteristics of the French, from their apparent obsession with death, gathered during her visit to the Père Lachaise Cemetery, to the elegant silhouettes of the smart French ladies which, she wrote, put her to shame. Above all, the diary is striking in her observation and appreciation of the natural world, its beauty and how modernity was, already in 1913, threatening to destroy it.

Her first lines, written as the boat train travelled through Kent, remark on the wildflowers growing on the railway embankment: 'Kent is superbly kind, a great mother with her purple milkmaids (cuckooflower) and primroses to greet us on the banks. Above all her gentle fields, green under the wide grey sky.' In France, 'What struck me most was the beautiful richness of the green, soft and almost moss-coloured. The soil is also rich and red, the budding trees often brown.' She is a painter, making notes before touching brush to pigment, responding as much to colour variations as to detail. But the French houses, observed from a train window as she travelled from Calais to Paris, were 'entirely out of harmony with the surroundings'. Other journeys 'were spoilt by the number of posters, that stood in a procession, field after field ... disgusting irreligious abominations ... they will post their bills on anything and everything'; and then, six words that sum up, for her, the contrast between kempt, clipped and elegant France, with the moors of her home: 'I saw nothing wild in France'.

Her quite extreme response to the defacement of the natural environment is striking in a just-turned-nineteen-year-old, and hints at the vigour with which she would fight for the countryside as an older woman. Already, and before the great tragedy of her life would call upon the rocks and turf of the Peak to save her, she is a woman who prefers wild places to elegant shopping streets. The diary also reveals a highly romantic sensibility, and hints at a beloved, or an intended at least. In the Forest of Fontainebleau she thinks of the writer Robert Louis Stevenson, who began a passionate love affair while he was there and Ethel succumbs 'absolutely to my own weak and dear imagination ... I became obsessed with all sweet and romantic thoughts ... my eyes are hot for tears, and I can only ask for courage, "to labour and to wait".' The final section of the diary records her thoughts as her home-bound train steams through the English countryside. She is relieved, excited and happy to be back

> in the only place in the universe worth living in ... green curving lanes, with hawthorn hedges sloped here and there between the fields ... a cottage ready smoking for the evening meal. Cows, brown and peaceful ... and trees stood with their irregular forms against the quiet evening sky. Oh the homeliness of England, it is like a free and peaceful garden, where everyone may turn in and rest.

This highly romantic and idealised depiction of the English countryside shows that she was not only a good student of Wordsworth, John Clare and Coleridge, but the 'garden' is also the Garden of Eden and shows how her feelings for nature are closely tied with her religion, still devoutly Methodist. Within a few short years that belief would be tested to breaking point, her record, 'blotched and barred by Scarlet sin'.

And so, in the autumn of 1914, to Westfield – 'Castle Adamant' as the students called it – in Hampstead, north London. The mansion was built in classical style in 1840, with a tall pillared portico in the centre like the entrance to a Greek temple. Behind this airy façade lurked a rabbit warren of rooms and corridors, always too cold and too dark, according to former students' memoirs. Although Ethel could see the ridges of the Chilterns from the attic rooms, the far horizon was no substitute for the tawny hulks of Kinder Scout

4.3 Portrait of Ethel Bassett Ward painted when she was 21

or Blacka Moor, which glutted one's whole view. It was an inauspicious time to be starting at university: many young women immediately left that autumn, to volunteer as nurses. Those who stayed had evenings punctured by blackouts and zeppelin drills, 'midnight alarms that called us from our sleep to thread the dark corridors by the light of dimly burning lanterns'.

As well as writing essays, the young women spent evenings knitting socks and blanket squares for the troops, and during the winter volunteered to sweep snow from the streets of Hampstead, in the absence of the municipal workers who had gone to the front. In the summer they went to help with the strawberry, apple and damson harvests in Dorset and Warwickshire. The school magazine, *Hermes*, reported that in the summer term of 1915 the students picked '10,000 lbs of strawberries that would otherwise have been lost'. Ethel studied Classics, Mathematics, History, English Language and Literature, French, German and Botany under the inspirational Marian Delf. Delf took the young women out to Hampstead ponds, in their long dark skirts and their scholars' gowns, to study the flora and fauna, and take specimens of algal plankton back to the new botany laboratory on the top floor of the college. One woman who attended Westfield during Ethel's time there remembered the quiet and 'very studious atmosphere'. There never seemed to be enough food. Marian Delf, who left Westfield to go to Cambridge in 1915, recalled the 'spartan conditions' of the college, although she had been given the budget to purchase a series of models of extinct fossil plants and a microscope for the students, at the end of 1914.

As it was, Ethel only stayed for three terms, taking a full honours certificate but returning home after the summer term in 1915. By then, it was clear that the war that was supposed to be over by Christmas 1914 was going to be long and brutal. People were already being killed by incendiary bombs dropped from the silken leviathans above them. The same zeppelins that provoked the Pilley family to holiday in Wales that year forced Ethel back to Sheffield, and to abandon further education. Back home in Sheffield, Ethel set to work, serving on the Sheffield Prisoners of War Help Committee and fundraising for donations of Red Cross parcels.

The 'love that fell so soon'

Six months after she left Westfield, Ethel was married. Henry Burrows Gallimore, nine years older, was from another Nonconformist industrial Sheffield family, of electroplate manufacturers. 'There could not have been a more suitable match': the Gallimores, like the Wards, were members of the Fulwood Wesley Chapel. Henry's father, Henry senior, was President of the Sheffield Temperance Electoral Association, and a leading promoter of vegetarianism. Henry had attended the Leys School, Cambridge, founded in 1875 with the specific purpose of educating the sons of Methodist ministers; he then studied modern and medieval languages at King's College Cambridge, graduating in June 1907. He volunteered for service in August 1914, having commanded a company of boy scouts before that and was created a Lieutenant in the Royal Field Artillery.

Ethel and Henry married at the Fulwood Wesley Chapel at the end of February 1916. There were few flowers, appropriate for a wartime wedding, although the small display of white tulips, red poinsettias and blue hyacinths 'charmingly suggested the national colours', reported the *Sheffield Independent*. Her dress was of ivory velvet and silk, trimmed with pale pink ribbon and she wore a veil of Limerick lace, lent to her by her aunt. Len, Ethel's older brother who by then was stationed in France, was sent photographs and cake. Their wedding present from Henry's parents was a case of electroplated silver cutlery. After a short honeymoon spent walking in the Lake District, Henry joined his regiment in France. He was killed on 26 May 1917, 'in an act of exceptional bravery' after trying to extinguish a fire in a gun pit before it reached the ammunition store. His death notice described him as 'possessed of a charm and manner that endeared him to everyone with whom he came in contact' and 'dearly loved husband of Ethel M. B. Gallimore'. They had been married for 15 months, during which time she had barely seen him; they had not even set up house together, Ethel still giving her address as her childhood home, Endcliffe.

She was not, of course, the only young widow in 1917. She joined the seemingly endless train of broken-hearted women who lost their husbands, fathers and brothers in the Great War. But Ethel fell hard and far and fast. She wrote later, in her prose poem *Pride of the Peak*, that she was smitten 'with such o'erwhelming sorrow' for the 'love, that fell so soon', that she 'begged' her own life should 'cease before each loathed morrow'. After the emotional pain came the physical agonies 'from nature all unfilled and grieving slow'. Yet gradually, with Gertrude often by her side, Ethel began to walk out into the hills of her childhood, relishing the 'heavy mile', the 'slanting balls that beat across my cheek with blasting blows'. They were hard years and it seemed that Ethel was trying to punish herself, choosing the mistiest days, the strongest winds, the foulest weather, to walk out in. 'I can't see why you want to go', said her mother. 'You can't see anything, what can you see?' asked her father. 'Mist', replied Gertrude. Landlords in remote village inns and tea shops began to recognise her. Other ramblers also became familiar with the tiny, dark-haired figure marching through the storm in tweed coat and jodhpurs. One day, said Ethel, when the rain was 'siling down' and she was wandering the moors around Longshaw, she sought shelter at the lonely Fox House Inn on the Hathersage Road. 'The Landlord said "Oh it's you! I might have guessed it was your weather!"' as he made her a steaming cup of tea.

Gradually, 'mid the greenery', she began to hope. In the sunshine at the top of Win Hill, she learned how to smile again. She walked and she walked, and she began to write. She wrote poems of the places she passed: the 'awful, lifted floor' of Kinder; the 'spreading arms all black and toothed and belching dreadful blast' of Jaggers Clough; the 'high end of the heavenly stream ... beauteous, so aloof, sublime unfound' at the source of the Dove. In her poetry she declared her trespassing all across the Peak, from Froggatt Edge, to Bleaklow, stressing her determination in her language not to let 'Keep Out' signs or gamekeepers stop her: 'I *will* go up, I *will* go up all alone/Up to the moors ... beside the grasses pale and by the sedge/On high above the cliffs of Froggatt Edge.'

During this time, two opposing phases began to turn in her soul: her faith in God gradually faded into agnosticism and her faith in nature as a source of spiritual fulfilment grew in its place. She journeyed to villages across the Peak District, in order to write about local customs, such as well dressing, and the old stone buildings, which, 'like the nests of birds should be a part of earth, the offspring of her flesh and bones'. It was here she began to refine those thoughts, first recorded in 1913 in France, on how human engineering, from roads, to bridges, to houses, should relate to the natural landscape, not fight with it. These ideas would become a major part of her thinking on how land could be protected, and how, when houses and roads must be built, they should be in harmony with the stones on which they are laid, and the colours of the hills against which they stand.

Letters from this time are postmarked Rose Cottage, Ashover (where her mother's family lived), the Marquis of Granby inn, Bamford and the Fox House Inn, Hathersage, each letter marking a temporary resting place during her apparently ceaseless movement through the Peak, responding to the urge to be in, and of, the land: 'Nothing can hold me, nought my freedom reins', she wrote. 'I am mounting like a bird unto the moors.' Always, she would return to Endcliffe Vale House, and Sheffield. While she gradually lost her faith, living within a deeply religious household, where Methodism ran in her family's veins, it was hard to disentangle herself from the social duties of her church, and nor did she want to. The local papers published notices of events held in the house and grounds and hosted by her mother, with she and Gertrude helping: the London Missionary Society annual fête, a baby show to raise money for the Holy Trinity Church, violin recitals in aid of wounded soldiers or unmarried mothers. It was in these early post-war years that she and Gertrude, even as their father grew richer, developed their keen sense of the social inequalities that beset England, and their home town of Sheffield. They joined progressive causes and campaigned against poverty. Older brother Len, still stationed in France, sent a letter home in January 1919, in which he joked about his sisters' socialism. Asserting his own rosy-tinted patriotism for a country he had barely seen for four years, he wrote: 'Good old England! How much superior you are to everything else in the world! So, Eppy and Gag, put that in your pipes and smoke it (or whatever the feminine equivalent is), as I know them's [sic] not your sentiments.'

In 1920, Ethel was, along with her sister Gertrude and younger brother Alan, invited to become a member of the progressive Sheffield Educational Settlement. The Settlement, in Shipton Street, north of the centre and in the 1920s made up of close-packed, unhealthy Victorian terraces, was founded in 1918 by the YMCA, with the Quaker philosopher and Fabian Arnold Freeman as its warden. The aim of the settlement, quite simply, was to 'establish the kingdom of God' in working-class Sheffield, through the dignity of skilled work, healthy, airy homes, rambling in the countryside on Sundays and 'schools that would win the approval of Plato'. In short, the Sheffield Settlement (along with others established at the same time throughout the country) was a Utopian vision to improve the lives of the poor and disadvantaged in the decades before the Welfare State took over this responsibility. Volunteers offered classes in public speaking, needlework, foreign languages, history, folk dancing and elocution. The list of invitees to become council members ranged from prominent national Fabians, including Sidney and Beatrice Webb and H. G. Wells, to leading local liberals. Ethel replied to her letter of invitation in February 1921, saying that she would serve on the council 'with pleasure'; although, she added, 'I am rather alarmed at the sound if it.'

In fact, she and Gertrude, who was also invited, didn't stand for election as full council members, but offered themselves as 'service members' – supporters, cheerleaders, volunteers – as they did not think themselves suitably qualified to help with the business of day-to-day running of the settlement. It was, she wrote to Freeman, 'an undeserved honour'. And so, she raised money, donated flowers and gifts for fundraising, and wrote to Freeman, sympathising when yet again the settlement was criticised in the press. Its socialist and pacifist principles were not popular with many members of Sheffield's industrial classes. Through the settlement, Ethel discovered a purpose, and learned of the hard graft and determination in the face of obstructions and challenges that were needed to make change. In an essay of appreciation of Arnold Freeman for the settlement's thirtieth anniversary she wrote that it was distinguished by its friendliness, lack of snobbishness and pettiness, and was 'a friendly haven from the dreariness of modern industrial life'. But more than that, for her it was the 'spark of fire' that she received, while a young, grieving widow of 26, that would 'illuminate [her] whole life'.

Also invited to serve the settlement was G. H. B. Ward. In between sitting at committee meetings and urging the local health councils to provide more country walks for Sheffield's children, he was organising midnight trespasses on Kinder and Bleaklow, baiting the gamekeepers who, since the end of the First World War had been keeping stricter watch over the moorlands. His Clarion Ramblers were regularly raising funds to help pay the fines of walkers caught by the dukes' keepers: the decades-old game of cat and mouse of which both parties were heartily sick. G. H. B. and Ethel's joint service at the Sheffield Settlement marked the start of a working partnership that would last another nearly 40 years. Ward would be a great influence on Ethel, encouraging her poetry and her activism. Ward, nearly 20 years her senior, encouraged her to establish the Society for Protection of Local Scenery. They had great admiration for each other's different, but complementary work. He admired her quiet determination and her literary abilities. He disseminated snatches of her poems to members of his rambling groups in the years before they were published as *Pride of the Peak*, and they were carefully copied, along with illustrations, into ramblers' walking journals. One young working-class rambler, George Willis Marshall, transcribed a verse about her trespassing ascent of Kinder at winter time, three full years before it was published, evidence of the circulation of her words through Ward, who often walked with young Willis and his friends. Her dauntless spirit in the face of foul weather, but also in the face of her own inner sorrows, provided encouragement to the other ramblers: 'With all the strength that grief has brought, I dare', she wrote of her fears of attempting to climb the 'huge peaty plateau' of Kinder, where walkers often died.

Pride of the Peak

Once it was published in book form, Ward promoted *Pride of the Peak* in his annual *Sheffield Clarion Ramblers Handbooks*, recommending it as a gift 'to a rambler who knows that Derbyshire Dales and moors mean something more than walking so many miles a day'. In another edition of the *Handbook*, he printed an excerpt of her verse on Kinder, calling it 'the first high poem of Kinder ... some day it will be ours, and the lock upon it rusted away'. For her part, Ethel reflected Ward's philosophy in her poems: Ward had long argued that the existence, throughout the Peak, of ancient way markers – old stone crosses, many destroyed by gamekeepers trying to erase age-old rights; stone and timber poles marking the way in case of deep snow; furrows denoting old trackways – were all evidence that travellers had, for centuries, free passage and rights of way across the entirety of the moors. Ethel underlined this in her poetry: 'The packhorse path arises, til a pole/Stands high, that marked the track beneath the snow.' She described the long barrows, the circles of enormous flat stones, the 'many green and weathered burial mounds, with hallowed rings of trees', all across the high moors and the riverside meadows. 'Men lived here', she declared, since the dawn of time, in country that was now fenced off by usurping landlords. But she could still see these early inhabitants of the Peak, and feel their presence, when she slept beside a tranquil river, or beneath a cliff. Sometimes, in her dreams, she saw their spirits mounting from the waters, joining hands and singing.

When it was published in 1926, *Pride of the Peak*, dedicated to the people of Sheffield, received praise in both local and national publications. The London *Westminster Gazette* admired her 'remarkable expression of pantheistic philosophy' and her 'equally remarkable truth of topographical detail', suggesting that this new form of regional poetry should make the capital look to its laurels. The *Sheffield Daily Telegraph*, describing Ethel as 'well-known to Sheffield readers', praised her 'fine poetic sense' as well as her insistence on using local dialect, with words such as 'cruddle' (to cower, bend down), 'franzy' (fresh, wild) and 'punder' (to be blown, or 'whiffed away' by the wind), all translated and preserved in a Glossary at the end. This was all good and gratifying. But by late 1926 Ethel had no more time for poetry.

The 'daring little Sheffield committee', as G. H. B. Ward called it, continued meeting through 1924, 1925 and 1926. It examined proposed new limestone quarries in the hills; it hired, for 100 guineas, an engineering firm to investigate an alternative motor route through the Winnats; it urged local councils to do more about rubbish tipping in local beauty spots. Ethel joined with the Society for the Protection of Ancient Buildings to work to ensure that all the old stone bridges in the Peak District should be scheduled as ancient monuments. Ethel funded the building of a new oak footbridge across the Derwent near Hathersage. She, her brother Alan and sister Gertrude indeed paid all the administrative and secretarial costs of the committee (£250 a year) for its first 13 years. Her father, and then after his death in 1926, her mother, provided meeting and office space at Endcliffe Vale House free of charge for the next 33 years. The committee was Ethel, and Ethel was the committee, and it gave her a reason and purpose to live.

At the end of 1926 a new rural body, with a more campaigning and activist remit than the National Trust, was formed, reflecting the new countryside activism facing down the threat of the motor car and ribbon development along new motor routes. The Council for the Preservation of Rural England, or CPRE, held its inaugural meeting at the Royal Institute of British Architects on 7 December 1926. Comprising all the urban and rural district councils of England, the Town Planning Institute, the Royal Society of Arts, the Commons and Footpaths Preservation Society and the National Trust, the *Times* described it as 'a body of societies and councils ... such as has never before been brought together for a great common purpose'. Ethel, with her notebook and pen, was there, a slight, neat figure, quietly moving among the grand architects and politicians and heads of national organisations. Somehow, she secured an invitation that her little committee should become affiliated to the CPRE, at the body's very first round of inviting associates. Others invited were august, learned and major national organisations: the Ancient Monuments Society, the Linnean Society, the Boy Scouts and Girl Guides Associations, the National Federation of Rambling Clubs, the RSPB. They even spelled Ethel's committee name wrong, listing it as 'the Scenery Preservation Committee', but that it was on there at all, a 12-strong local group from Sheffield, was nothing short of miraculous. 'She had this quietly persuasive way about her', says Jean Smart, who worked with Ethel for over 20 years. 'She could charm the birds from the trees and get people to do anything for her.'

Building footbridges across rivers and campaigning against new roads was all well and good but Ethel and her little society needed something substantial to get their teeth into, to make its mark. Throughout the society's early years, the committee determined its view of the countryside around Sheffield from the evidence it amassed: that the wild open spaces of the Peak were not safe in private hands: hard-up dukes kept selling off small pouches of their estates for buildings and golf courses, or to mineral speculators. The moors and heather, controlled for only one thing, the breeding of grouse, were not being managed well. A survey of trees on the Duke of Rutland's land found that they were in a terrible condition and in urgent need of radical arboriculture and regeneration. To be safe, the land had to be held in public hands, managed for the benefit of all wildlife, and be given special protective status. Looking back at the committee's early years in 1951, Ethel admitted that from the very start, she had always had, as its 'grand purpose', the aim of slowly acquiring parcels of land, merging and overlapping their boundaries like raindrops forming a puddle, in order to protect it under a public shield. But how to do this when the dukes loved their grouse shooting so much? And lo, death and taxes produced the opportunity Ethel was looking for.

The announcement was made in the *Times*, on 30 March, 1927, by estate agent to the aristocracy, John D. Wood and Co., of Grosvenor, London. The advertisement announced that 'by direction of his Grace, the Duke of Rutland', the Longshaw Lodge Estate and its 'well-heathered' shooting drives including Blacka, Clod Hall and Totley moors, supporting 3,000 brace of grouse, in total some 11,400 acres, was on the market. Just six miles from Sheffield, Longshaw was a plum. Accessible by bus and train to Grindleford Station, the wooded slopes led walkers out onto open moorland and the endless horizon, a sea of sphagnum and heather, topped by the rocky plateau of Higger Tor; air to breathe and views as far as the eye could see. The *Manchester Guardian* opined that 'it would be difficult to find in the whole country a more beautiful tract of unspoiled moorland'. G. H. B. Ward and his Clarion Ramblers had been having run-ins with the eighth Duke and his land agents at Longshaw for two decades. Testy letters from the estate office to Ward first denied any access at all, then, thanks to the 'kindness' of his Grace, small parties of fewer than six walkers (no dogs, no cars, no picnics) would be allowed at certain times (three wintry months, January to March) outside the breeding and shooting season if they applied for permission beforehand. The Duke himself was rarely at home, preferring to reside either at his London house or at his other estate at Haddon. 'I do not want it spread broadcast in guidebooks and papers that the drives are in anyway or at any time open to the public', wrote the land agent. 'Parties over six, if met by the keepers, will be liable to be turned back.' And so the ramblers walked at night, or in the dark, or faced down keepers and their dogs to enjoy the rare pleasure of walking into the wild.

On 8 May 1925, the eighth Duke, Lord Henry John Brinsley Manners, died at his London residence, of pleurisy. Already the family finances had come under considerable pressure and the old earl had sold off land in Leicestershire for £500,000 after the First World War. The ninth Duke, Lord John Henry Montagu Manners, still owed a fortune in death duties and so put Longshaw Lodge, its formal gardens, parkland, farms and moors up for auction. It was vital that Ethel and her committee move fast: already some of the parcels of land had been sold and earmarked for development. The prospectus boasted the woodland 'afford[ed] several beautifully placed building sites'. But to buy up even a few hundred acres would cost thousands of pounds the committee didn't have, and time was running out.

A cunning plan was needed. It was now through Ethel's connections, via the Sheffield Educational Settlement and the Sheffield Council of Social Service, whose members, including Ethel, overlapped, that Ethel persuaded Sheffield City Council to buy the vast bulk of the estate. Sheffield was growing, and its inhabitants needed a reliable supply of fresh, clean water. The catchment area of the high moorland just west of the city would be a perfect solution to the problem, Ethel argued. The council would then, through a separate agreement, sell 747 acres, including the Lodge and its grounds, to a body constituted for the purpose of raising the £14,000 needed to buy it, called the Longshaw Committee (Hon. Sec. Ethel Gallimore). This committee would then donate the lodge and land to the National Trust for its safekeeping in perpetuity.

Ethel and her siblings contributed the lion's share of the money, but by the end of 1927 they still needed to find nearly £5,000, and Ethel, wealthy widow though she was, could not bridge the gap alone. She approached everyone she knew and many were indeed helpful. Many others, however, were suspicious, particularly when the stated ultimate plan for the land was to make it openly accessible to everyone, including the 'hatless, yellow-jerseyed, raucous, slung-with-concertinas' working-class youth from the cities, as *The Times* sniffily described the new breed of rambler. What a preposterous idea. When Ethel approached Miss Tozer, the wealthy spinster daughter of a Sheffield steel magnate, for the last £1,000, Miss Tozer exclaimed: 'I'm told you are all *Bolsheviks* – are you?' Despite the setbacks, the money was finally found (with the National Trust finding the last £570), and the deeds to Longshaw were handed over to the National Trust at a short ceremony held at Longshaw on 27 June 1931, at 4.15 pm. Nearly 750 acres of open land for all and anyone. Horizon, oxygen, freedom. It was for Ethel's committee the first major victory. Groups of ramblers, led by G. H. B., organised voluntary working parties of wardens to maintain paths and fences, dig drains and plant trees, a tradition that lasts to this day.

Access battles and mass trespass

As the 1920s rolled into the 1930s, that 'political decade', where extremes of left and of right tore at the delicate fabric of European alliances and domestic politics, even the hills and moors of the Peak were not immune to the vast tectonic movements of political and social thinking. Ideas that Britain's vast wealth of lovely landscapes should be available to more than just farmers and a few grouse-shooting elites began to circulate more widely. An Access to Mountains Bill, giving the public the right to walk across areas of uncultivated moorland and mountains, had been regularly but unsuccessfully introduced by Labour MPs Charles Trevelyan (1928) and Ellen Wilkinson (1931) and the Liberal (later Labour) MP Sir Edward Mallalieu in 1932. The promises made to the men who left the pits and factories of the north to fight in the First World War, that they and their families would enjoy 'Homes fit for Heroes' on their return, appeared to have been broken. There were bread riots and hunger marches, from Cardiff in the west and Jarrow in the north. While some authorities did build new suburbs, these were largely seen to have failed, sprawling and isolated from areas of work, and many people were still living in inner-city slums. From their tenements, they could see, on a sunny day, the mirage of high moors and mountains just a few miles away, but which they weren't allowed to enjoy.

Health surveys of working-class children in the north of England during the 1930s found them to be still 'rickety, pigeon-chested and stunted', and many medical experts prescribed greater access to the tantalising fresh air and scenery on their doorsteps. Papers like *Left News* promoted rambling as a cheap, healthy activity; the *Country Standard 'For Peace and Socialism in the Countryside'* (price one penny), an agricultural paper aimed at farm labourers, like the *Clarion Handbooks* specifically entwined left politics and rambling. The Clarion Ramblers and other working-class walking groups were now joined by the Communist-influenced British Workers Sports Federation, members of which led the famous 1932 Mass Trespass on Kinder Scout, which resulted in five young men receiving what were widely seen as overly harsh sentences for 'riotous assembling' and actual bodily harm (a gamekeeper was injured in the scuffles). G. H. B. Ward, who did not take part in the trespass, described it as a 'brave but badly planned Communist raid'. He and Ethel later tried to broker a truce, in a hotel near Sheffield railway station, between ramblers and moorland owners that would allow certain rights of access, but the landowners doubled down and refused to budge.

'To consider if it is desirable ... to establish one or more National Parks'

Public opinion was demanding the landowners and gamekeepers change their attitude. These new ideas about sharing public access to beautiful, publicly protected landscapes prompted, in 1929, the minority Labour government, under Ramsay Macdonald, to establish the National Park Committee, under the chairmanship of Christopher Addison MP. Its remit was to 'consider if it is desirable and feasible to establish one or more National Parks in Great Britain with a view to the preservation of natural characteristics including flora and fauna and to the improvement of recreational facilities for the people'. Ethel of course saw the opportunity to make her dream for the Peak come true and in 1930 proposed that her society, which had recently changed its name to the Sheffield and Peak District branch of the CPRE, should work towards making the case that the Peak should be a candidate for one of the new National Parks.

The Addison Committee took evidence for two years, from interests on both sides, including local authorities and landowners, as well as rambling and other groups from across the country: the Lake District, Dartmoor, the Norfolk Broads, the Forest of Dean, Snowdonia all made their case. Dovedale, straddling south Derbyshire and north Staffordshire, asked for Ethel's help in preparing their suit, which she happily gave, even though she always felt that Dovedale and the Peak's claim would be stronger if presented as one. The Addison Committee also considered the needs of industry, particularly quarrying and its associated businesses, and whether the countryside around these quarries and mines should be considered too far destroyed already to be deserving of protection. This issue was pivotal in the Peak: already large areas around the town of Buxton were being quarried for the valuable limestone in the ground and now parts of the eastern Peak, in the Hope Valley near Sheffield, were being opened up to the cement industry. The Hope Valley Cement Works, with its puffing chimneys' cloudy excretions visible for miles, had been opened in 1929. Would this monster be enough to derail the Peak's claims?

The Addison Committee's report, published in 1931, made the landmark recommendation that there should indeed be created a series of National Parks, as well as other, regional ones, the latter enjoying a lower level of status, protection and access. Then came the hammer blow for Ethel. The report listed its recommendations for land to be given National Park status: the Lake District, Snowdonia, the Cornish coast, Pembrokeshire coast, the Norfolk Broads, South Downs and Dovedale. The Forest of Dean, in Gloucestershire, should too have a form of special protection. In the secondary, regional category, the report recommended Cannock Chase, the Forest of Bowland and 'the high Peak' area of Derbyshire, representing a fraction of the land that Ethel dreamed of comprising the Peak District National Park.

It was a victory for the grouse-shooting dukes, the cement industries who eyed the Peak's limestone deposits with acquisitive glee, and the Dovedale campaigners who had rejected Ethel's suggestions that the Peak and Dovedale should combine forces to make their case stronger. This was a severe betrayal. To rub salt into her wounds, for the next few years Ethel could barely open a paper without reading a letter, opinion piece or column by Frederick F. A. Holmes, who spearheaded Dovedale's case, crowing about the valley's cause. That Dovedale was beautiful was beyond doubt, but their park plan was for a paltry *16 square miles*, whereas the Peak's proposed area was more than 500 square miles. What could that tiny patch of countryside, so mean and low in its aspirations, offer the people of Sheffield and Manchester and the other industrial towns, for recreation and natural beauty in the heart of England? This wasn't about access, it was about one man's vanity, and appeasing the landowners. But the fight was not over yet, not nearly. Successive government crises during the 1930s, the financial slump and then the growing shadow of another war forced the shelving of the National Parks idea for two decades. Ethel carefully removed her gloves and began, quietly but determinedly, to fight.

Wangari: the Aberdares, Kansas and Nairobi, 1940–77

'Watch Mary Jo! She's going to do something special one day'

The 1930s marched towards war with a terrible inevitability. This time the conflict that broke over humanity's head affected every corner of the globe. Even where there was no actual fighting, its violence and privations were felt. Deep in the folded green foothills of the Aberdare (*Nyandarua*) Mountains in central Kenya, a young Kikuyu girl watched great walls of dark grey smoke churning up into the sky above the forest. It was a sight she would never forget. The colonial administration, in need of more agricultural land, military camps and timber for the war effort, approved the clearing and felling of large sections of forest: millions upon millions of tons of wood were cut during the 1940s. Trees over 100 feet tall, stinkwood, ironwood, dizzying *newtoniae* with their flaring buttressed trunks; the figs, their braided roots curling above and below ground, and all embroidered with liana vines, were being cleared. The British army, fighting in north Africa, and later, Burma (Myanmar), needed to be fed. European farmers, in control of much of the best agricultural land in the central highlands, lobbied the government in Nairobi hard to be able to plant more acres of maize, wheat, pyrethrum daisies and sorghum. Plantations of tea, coffee and sesame expanded, bright green waves rippling across the hills. The soil of central Kenya: rich, dark red, fertile, that had provided everything required for animal and early human life, was in trouble.

The first species of *Homo* appeared and lived near the East African Rift, longer than anywhere else in history, hunting and eating the lush natural pantry for nearly 2 million years. Still, a European visitor in 1893 saw a 'country of teeming abundance where in a few days I obtained many thousand pounds of food'. For millennia the pastoralists, hunter-gatherers and farmers had lived lightly on the land, keeping the fragile balance between rain, soil, flora and fauna that had, miraculously, nurtured our species in its most delicate, newborn state. For thousands of years the glaciers on Mount Kenya covered its summit, shining in the equatorial sun. The Kikuyu called it *Kirinyaga*, or *Kireira*, 'mountain of whiteness', or 'place of brightness', and believed their God, *Ngai*, lived there, providing his people with all the abundance the land gave them.

The farming Kikuyu had cut the forest with their hand tools, to create fields and homesteads, moving on when the soil became exhausted, but their population was small and they were careful to retain large areas untouched, for protection from other tribes and for a home for their God. Then came the Europeans, down from the north, and up from South Africa. By the end of the first decade of the twentieth century, Europeans had occupied more than a quarter of a million acres of forested land, much of which they cleared for farmsteads. Thirsty eucalyptus, or blue gums, were deliberately placed in marshy areas to soak up the water and dry out the soil, to prepare the land for commercial crops. Those marshes were the source of the shining mesh of lakes and rivers that encircled the Aberdares, and were the liquid larders for a host of wild mammals, birds and insects. By 1960, 2 million acres of formerly open grassland had been enclosed in paddocks. The trees, whose root systems anchored the land, whose fallen leaves were the source of the rich, brown hummus, and whose great green moist mass captured the precious rains, began to disappear faster. The Christian missionaries, too, had played their part, targeting for destruction the sacred fig trees beneath which the Kikuyu worshipped *Ngai*. If the fig trees were no more, so thought the missionaries, then the Kikuyu would worship the Christian God.

Before the outbreak of the Second World War the colonial administrators had begun to notice, and to worry and measure. Lakes and rivers were silting up; the soil was drying and cracking. The colonial administration created Crown Forest reserves, developed tree nurseries to supply the plantations of eucalyptus and cypress, and appointed a Conservator of Forests, but always in the balance between conservation on the one hand, and the commercial needs of the colony on the other, the latter came first. The Europeans were, in fact, very careless with Kenya's precious forestry resources. The 572-mile-long Mombasa to Uganda railway, opened in 1901 and instrumental in the settling of the so-called White Highlands, initially ran on Kenyan firewood. By the outbreak of the First World War the locomotives were guzzling more than 50,000 tons of wood a year. Although coal was brought in from South Africa to give added power to the mainline engines, branch lines still ran on wood until 1955. It was a standing joke among railway men that if you were working on a bend when the train was coming, you stood well away in case you got hit by a carelessly loaded log flying off the fuel truck. The boilermen complained that on the uphill haul west of Nairobi the engine consumed so much wood it was like the entire forest of Kenya was flying up the chimney. The settlers, of course, blamed the irresponsible Africans for overgrazing and for refusing to take part in hillside terrace construction to slow the escape of water. Recent studies, however, that have measured soil samples going back decades, have dated the beginning of significant erosion to the early years of the twentieth century when the settlers began to arrive in large numbers.

The young Wangari Muta, who watched the grey smoke roiling up over that wall of green and loved to see the wind blow across the Europeans' wheat fields, which 'stretched as far as my little eyes could see', did not yet know of the ecological time bomb that men like Mr Neylan, whose farm she lived on until she was seven, had planted. How could she know that after that time bomb exploded, when soil erosion, failing rains and deforestation would threaten human and animal life in Kenya, she would start a movement that would plant millions of trees, return the damaged land to the wild and help arrest Kenya's slide into desert. What would she have thought if someone had told her that when she was older, planting saplings would be seen as an act of civil disobedience. Back then, she stood in the long grass, a bunch of sweet yellow *managu* berries in her hand, a load of firewood on her back, and marvelled at the wind as it chased across the endless field of golden wheat.

For the first few years of her life, Wangari Muta, born in April 1940, lived on a settler farm at Nakuru District, in the Great Rift Valley, with her brothers, sisters and mother. Wangari's father, Muta Njugi, a distant but kindly figure. with other wives and children, drove trucks and tractors for Mr Neylan on the farm. Wangari, the eldest daughter, helped her mother Wanjiru Kibicho in their homestead, looked after the younger children and listened as her mother told the Kikuyu folk stories, rolling back through the fog of time and memory when ogres and dragons stalked the forests hunting for children to eat or girls to marry. She learned such morals as to share some of the grain she grew with the wild birds, otherwise they would punish her and that if anything was done to displease God, then the rains would fail and the people would go hungry. Nature and man were in delicate balance.

When she was seven, Wangari, with her mother, moved back to her mother's family's home, the village of Ihithe in the foothills of the Aberdares near Nyeri. It was a strange and wonderful shock, to move from the hot plains of Nakuru to Ihithe, where the earth was so moist she could scoop up balls of it and work it, almost like clay. When she rubbed it between her hands, 'you could almost feel the life it held'. Here 'the landscape [was] full of different shades of green, all springing from soil the colour of deep terracotta – smooth and dark and richly fertile, but mostly hidden behind the mass of wet, fresh vegetation'. Beyond the homesteads 'was the thick, deep green of the Aberdare Forest', an apparently endless tree canopy, loud with the shouts of monkeys and the calls of the birds: silvery-cheeked hornbills and the red and blue Turacos.

Wangari's brothers attended the local Presbyterian-run primary school and Wangari stayed at home to help her mother. By now she was walking several miles each day to collect fallen branches and twigs from the stands of trees left uncut by the Kikuyu farmers. The Kikuyu had a sacred relationship with the forest and preserved patches of the old wild where the buffalo, leopards and elephants still lived, among the Nandi flame trees, pepperbarks and acacia. Wangari also tended her own small field of sweet potatoes, beans, maize and millet on a pocket of land given to her by her mother. Her curious nature however was already beginning to show, and she would lift the tiny seedlings out of the soil and gaze, fascinated at the split husks and the curled, waxy monocotyledons and dicotyledons; those fine hairy filaments on the semi-translucent roots, branching and bifurcating in their endless quest for moisture. When the maize cobs ripened, she watched delightedly as the birds flew down and pecked the grain. When her beans flowered, her little field was a ceaseless sea of insects. She loved the land and felt a deep kinship with it. Her favourite time of day to tend her little plot was dusk, when a light breeze signalled the sun's descent. She would only stop weeding when it was so dark that she could no longer tell the difference between weed and seedling and then she would make her way home through the steep ravines to the noise of the rivers and streams as they raced along the valley floor to join the Gura River. Climbing out of the shady gullies and onto the ridge where her home stood, she was greeted by a sky 'exploding with stars and the Milky Way spread across the heavens'.

In the daytime she would play by the little streams, 'narrow, fast-moving and clear … the water made a whooshing sound as it hurtled over the stones on the riverbed'. The streams seemed, miraculously, to spring from the roots of the wild fig trees, the huge Migumo (*Ficus natalensis*) with 'bark the colour of elephant skin' and a dense canopy. The Kikuyu revered the fig trees and never cut them, and, even in the cultivated areas, every so often an arboreal giant would provide shade and fruit for humans and animals alike. An abiding memory was her mother's admonishment to never collect firewood from the fig. 'This is a tree of God', she told her daughter. 'We don't cut it, we don't burn it, we don't use it. They live for as long as they can, and they fall on their own when they are too old.' The fig trees' roots broke through the rocks below and springs would bubble up, eventually forming streams where frogs would live and once a year the water was full of the slippery, pearlescent eggs that the young Wangari tried to catch to make a necklace with. And then the teeming black tadpoles that broke through the jelly, wriggling specks that eventually and miraculously would begin to sprout limbs. She spent her happiest childhood days by those streams, she would later say, learning about metamorphosis and the life-cycle of amphibians without even knowing it.

It was a chance question from her older brother Nderitu, who asked her mother why Wangari, clearly as sharp and bright as her brothers, didn't go to school like he did that prompted her mother to reply: 'There's no reason why not.' Nderitu's question changed the course of her life. Her uncle agreed to pay the fees and so, at eight years old, Wangari Muta walked the three miles each way to the primary school with its beaten earth floor, mud walls and tin roof, where she learned her letters, and numbers, then maths, Kiswahili and geography. When she was 11, she started to learn English.

The young Wangari was studious and exact. Her mother said she was like her grandmother, an organisational powerhouse, collecting her firewood and crops in neat piles by the side of the fields when other children would throw them down any old how. She worked hard, did all her homework, passed her primary school exams with top marks as well as making time to tend her plot and help her mother. In September 1952, a 12-year-old Wangari walked, barefoot, to Saint Cecilia's Intermediate School at the Mathari Catholic Mission on Nyeri Hill, which was run by Italian nuns. The building was of stone and during the winter the cold damp walls made life miserable, but she came top of the class again. She did so well at her intermediate school that again, breaking with tradition, she was selected to attend a secondary boarding school run by Catholic nuns, where she encountered science, and where all those observations of plants and animals she had made as a child found name and form. Her grades ensured she gained a place at the selective Loreto Girls' High School, Limuru, where she came top of her year every year for each of the four years she attended, but she still had time to learn the jigs the Irish nuns taught her.

The boarding schools were quiet places of study and safe havens from the violence outside their cold stone walls. This was the time of the Mau Mau insurgency (1952–1960) against British occupation. The British responded with a brutality that still haunts modern Kenya, torturing and executing thousands of Mau Mau fighters and causing the death by disease and starvation of hundreds of thousands of Kenyans through their 'villagisation' policy. The British forcibly moved Wangari's mother, with her younger children, to one of these 'emergency villages', where they lived for seven years, unable to return to their home and land. Wangari learned to fear the British as well as the Mau Mau. The British arrested and interned her in a camp while she was on her way to visit her father.

Now it was the turn of the British to associate the forest with the wild, barbaric, even demonic, men of the insurgency. Good Africans stayed in the barbed wire-encircled villages, or so the British propaganda would have it. These villages were cut off from the forest by trenches 50 miles long, 10 feet deep and 16 feet wide. Within these villages, women and children were domesticated, visible, watched. The forest was painted as the primordial, savage space of the Mau Mau, the bad men who lurked in the shadows, made blood sacrifices, raped young girls. The nuns apparently however hadn't read the colonial information office's memos. During Mau Mau raids Wangari and the other young women were sent to hide *in* the forest, which the nuns considered safer than in the buildings: 'we would be rushed to the bushes whenever we heard anything'. Once, from her hiding place, she watched a leopard, illuminated by the moon, pass silently by the group of girls and a sleeping baby. Under-growth, thickets, forest, the dense wild places on the boundaries of so-called civilisation represented for these young girls not the dangers suggested in myths or colonial propaganda, but a bower of protecting greenery.

Undeterred and ever committed to her studies, Wangari graduated top of her year at Loreto Girls' High School, passing the Cambridge School Certificate with a First Division. But graduating top of her year, for a girl in 1950s Kenya, was a problem. Clever girls were viewed with suspicion. She refused to con-template the only two acceptable professional paths open to women at the time: nursing or teaching. The organisms of the natural world still held fascina-tion for her, and she wanted to study further. She wanted to go on to higher education, initially to study chemistry, but how?

There was only one university in East Africa at the time, Makerere in Uganda, and, like Oxford and Cambridge, its shining possibilities were far from the grasp of a young Kikuyu girl who had grown up tending maize and millet. Of the 630 students who studied there in 1955, only 63 were from Kenya, and none of them were women. By 1960 just one Kenyan woman had graduated from Makerere. Women were not supposed to study beyond school. They were the backbone of Kenyan farming society: they tended the crops in the field, fetched water and firewood, cooked and looked after children. They were kept deliberately under-educated. But Wangari was determined and confident, and a miraculous confluence of events, combining Britain's withdrawal from its colonies, an Irish-American senator's philanthropy and a Kenyan trade unionist's ingenious idea, provided the opportunity she had hoped for.

On 15 September 1960, Wangari found herself on an aeroplane taxiing across the tarmac at Nairobi airport. Thousands of people had turned up to wave off the aircraft and its cargo of a hopeful future. It was the Year of Africa, with no fewer than 17 sub-Saharan countries gaining independence from their colonial masters, and Kenya's freedom would not be long in coming. Wangari was about to make the then four-day journey, in a regularly stopping twin-prop, to New York via Benghazi, Libya, then north to Luxembourg and Reykjavik, Iceland, before crossing the Atlantic. She had, along with 287 other students (53 of whom were women), joined the 1960 'Kennedy Airlift'. The plan was instigated in 1959 by then US Senator John F. Kennedy and Kenyan nationalist and trade unionist Tom Mboya to educate the future leaders of a soon-to-be-independent Kenya. The country would need civil servants, engineers, lawyers, university lecturers, medics, as well as politicians, once the British withdrew. It was also the height of the Cold War and better that young African brains be shaped and educated in America than in the USSR or its satellites. Several thousand Kenyan students did also travel to other countries for their higher education, including the Eastern bloc, USSR, India and western Europe, but it would be the ones who studied in America that would take up the plum jobs when they returned after *uhuru* (freedom).

As she sat on the plane, Wangari saw the grasslands of northern Kenya give way to the scrub of the Sahel and the sands of the Sahara. She would later discover how her country was at the very limits of habitation, a liminal region, despite the snows of Mount Kenya and the dripping green forests of the Aberdare range. Those northern grasslands, fading from green to gold; the acacia trees becoming ever more sparse and stunted; north of Kenya and Lake Turkana, the rivers and lakes dwindling to isolated watering holes. Soon the hardy Tamarisk and the miraculous *Maerus*, a small, twisted evergreen apparently living off dust and air, were the only trees to be seen; the great herds of the grasslands – elephant, wildebeest, zebra – diminished to the occasional oryx and dama gazelle. And then came the sands, that vast expanse of dead land: the plane, it seemed, slowly crawled across them for hours and hours. At one point Wangari fell asleep, and when she woke up, hours later, the endless yellow windblown dunes were still there below.

The Sahara was, in the 1960s, expanding, pushing north and south as the rains failed across the Sahel and human activity extracted every last nutrient from its dusty margins. The desert was once covered in Mediterranean forest: holm oak, juniper, the aromatic mastic; home to myriad species of flora and fauna, as well as herding pastoralists. But over a period of several thousand years, it had dried out and through the twentieth century it would expand by more than 270,000 square miles, mostly through its southward creep across the drying Sahel towards Kenya. But the young student, in 1960, wasn't turned on to ecology, yet. Progress and modernity excited her. In an article she wrote for the *Mount Mirror*, her American college magazine, she would praise the new oil and steel refineries, the manufacturing, the cement works springing up across Kenya. These were all signs that Africa was no longer 'the dark continent', she insisted, but a forward-looking region of growing numbers of independent nations capable of self-governance, although the horrors of the slave trade were still alive in people's memory.

America

After landing in New York, it was a two-day journey by Greyhound bus across the central states, where at one stopover diner operators refused to allow the young Africans to drink Coca-Cola inside their premises and so they went thirsty. Her final stop was Atchison, Kansas, a bustling town sitting on a wide, slow bend of the great Missouri River, part-way along its gargantuan journey from the Rockies to the Gulf of Mexico. Mount Saint Scholastica College (now merged with Benedictine College) was a Catholic institution in a campus of elegant red-brick Victorian houses, with their interior and exterior grandeur still intact, and a later large administration (the 'Ad.') building, with gardens flowing around them and shaded by hickory, black walnut and sugar maples. Wangari, and fellow Kenyan Agatha Wangeci who arrived with her, also on a scholarship, were two of only five black women students at the college. It would be her home for four utterly transformative years, sheltered and nurtured by the Benedictine nuns, whose order had established a convent there in 1863.

Always open to new experiences, Wangari straightened her hair using a hot comb, visited Washington D. C. and toured the White House. She learned American country music and performed for the astonished other girls the

5.1 Wangari c. 1960s

Irish jigs she had learned from the nuns in Kenya. She watched the celebrations in Nairobi as Kenya gained independence from British rule in December 1963 and Jomo Kenyatta, once imprisoned by the British, became Prime Minister. She watched, on television, again and again, the news of Kennedy's assassination, after which the college was closed for several days, leaving only Wangari and Agatha and other foreign students on a campus quiet and in mourning. In the close, sweltering summers she took a job at a Kansas City hospital, assisting in the tissue-processing laboratory; she learned dexterity with the microscope and how to spot tiny cellular changes that signalled disease. She went for walks along the Missouri's wind-blown bluffs, watching the busy tugs and barges along the river. The trees were sensational. The maples, when they lost their leaves in the first autumn she arrived, were so different from the ever-green trees of Kenya, which shed uniformly throughout the year. Wangari was amazed at the colours: magenta, rose madder, russet, yellow and copper, lying in colourful piles around the college gardens and along the riverbanks.

During a class in Wangari's first December, it started to snow, slowly and silently outside the classroom window, the huge and multi-structured flakes making the air white as they fell to the ground. For the rest of the lesson she stared, transfixed, at the quiet silting of barely frozen, crystalline shapes, until the bell rang and she flew down the steps to the lawn below and held out her arms, face upturned to the heavens. 'I will never forget her excitement at the snow', says Florence Conrad Salisbury, her best friend at the college. Florence and I are talking on a rather poor Zoom connection; she's coughing a lot because the smoke from the Canadian fires of summer 2023 has travelled hundreds of miles and infiltrated into her home in McLean, Virginia. The irony that, during this catastrophic heatwave that is destroying millions of trees, we're talking about a woman who tried to prevent ecological collapse by planting them, isn't lost on us.

'I will never forget Wangari seeing snow falling for the very first time', she says. 'We were sitting in class when big, lush, white flakes began to fall. She could hardly contain herself as more and more fell faster and faster. The instant the class dismissed she dashed from the room, down the steps, and out the front door of the Ad. Building, scooping up snow, throwing it in the air, rubbing it onto her face and arms, squealing with delight. It is one of my happiest memories.' Florence's eyes light up as she describes her new friend's wonder. Wangari wanted to examine the snow, play in it, feel it on her skin: responding to the natural world with a perfect combination of delight and scientific inquiry. During the holidays Wangari stayed with the Conrad family, learning to bake using an oven rather than open fire. Florence's mother, Mildred, with whom she formed a special bond, sent her banana bread and cookies during term time.

Wangari's own mother couldn't write, so they communicated via letters she wrote to her brother Nderitu, now a schoolteacher in Kenya. At the Mount she majored in biology, learned micro-anatomy and how to use the latest biochemistry equipment, including a photoelectric colorimeter that tested the glucose concentration in blood. She also studied government, speech, zoology, religion, psychology, German and English, and many other subjects. She acquired not only the skills and qualifications to equip her for a life in the sciences, but also a steadfastness and self-reliance that would see her through her darkest days of persecution that lay ahead. In a letter she wrote to the nuns in the 1990s she acknowledged this. She told them that what she admired in the nuns was that they were 'people who do not lose sight of their goal and their purpose', even when challenges and obstacles try to throw them off their path. She was grateful for their stability: 'I have gone through so much and yet you are still there, steadfast and unchanging', she wrote, adding: 'Your prayers have sustained me and have gave [sic] me light along my paths when all else was dark.'

Sister Thomasita Homan was a young nun at the Mount completing her teacher training, and just a year older than Wangari. She watched Wangari, rarely seen without a book in her hands, sitting on a bench under a large sugar maple near the dorm. Sister Thomasita first heard of the new Kenyan student, apparently so much at home, so far from home, through her biology teacher, Sister John Marie Brazzel, who told her: 'Watch Mary Jo! [Mary Jo was the Catholic name she chose on confirmation] She's going to do something special someday!' Years later, when Sister Thomasita became Alumni Director, she remembered the bright, studious and enthusiastic young Kenyan who was making a name for herself by planting thousands of trees and advocating for women's rights, and tried to trace her to award her their annual prize for most outstanding alumna. But by then, Wangari was in hiding, an exile in her own country.

Florence Conrad Salisbury remembers a diligent, studious and mature young woman, with a huge sense of fun, who was either to be found in the library, biology laboratory or on a bench in the gardens, sunning herself. 'She loved to be out of doors and she would go on long walks through the gardens and out into the fields, when she came to stay with us', says Florence, who was studying elementary education, and who later became a teacher. 'Whether in a tiny room or huge auditorium, she would light it up; she was fearless, always stood up for what she believed and would never back down. Later during the Moi years, I was terrified for her safety; some days I would become overwhelmed with concern, just knowing something was wrong, and I would hear the news that she had been imprisoned again, or beaten up and my heart would break for her. I wrote and wrote but she never got a single letter from me.' After graduating with a BSc in Biology, Wangari won a further scholarship to study for a Master's at the University of Pittsburgh, in Pennsylvania. There she refined and specialised her investigations into cellular anatomy. She spent her time looking inwards, at life's smallest yet most complex building blocks, at cells on microscope slides, her fascination for the natural world a long, unbroken connection from those days as a child when she watched frogs' eggs turn into tadpoles in the stream under the fig tree near her home.

As well as learning through studying her academic subjects, the young student also learned something of protest and campaigning. This was 1960s

America and the country was ablaze over the civil rights movement. She watched images of the Freedom Riders being attacked on their tour of the southern states, the March on Washington and Martin Luther King's immortal 'I have a dream' speech. Although Atchison was a segregated town, she was protected from racial harassment in the small, close-knit college, which was more like a family to her, the nuns her sisters, mothers, friends. Later she would say that although at the time she watched and read about these events of the civil rights movement with a kind of semi-detachment, she realised they were sowing a seed deep within her, about her sense of justice and respect for human rights. 'What you are observing, what you are reading, what you are seeing influences you, sometimes in your subconscious and I'm quite sure that the civil rights movement … greatly influenced my sense of justice, my sense of the need to respect human rights, my sense of respecting the rule of law.'

Wangari would say that being removed from her society for nearly six formative years gave her a certain independence of thought and a greater propensity to question authority than many of her fellow Kenyans. 'You suddenly see it, and you see it so clearly, so you're passionate about it, and sometimes people here don't understand what burns you.' She was not starry eyed about the US, however. How could she be about a country that refused her a Coca-Cola in a diner because of the colour of her skin? She also returned to Kenya wary of extreme radicalism. Her one experience of this came when she attended, at a colleague's suggestion, a Nation of Islam meeting in Kansas. Wangari, a devout Catholic and a stickler for accuracy, was shocked by what she heard: that Jesus had attended the University of Alexandria and had lived for several years in Africa. She learned that just because people shouted about their beliefs and grievances, it didn't always mean that they were right.

Back to Africa

As she completed her Master's dissertation, scouts from the new independent administration in Kenya visited her in Pennsylvania. It was time for the Airlift students to come home to fulfil their unspoken contract to be the backbone and energising force for the new Kenya as it faced the task of building a nation after years of colonialism. She was offered a post as Research Assistant to a Professor of Zoology at University College Nairobi (later the University of Nairobi) and returned to Kenya in January 1966, brimming with confidence and excitement, thinking 'the sky is the limit for me'. It never occurred to her that the multiple ills of sexism, ethnic rivalry and corruption would derail her dreams. During those early post-independence years, Kenya, and particularly Nairobi, the beautiful 'Green City in the Sun', were intoxicating in their promise for the newly returned graduates. Getting a good job in the civil service, academia, the media or commerce 'was largely a matter of showing up', said one returnee. One Airlift graduate, Hilary Boniface Ng'weno, who returned from Harvard to take up editorship of the *Daily Nation* newspaper, recalled later, 'You could literally choose what job you wanted.' He should, of course, have added the caveat, 'If you were a man.'

Women's subjugated status in Kenyan society was woven into the fabric of custom and culture. A handful of women arriving with their university degrees and western qualifications was not going to change much, perhaps for decades. On the morning Wangari presented herself at the College, employment letter in hand, she was told the post was filled and the letter not valid. The job had gone to a man, of the same tribe as the Professor. It was an utterly bewildering moment, forcing her to confront the vast gulf between her optimism and reality. She did, after several months, gain a post in the smaller and less prestigious Department of Veterinary Sciences. As well as working as a research assistant, and later teaching as an assistant lecturer, she studied for a PhD investigating the anatomy of bull testes and in 1971 became the first Kenyan woman to be awarded a doctorate. In a revealing citation for her much later honorary doctorate, conferred by the University of Nairobi in 2005 and perhaps acknowledging its own role in her earlier mistreatment, the anonymous author wrote: 'Professor Maathai's life has been one of many firsts and though her entire life has sparkled with them, *there are many who, for long, never appreciated the glitter.*'

In 1969 she married Mwangi Mathai, former Director of the Kenya branch of Colgate-Palmolive and now a political activist concerned particularly about the problem of male unemployment in postcolonial Kenya. Wangari supported his successful campaigning to become an MP in the 1974 elections. She continued veterinary studies, into East Coast Fever, spread by ticks, in cattle. They had three children, Waweru, their eldest son, Wanjira, a daughter, and their youngest son, Muta; they set up home in a shady compound on the Lenana Road, and later the slightly grander Kabarnet Road in Nairobi and for a while it looked as though she might settle down into the routine of mother, politician's wife and academic. History had other ideas, however.

What first spurred her to action was not the environment, but the way women were treated at the University. Wangari was only one of two, and later three, women academics at the University and the new female lecturers were paid less than their male colleagues, and not given University accommodation or health benefits. A sense of injustice erupted and she understood that she was not the kind of person meekly to accept such blatant unfairness. Wangari joined the Association of University Women of Kenya, established just before she returned from the States and part of a network of thousands of women's groups across the country, all agitating for greater equality. Kenya's women had quickly realised that independence 'did not translate into social and economic improvement' for them and their children. By 1978 there were more than 8,200 women's groups across Kenya, with more than 326,000 members, with interests ranging from neonatal health, girls' education and community finance, to business and farming. Two umbrella groups, the National Council of Women of Kenya (NCWK) and *Maendeleo ya Wanawake* ('Women's Progress') acted as apex groups, amplifying women's voices and forcing the Kenyatta government to listen to their concerns. Wangari joined the NCWK with her eye on agitating for better working conditions for women academics. It was 1974 and women across the world were preparing for the first United Nations Women's Conference in Mexico, held in 1975. The NCWK met to discuss the items they would like to propose for the agenda and it was at this point that a truth struck her. As well as professional women, there were representatives from rural women's groups across the country at the meeting. When she heard their stories, her problems at the University appeared nothing so much as 'trivial minutiae'. She wanted a pay rise. They were asking for the means to life itself.

'They were asking for water. They were asking for food. They were asking for energy, which was mainly firewood. And they were saying they have no income.' Most shocking to Wangari, many of the women who spoke at the meeting came from the Aberdare Highlands, where she had grown up. They arrived, malnourished and exhausted, from that land where, as a child, she had fetched good, pure drinking water from a nearby stream, where the great Migumo trees provided shade, springs and a habitat for her beloved tadpoles. 'It struck me that in that period of less than ten years, so much change had taken place in the environment, that water was no longer clean ... all these wood lots had been cleared away for tea and coffee ... the stream where I used to play with tadpoles dried up, and the fig tree that my mother had talked about had been cut to make way for tea.' What had happened?

After Kenya became an independent nation in 1963, colonial values and policies were not 'turned off like a light switch'. Many Europeans kept the top jobs in the civil service, that had been designed to engineer the whole country to operate in favour of Europeans over Africans. The new nationalist government continued to pursue the export-oriented agricultural policies of the colonial government. Jomo Kenyatta's priority was growth, rather than social justice and redistribution. Foreign investors and multinational corporations were encouraged to stay, even as thousands of white settlers fled. Of the more than 1 million acres of Kenyan farmland that had changed hands since independence, 70 per cent was bought by Europeans and elite, land-rich Kenyans. Kenyan commercial farmers planted more and more tea and coffee: low-growing smooth bright green waves following the denuded contours of the hills where once towered trees. The Kenyatta administration urged small-scale farmers to intensify production, to plant 'an extra row of maize, work an extra hour a day, plant the recommended seed and follow the advice of the agricultural officer'.

Deforestation continued apace under both Kenyatta and his successor Daniel arap Moi, so that by the late twentieth century just 2 per cent of Kenya's land mass was classified as virgin forest, well below the UN-advised minimum of 10 per cent needed to preserve ecosystems and protect humans and animals alike from pollution and desertification. Habitats that once brewed soups of pollinators literally vanished. Levees that used to run clear silted up. When it rained the 'topsoil left the land in red streams, tens of thousands of tons flowing irretrievably into the Indian Ocean'. The wild was in retreat. The forest, the source of life, legends and the resting place of the Kikuyu god, was disappearing.

It was then, with the combined influence of her biological science back-ground, her understanding of the Kikuyu connection with nature and the over-layering of Christian morality, that Wangari realised several things at once. She saw that extractive, commercial farming practices, the immorality of landowners not recognising their responsibility to either the land or its people, and the loss of connection between humans and the natural world had wrought this ecological disaster on her once-fertile homeland. She also saw that women were the key to reversing the disaster, but that social, political and religious conditioning had rendered them powerless and stripped of agency. They walked further for increasingly unclean water; they worked harder for decreasing harvests and watched their children suffer and die from lack of nutritious food.

Along with women from several other groups, including the colonial-era Women's Guild, Wangari formed a sub-committee of the NCWK to promote environmental protection and local employment through planting trees: trees that would anchor the soil, provide shade, attract birds and insects, and also, if the right varieties were chosen, provide fruit to add to the women's and their family's nutrition. She invited her friend and fellow academic Vert Mbaya to join the committee, which she did. Vert, a biochemist, would shortly be 'digging holes in the dirt under the hot sun' on their various early tree-planting forays, the beginning of her own involvement with the Green Belt Movement (GBM) that would last the next half-century. 'She could get people to do anything', laughs Vert over her 'kinda crazy' and crackling phone line. 'But we always had fun doing it.'

Not really knowing where it would lead, and always the questing scientist, Wangari formed a company, Envirocare, initially to help find jobs as gardeners for Nairobi's unemployed. She started experimenting at home, with tins that she drilled holes in the base of, soil and tree seeds. Turning the compound of the family home into a miniature botanical laboratory, she collected seedlings from the Karura Forest at the northern edge of Nairobi, a remnant of the 'super-forest' that once covered most of highland central Kenya, working out which species thrived best. Her daughter, Wanjira Mathai, remembers home when she was seven and eight years old, as 'being surrounded by vegeta- tion ... we filled our compound with trees and shrubs, she was constantly planting'. The Kenya Forest Department, which was responsible for Karura, allowed Wangari to use part of their tree nursery to propagate and nurture seedlings. She would walk the forest paths, out of the city and into the wild, to her patch of nursery alongside the rushing Karura River. As she had done as a child when she walked to her field of maize and sweet potatoes, she carried her tools and seedlings with her, feeling the red mud underneath her fingernails once more. When she took her children into the forest with her and it rained, she would say: 'Look, we are not wet, and all the rain is getting caught by the trees' leaves and then it will trickle slowly down the trunk into the belly of the earth ... and [come] back to us as rain.' Wanjira says: 'I found that beautiful, beautifully symbolic of just how much work our trees do for us.'

The early 1970s saw not just the birth of the modern women's movement, but also the environmental movement, at the UN Conference on the Human Environment in Stockholm in 1972, where for the first time the idea of human rights was linked to the health of the environment. The conference declared that an adequate environment 'of a quality that permits a life of dignity and wellbeing' was a fundamental human right. This was exactly what Wangari saw lacking in those malnourished children and the women who walked so

5.2 Karura Forest

far for such poor-quality water, and her ground-breaking ideas meshed with those of the early environmentalists.

Nairobi at this time, still forming in the tumult of post-independence, was an exciting place, 'a melting pot of ideas'. The city grew rapidly after *uhuru* as it became a major regional hub and Africans returned home to begin the job of nation building. The *New York Times* East Africa correspondent described it in 1967, the year after Wangari returned: 'tall hotels and modern office buildings have sprouted from an underbrush of close-packed Indian shops and tin-roofed shacks, and African policemen direct the choking traffic with cool efficiency'. Kenyatta, now President, encouraged indigenous music, dance and literature. He also pulled in foreign investment, attracting multinationals and their employees, so although many Europeans had left immediately after 1963, many now came in and out on short-term contracts.

Development and concern for the environment were part of this mix, and several environment-focused organisations set up in Nairobi under United Nations Environment Programme direction, including the Environment Liaison Centre (ELC), in the wake of Stockholm, to promote conservation and environmentally friendly development in sub-Saharan Africa. Oscar Mann, Kenyan-born son of European professionals, a veterinarian and architect, and who had been working in various technical and environmental projects in Nairobi in the early 1970s, was asked to be Director of the ELC. He accepted immediately and set up in a small one-room office near the old Post Office in central Nairobi.

Desertification and deforestation were urgent problems in Kenya. The *Daily Nation,* one of the country's leading newspapers, was full of stories of illegal charcoal burning that cleared whole forests in months; and of the concomitant flash floods, mudslides and then dried up riverbeds that were the direct and visible consequences of a forest suddenly vanishing. Schools and churches encouraged their local communities to conserve what was left. Wangari's elder brother, Nderitu, now headmaster of Kianyaga High School, organised the children to plant grass, flowers and trees into the once-bare and dusty schoolyard until it had become a 'green oasis' alive with butterflies and bees. It was into this fast-moving stream of ideas, talk and action that Wangari, at first cautiously, dipped her toe. She and Oscar met through the network of environmental meetings and discussions taking place across the capital: she was struggling to establish her tree-growing and -planting business, he was looking for a local manager, and she joined, initially on a voluntary basis. '[He] literally drafted me into the Environment Movement … a whole different world opened up to me', she later said. Oscar Mann remembers his new colleague as 'a calm and quiet lady with a lot of energy that could become fiery. She was very good at directing people.' Her knowledge of biology, too, was vital in the ELC's work on biodiversity.

Wangari attended the United Nations Habitat Conference in Vancouver in 1976, where she met and networked with other women from across the world, all concerned with the unchecked growth of cities, seeing the need to create green spaces and protect forests on their edges. In the cool green surroundings of Vancouver, mixing with leading women thinkers, including the anthropologist Margaret Mead, the economist Barbara Ward and Mother Theresa of Calcutta, provided, she later wrote, 'just the tonic I needed' after weeks of struggling to water seedlings and trying to get her Envirocare business off the ground. She returned from Vancouver heady with excitement at the possibilities of the growing consensus around the centrality of the environment to all human endeavour, and how she would expand her tree-planting plan, not just in down-at-heel parts of Nairobi, but on forest margins and, in bands a thousand trees wide, on the boundaries of Kenyan farms, providing shade and windbreaks and encouraging birds and insects to return. She would mobilise local women, and they would be paid for every seedling that grew into a healthy young sapling.

Still under the auspices of the NCWK, she first called the movement 'Save the Land *Harambee*', the word, literally meaning 'Let us pull together', a favourite of Kenyatta's, denoting community energy and self-help. She had chosen this word deliberately. She was clever, she was careful, she was strategic. The Kenyatta government had become increasingly authoritarian, and critics and opponents were regularly rounded up and imprisoned. Tom Mboya, the Airlift architect, had been gunned down in the capital in 1969, and although the assassination was never directly linked to the President, the murder sent a chill through educated Nairobi. After another prominent opponent, the populist J. M. Kariuki, was found murdered in the Ngong Hills in March 1975, the Nairobi *Weekly Review* opined: 'Kariuki's death instils in the minds of the public the fear of dissidence, the fear to criticise, the fear to stand out and take an unconventional public stance.'

And so, at first, Wangari did not criticise or oppose. She observed. She made alliances with the Forestry Department. She made connections with the media, which covered her early tree-planting work, garnering interest and donations. The NCWK also donated start-up funds and shared a disused prefabricated office building near to the university, where she set up her headquarters. But Wangari returned from Vancouver to Nairobi in the middle of a drought. Her seedlings died and her marriage faltered: Mwangi was tired of his wife being so much more qualified, successful and focused on her work than he thought a good Kenyan wife should be. He was also fed up with the family compound being full of tree seedlings. 'Nobody warned me – and it had never occurred to me – that in order for us to survive as a couple I should fake failure and deny any of my God-given talents', she later wrote. Within a year, the marriage would be over and despite all her hopeful early steps in conservation and rewilding, nothing lasting or transformative had yet got off the ground. Of the first seven trees planted in a park in Nairobi, at a World Environment Day ceremony in June 1977 at what was supposed to be the triumphant start of Save the Land *Harambee*, five had died. Where would she go from here?

Part II

TREES

6

Mina: northern Labrador and London, 1905–8

I mean to try to face the other life as bravely as I can

It was 6 January 1908: Epiphany. A cold, clear day with temperatures in London struggling to get above freezing. Grey slush sprayed out from under the horses' hooves and carriage wheels. The Royal Geographical Society's lecture theatre at 6, Burlington Gardens, Mayfair was full of children attending the series of Christmas and New Year lectures, a longstanding tradition of London's learned societies, some of which continue to this day. As it happened, just around the corner, three minutes' walk away at the Royal Institution, a 13-year-old Dorothy Pilley was attending a lecture on astronomy, hearing about the trajectory of meteorites and the origins of shooting stars. The Burlington Gardens lecture hall, built for the new London University some 40 years previously in the grand Palladian style, was three storeys tall and decorated with classical sculptures and friezes depicting the muses celebrating the study of Music, Mathematics, History and Art. It was a grand, airy space and someone struggling to project their voice may well have got lost in the sheer scale of the room.

Into this chamber swept a tiny, fur-clad woman, looking like the Snow Queen from Hans Christian Andersen's fairy tale. She told the rapt audience of her 600-mile journey across northern Labrador, of the icebergs as big as houses floating past her, how she woke one night to find mice scuttling across the roof of her tent, how she witnessed the great caribou migration, met two different groups of First Nation Americans and mapped the source of the 'Nascaupee' River. The *Daily Telegraph* reporter who attended described the 'plucky' lady's 'delightful' talk as 'interesting, at times almost a thrilling tale'.

Mina Hubbard, who had taken elocution classes to help her public speaking and anglicise her Canadian accent, had spoken of her journey before in a series of lectures beginning, just a few weeks after her return from Labrador, at Williamstown, Massachusetts, where she had been living. That first lecture, in December 1905, was mostly before a small crowd of friends and local Methodist church ministers who wished her well, and was judged 'forcibly and entertainingly delivered ... without being made in the least tiresome' by the local reporter. But speaking under the auspices of the august Royal Geographical Society was something else. For starters, in 1908 women were not even permitted to be Fellows. Women had momentarily been admitted in 1892 but were banned the following year after too many of the member-ship, particularly the naval explorers, objected on the grounds that women's brains and bodies were unsuited either for arduous exploration or for careful scientific mapping. The modern phenomenon of wealthy, American 'female globe-trotters' was described as 'one of the horrors of the latter end of the nineteenth century' by prominent Fellow and future RGS President Lord Curzon. While other women explorers had refused to lecture at the society while their sex was not permitted the honour of Fellowship, Mina had a different point to make.

In the four years since she learned of Leonidas's death, she had undergone a transformation from a 'very helpless and sad' woman who would never have believed she could undertake such a journey, to someone who had discovered within herself deep reserves of determination and resilience. She wanted to inspire the young listeners to go on and make something of their lives, and not be put off by the kind of ignorance and prejudice she had endured. By the time she entered the lecture theatre in Burlington Gardens, Mina had grown in confidence, and also had the aid of more than 100 lantern slides made up from the photographs she had taken on her journey, depicting the tumbled, round hills, dark lakes and spruce forests. After her first talk in Williamstown in late 1905, where she barely remembered what she said or for how long she spoke, she had written and spoken of her travels many times. Each appearance was one in the eye to the doubters and critics: her forceful presence and the sure way she spoke convinced people: she was there and she had indeed done all those things she said she had. By the time she reached Burlington Gardens she had already spoken in England, having delivered a very similar lecture to the Manchester Geographical Society just a month before. She regaled the children with stories of bears and wolves and told them of the beautiful flowers that decorated her path. She called Labrador 'the land of rainbows', describing how she had never seen so many, so intensely chromatic, shimmering in the haze of waterfalls and arching across the hills.

Who knows how many young minds Mina inspired that day. Just a few years later, a 19-year-old Dorothy Pilley would be sitting in that same lecture theatre, listening, entranced, to another Canadian woman talk about the wildflowers of Vancouver Island, illustrating her descriptions with images on magic lantern slides. That night Dorothy wrote in her diary: 'She read her lecture and most poetical it was. I longed to go exploring as she had done, her slides were too beautiful.' If Mrs Julia Henshaw could climb to heights of over 10,000 feet, wear hobnail boots under her skirts and stride through high-altitude Alpine meadows, then why couldn't any woman? And, indeed, later that same year Dorothy would finally put hand to mud and moss and rock, disappearing alone into the Welsh hills to discover her life-sustaining love of the mountains.

By early 1908, Mina had already gone a long way in countering the prejudice and suspicion that had surrounded her decision to make her journey three years earlier. *Outing* magazine continued to ignore her, of course, instead reporting the 'successful penetration' of Labrador by Dillon Wallace in its typically masculine language. Several New York newspapers at first continued to question her motives and her claims, couching their reports of her return with weaselly words designed to sow doubts over the veracity of her statements such as: 'Mrs Hubbard Returns: *she says* she succeeded'. However, the respected travel writer William Brooks Cabot had been much impressed by Mina's journey, becoming one of the first to use her map in his own travels that criss-crossed her route for several years between 1905 and 1910. In the summer of 1905, he had been on his own journey around the Ungava coast and met three Innu travelling between their camps on the George River and the Hudson's Bay post at its mouth, trading furs and skins for ammunition and tobacco. Cabot established that the men had met Mina on the George River, within days of his encounter with them. Cabot was thus one of the first to be convinced that Mina had indeed successfully concluded the journey, and, as it turned out, well before Dillon Wallace. In his record of his years travelling the Labrador interior, Cabot describes Mina's journey as 'the most important work done since Low's return [in 1897]' and says 'her good travel map' was appreciated by explorers such as he. The American Geographical Society published her map in its 1906 *Bulletin*, dedicating ten pages to her photographs and detailed descriptions of the geography, geology, and plant and animal life she encountered. In this, the official record of North American exploration, she described how the fragrance of the small white Labrador Tea flowers and their aromatic evergreen leaves filled the air, and 'the dainty pink bells of the low cranberry showed in the carpet of glossy green, and near the water along the low drift shores, the pink almost rose-like blossom of the dewberry', conveying her feminine sense of enchantment even in the journal of a learned society.

Perhaps even more important than the imprimatur of Cabot and the American Geographical Society was her article commissioned by *Harper's Monthly Magazine* for its May 1906 issue. *Harper's* in 1906 was the giant among giants of the flourishing literary and cultural periodical magazine world of early twentieth-century north America. One of the widest read of the so-called genteel literary magazines, entertaining readers with its mix of fiction and articles about travel and adventure, *Harper's* made, and broke, reputations. Herman Melville, Thomas Hardy and Joseph Conrad were among a galaxy of north American and European literary stars it published within its pages. Mina had been sent letters of introduction to both the editor of *Harper's* and the editor of another leading periodical, *Century Magazine*, by a friend of her husband, another writer and polar adventurer, Herbert Lawrence Bridgman. Knowing that editors of such respected journals would be taking a risk in publishing the testimony of someone whose claims had been so widely questioned, Bridgman personally vouched for her honesty, writing to Richard Watson Gilder, editor of *Century Magazine*: 'I wish ... to commend her to your absolute confidence, a suggestion which is based on a pretty thorough knowledge of character and of record ... I trust that you and Mrs Hubbard will find each other's acquaintance of value.' This letter, on Bridgman's own *Standard Union*-headed notepaper, was written on 24 November 1905, just two days after Mina had emerged from the wild, after months of silence. It shows how quickly she acted to galvanise her own networks and how apparently determined she was to place her travels on record. It also shows she knew that, without a man to vouch for her truthfulness, all might be lost. *Harper's* pipped *Century* to the post in commissioning her and, with magazine lead times being what they are, must have taken her on within days of her reaching Williamstown.

Mina's article, 'My Explorations in Unknown Labrador', is careful not to overblow her achievements. In an early part of the piece, she writes: 'the Indians (sic) who hunt that country make the journey from Northwest (sic) River post to Lake Michikamau by the Nascaupee route in twenty-one days and ... they do not consider it a hard journey'. Here not only is she careful not to boast of her success but underlines that she is by no means the first to navigate the Naskaupi, that Innu trappers and traders had been there long before her. She records her expedition in great detail, from the fact that the journey was accomplished in 'a few hours less than sixty-one days, forty-three days of actual travel and eighteen days of camp'; that the canvas-covered canoes were 'nineteen feet long, thirteen inches deep and thirty-four inches wide' and in her equipment she took 'five pairs of stockings – all wool. I also took a rubber automobile coat, a long Swedish dogskin coat, one pair leather gloves, one pair woollen gloves and a shirt-waister – for Sundays.' The whole tone of the article is careful, sober, scientific, aware, perhaps she had this one shot to convince general opinion that she really went where she said she did. It seemed to work. For a while she was fêted throughout the United States and Canada, and invited to give lectures across the region. Her friend, the journalist Helen Bridgman, Herbert Bridgman's wife, described Mina as 'that remarkable wife and widow' and 'the wonder of her hour in the fall of 1907'.

By 'the fall of 1907', Mina was already in London. She had arrived at Liverpool in May 1907 on a tide of publicity. News of her achievements had reached England and the publisher John Murray had paid her £100 (about £16,000 today) advance for a book contract. Ever since Mary Kingsley's sensational success with *Travels in West Africa* published ten years previously, women's travel books had made publishers lots of money, as well as making their authors famous. While her book, which would be called *A Woman's Way Through Unknown Labrador: An account of the exploration of the Nascaupee and George Rivers*, was in production, Murray took Mina on a whirlwind publicity tour. At intellectual London's clubs and societies, she would be guest of honour, sitting next to luminaries of the Edwardian literary scene, including Horace Vachell and Israel Zangwill, both of whom also had books coming out in 1908. She was a rare female guest at the belletrist dining society, the New Vagabonds Club, which counted the literary superstars of the day, Rudyard Kipling, Mark Twain and *Peter Pan* author J. M. Barrie as members.

She won the attention, and patronage, of the historian and suffragist Alice Stopford Green, who invited her to stay in her 'narrow, gaunt' home overlooking the Thames at Pimlico, providing a supportive base where she could finish her book. Green, a celebrated intellectual salon hostess, was well connected with radicals, authors, publishers and journal editors. She worked energetically to promote the work of her protégées. She counted the writer Arthur Conan Doyle, the campaigner Emily Hobhouse, the socialist economists Beatrice and Sidney Webb, and the famous explorer Henry Stanley, who 'found' Dr Livingstone in the African bush, among her friends. She collected women travellers: Gertrude Bell and Isabella Bird were close acquaintances. Her house was always full of writers and travellers finding a berth both calm and stimulating to complete their works in return for conversation and companionship.

Also suffering a painful widowhood after a short and happy marriage, as well as having Irish ancestry in common, it's understandable that Stopford Green hoped to find in Mina that companionship she craved. The explorer Mary Kingsley was her closest friend and after she died in 1900, Green had written her obituary in the journal of the Royal Africa Society. In the obituary, Green had particularly praised the way her friend had communicated her response to her journeying into the mangrove swamps of the Gabon, with her 'lucid sentences' and her 'distinct style created by a living mind'. As a friend, 'her conversation was extraordinary' – amusing, exciting, controversial and, on top of all this, she was the most kind, sympathetic and thoughtful friend anyone could want, wrote Green. Fascinatingly, Green wrote of her friend's response to the wild, that in even the darkest and most impenetrable of jungle swamps or the most terrifying of ocean surfs, Kingsley heard a voice calling to her saying 'this is your home'; that she was unafraid, as being in the wild, she lost all sense of her human individuality and became part of the trees and the swamps of which she wrote.

Mina was finishing writing her own book while staying with Stopford Green. Reading *A Woman's Way*, the influences of Kingsley, in those expressions of connectedness and of being in some way at home, are clear to see. And so, sitting in her room watching the brown sluggish Thames churn past, so very different from the Naskaupi and George rivers, Mina re-read her diary, fashioning the private record of her journey into the public account that would make the name of Leonidas Hubbard immortal.

North to Ungava

The river was racing past 'at railroad speed' underneath the bow of the canoe: deep and cold and so fast. She could see the rocks far beneath her flying by. The water was so clear it was as if they were airborne: they travelled 34 miles north that day, one of the fastest days of the journey. She noted that Job, who was steering her canoe, had a fierce look in his eyes: half thrilled and half terrified at capsizing at that speed. The closer they got to the coast, the more signs of First Nation Americans they found: from here a skilled paddler would 'sleep only five times' before reaching the sea and the trading posts. Time was running out, flying through her hands like the fast river: 'Now that the work is so nearly done, I don't want to', she wrote in her diary on 25 August, not

6.1 Mina doing her washing on the Labrador trail

specifying what she didn't want to, simply stressing the negative, like a child who is afraid. A few days earlier she had had her first encounter with a group of Montagnais women and children – their husbands were all away trading furs for flour and tobacco. Mina's first meeting with First Nation Americans was a fascinating moment: she, her travel companions and the women were initially terrified, afterwards becoming cautiously reassured, and then curious about each other. Mina's encounter with the Montagnais women, who rarely saw a white face and never a white woman's, puts Mina initially in the position of being herself a creature from the wild, for at first they are not sure whether she is a human, or some kind of monster. For the Montagnais women, their camp on the banks of the George River was temporarily home; everything beyond the circle of tents was strange and possibly dangerous. Their country was delineated in the minds of close-by First Nation American groups, and not to be trespassed into. Just a hundred or so miles further north, another group, this time Naskapi people, had a semi-permanent camp but they would not cross the invisible boundary into Montagnais territory. So, when Mina appeared quietly in her canoe, wearing extraordinary garb, including a long skirt and a green and red jumper, she aroused great fear. Mina's guides, particularly Job and Gilbert, were also afraid of the impending encounter, fearful that the encampment's 'conjurer' would order a massacre of the intruders.

Her transgressing the borders of the Montagnais country was a shocking, and memorable, moment for the women. In 1967, a group of researchers from Montreal University went to North West River to collect legends and stories from the Montagnais-Naskapi. Along with the legends of 'Aiasheu' (a story of female duplicity and sexual transgression), 'The White Whale' and 'The Woman who Killed the Bear', they also told the legend of 'Missus Hubbard'. The story, passed down over more than 60 years, from a woman who was there to her son, illustrates the Montagnais' fears and chief concerns. The teller, Edward Rich, told the researcher that his mother had met 'Missus Hubbard' 'deep into the bush' and that she had gone to find her husband: 'The English people thought that he had been killed by the Indians but Missus Hubbard didn't think that way. She didn't blame the Indians.' Rich goes on to stress: 'During their journey they met many Indians but the Indians never did any harm to them.' His mother, he says, was initially afraid of Mina, never having seen anything like her before, but, according to his mother, Mina called out: 'Don't be afraid, we are humans.'

This, the only recorded indigenous account of Mina's journey, shows that the Montagnais-Naskapis' chief concern was to stress that they, and the other First Nation Americans she met, had done her no harm – this is repeated three times in the short story. The way the story is told also shows they were used to being blamed for any bad thing that happened to white people in the interior. Rich's mother's chief emotion was fear at this possibly non-human being invading her and her children's domestic space where they were terribly vulnerable. Mina's diary acknowledges the effect her presence has on them: 'Much screaming and shouting. They were very much frightened. Their husbands were all away.' In her account of the meeting in her book, Mina gives voice to the women: '"Go away, go away," they shrieked. "We are afraid of you. Our husbands are away."' In reality, although George Elson had been teaching her Cree during their journey, she understood little of what the women were saying, and relied on Elson as her interpreter. In her diary and book Mina records that the women had some 'fine Eskimo dogs', decent crockery and clothing, and that once they were persuaded not to be afraid, they relaxed and allowed themselves to be photographed.

One fascinating piece of information is that the women, who never went to the coast, told Mina that it was a long way away, perhaps two months' journey, whereas the next group of First Nation Americans she met, just two days further up the river at Indian House Lake, a mixed-sex group of Naskapi, told her it was only five days away, which it was. This wide discrepancy suggests the women from the first camp had a very distorted and incomplete knowledge of their surroundings. Perhaps they only knew of the route east to Davis Inlet on the Atlantic side of the peninsula, the part of the coast where their husbands went to trade, and which was about two months' journey away. Whatever the reason, the men's and women's occupation of geographical space was very different. Studies of other nomadic hunting communities, both past and contemporary, show that while the men range far from the family or village base to find large game, the women's movements are restricted to a much narrower radius of their camp or village, where they hunt smaller game or forage for plants, and thus have an incomplete knowledge of the landscape. This may explain why the Montagnais women were both more scared and had less accurate knowledge of where the coast was, than the Naskapi.

As it was, Mina arrived at Ungava on Sunday 27 August, a week after her party left Indian House Lake. Those last few days on the river had slipped by too quickly. With every mile the George River became wider and faster as it tumbled towards the sea. Yet still, two days before they reached the coast, Mina was reflecting in her diary whether to turn back and retrace her steps inland. Truth be told her desire not to reach Ungava was as strong as her desire to get there. She wanted to arrive before Wallace, to get her story out and to restore the reputation of Leonidas Hubbard, explorer and adventurer. But life without Laddie, when she was back from the wild, was to her intolerable. 'I mean to try to face the other life as bravely as I can ... Only what am I going to do? I don't know.' Here, in the private confines of her diary, she reveals so clearly her feelings of straddling two lives: the ordinary life of the suburban New York widow and this 'other' life of rainbows and waterfalls, so close to Leonidas she can hear and practically feel him. It was with a mixture of relief and disappointment that she reached this part of her journey's end.

She was still many weeks away from getting home to Massachusetts but she and the men were safe now. The Ungava Bay trading post, set above a small south-facing cove and run by John Ford and his wife Elizabeth, consisted of a stone and shiplap house raised on stilts overlooking the marshy shores fringed with grey-green willows. There were outbuildings: a salmon smokery, a seal oil store and a long, low storehouse holding tools, spears, sledges, skins and dried foods to feed the tiny settlement's inhabitants through the long, dark winters. Inuit families from the far north were camping there and helping with smoking and packing salmon ready to load onto the *Pelican*, the ship that was due to pass through any day, and which would take Mina back into the world.

Although the post was running low on stocks, here was bread raised with yeast, sweet butter, marmalade and dried apples. They ate salmon three times a day. Mrs Ford kept a garden where she grew native soft fruits to make puddings with. Here they were in limbo land – not in the world of newspapers and society but neither in that magic world she had spent the past three months in. Symbolic of this change, while Mina was taken to sleep in the main house with Mr and Mrs Ford, George, Job, Gilbert and Joe camped away from the building, in tents. Relations with them were not so easy and uncomplicated now. There were misunderstandings between her and George, which upset her. As she made her way upstairs to bed in those darkening September evenings, she would gaze out of the window and see the lights in their tents, hear their music and singing, but not be part of it the way she had been on the smooth, flat rocks by the river. In a symbolic moment one of the Inuit's dogs tore up her own tent, and the skins she had been given as a gift by the Naskapi. She began to feel lonely.

Mapping her route

The *Pelican* was late that year, having been damaged on its long journey around the northern Quebec coast and in need of repairs, and Mina ended up staying at Ungava for nearly two months. While waiting to return to the world, she learned to steer a canoe on Ungava Bay, made socks and moss berry pudding, and wished she could be a man so she could take up service in the Hudson's Bay Company in some faraway post. During this time, she began writing up her account of her journey. By 25 September, a month after her arrival at Ungava, she had written 9,000 words and had in mind the forming structure of a book although she was not at all sure whether it was anything anyone other than herself would want to read. She also continued to take observations, checking and re-checking her calculations of altitude and latitude to confirm the accuracy of her readings. Her mapping skills bothered her. Sometimes she spent whole days worrying over her sextant, or her map. If she couldn't get this right, and correct the faulty map that had led Leonidas to his death, then what was the point of the past few months of privation and risk?

Mina's map was published in the American Geographical Society *Bulletin* in 1906, earning it the imprimatur of being the official account, and a testament to the care and accuracy of her work. But it is also a love letter and memorial to her husband. She named several landmarks after him: Mount Hubbard and Hubbard Lake are marked on it, Hubbard Lake being the first body of water her party reached after gaining the height of land. She also named a low chain of hills near to where Leonidas died Lion Heart Mountains, and the lakes just to their west, Disappointment Lakes. More than this, the map marks the routes of both the doomed 1903 expedition and the successful 1905 one. It thus tells a story, across two time zones, of disaster and death followed by redemption. Unusually for an official map, she marked with a cross the site where her husband died, and also where George Elson in his desperate attempt to save Leonidas's life, found a cache of flour. On the map, which has a scale of 25 miles to an inch, these two points are agonisingly close. Similarly, the outflows of the two rivers, Susan and 'Nascaupee' are seen as desperately close, just a few minutes' paddling around Grand Lake.

The map is a representation of Mina's longing, her 'what ifs' and 'if only'. As well as naming landmarks for her husband, she named several for her friends and relatives, including her three nieces Orma, Agnes and Marie, after all of whom she named a lake, eschewing the convention of naming landmarks after either kings and queens or military commanders and colonial governors. She also identified on her map no fewer than 11 indigenous portage and winter routes to the coast or around rapids, and marked the sites of three 'Indian' camps, the site of the first 'standing wigwam' she saw and an Innu food store, a large timber structure insulated with moss used as a larder to store seal meat. This act of providing evidence of indigenous presence on an officially sanctioned map is an important statement by Mina. While by this time European cartographers did occasionally record indigenous presence, it was haphazard and by no means on all maps. Equally important at the time, next to Lake Hubbard, she named Lake Elson, after her part-Cree guide to whom she owed her safe passage, acknowledging his equality with the white people she named on the map. Mina's map is thus a multi-layered document that celebrates

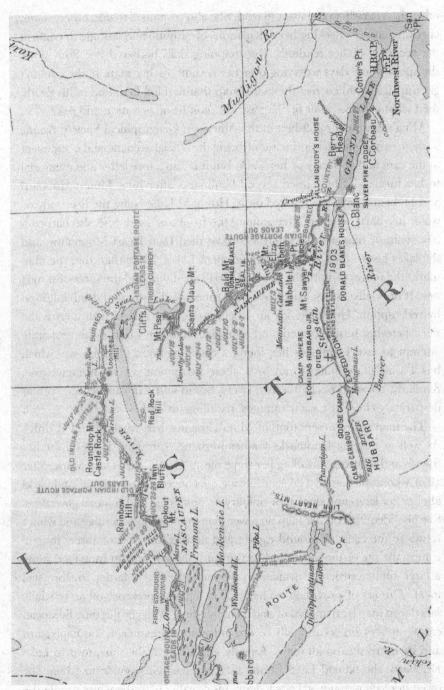

6.2 Detail from Mina's map showing the place where Leonidas died

her difference from official surveyors in the ways she viewed the wilderness through which she was travelling.

To help find her way Mina used a map drawn up by local First Nation Americans living at North West River post. While the learned societies required European mapping techniques for maps to be accepted as official records, colonial administrators had relied on native spatial knowledge and guides since they first arrived in conquered territory. Much indigenous geographical knowledge was cognitive rather than written down, leading to Europeans' 'mistaken view that Natives did not have formal concepts of their territories'. However, early treaties and agreements used maps, on deerskin, birch bark, occasionally paper or even in the earth or on snow, drawn by chiefs, to demarcate settlements and land occupation. First Nation guides, too, drew maps for the occupiers and there are several extant examples of colonial-era indigenous maps, many displaying supremely detailed knowledge of waterways, routes to the sea from far inland, tidal heights and ice-free channels. The Canadian explorer William Brooks Cabot wrote, somewhat in astonishment in 1912, that 'All Indian maps [are] made *only* to travel by.' While he admitted that this meant these maps 'are often better than ours' in terms of finding one's way between two points, the maps lack precise elevations or measurements for latitude and longitude. The maps often depicted distance as time taken to get from two points, rather than actual mileage, with wide, easy waterways contracted and difficult portages expanded.

While Mina may have been the first woman to have her map accepted by the American Geographical Society, she was not the first woman to create a map of the American north or sub-Arctic regions. In 1822 an Inuit woman named Iligliak or Iligliuk drew a map for British explorer Captain William Edward Parry, of the land and seas around Winter Island in the Canadian Arctic. The map does indeed, as Cabot said, foreground travel routes: sled marks, a series of dotted lines on the paper, show journeys of one day's length between overnight camps. One particularly long journey is annotated: 'These two long days' journey over the ice are performed in sledges with many dogs. The women seldom go,' indicating social, as well as physical, space: for Iligliuk and other Inuit women, the zone anywhere more than a day's sled ride between camps was out of bounds. This piece of cultural knowledge, marking 'where the women seldom go' on a text where mostly geographical features such as high tide lines and lookout points are recorded, shows how for Iligliuk landscape and culture are intertwined. Revealing other places of deep personal importance, Iligliuk marked on the map the place where she gave birth to her son, Ookatuk, and also the region where there were 'deer very numerous', knowledge intricately associated with Inuit survival.

Another elusive indigenous female voice was Shanawdithit, a Beothuk woman from Newfoundland who from memory created narrative representations of her people's territory and life. Combining geographical information with stories about her people's deadly encounters with English soldiers in the early nineteenth century, her images reveal much about her understanding of home and its being at the 'contact zone', that site of often violent clashes between two cultures. Shanawdithit was the last surviving member of her people. The Beothuk, part of the Algonkian Nation, were among the first indigenous Americans to come into contact with Europeans and were completely wiped out after 'two hundred years of haphazard genocide' by colonial soldiers, settler fishermen and European diseases. They painted their faces, bodies and furniture with red ochre, leading to invaders calling them 'Red Indians'.

Shanawdithit was taken captive, along with her mother and sister, both of whom died shortly after capture, in 1823. They were the three remaining members of the last surviving group of 72 Beothuk known to be living around Red Indian Lake in the centre of Newfoundland in 1816. The tribe had originally lived predominantly around the coast, only retreating inland during the winter. Over the years they moved into the central forests to avoid violent encounters with French and English fishermen who competed with them for the island's rich fishing stocks. They were thus forced to change their diets and hunting habits from mostly seafood to forest game over a relatively short period, contributing to their rapid decline.

After capture, Shanawdithit lived with a settler family at Exploits, near to Red Indian Lake for four years, where, it was said, 'at times she fell into a melancholy mood, and would go off into the woods … She generally came back singing and laughing, or talking aloud to herself' as if she drew sustenance from being near her home and where her family lived. While at Exploits she created several artefacts including sketches, deer horn combs and birch bark decorations. She made a scale model of a sea-going Beothuk canoe with high rear and stern prows, painstakingly planked and stitched and now on display in the Atlantic Worlds Gallery at the National Maritime Museum in Greenwich. Thousands of miles from home, enclosed in a glass case and smaller than I expected when I see it, it nevertheless exerts a huge power over the viewer. You could easily hold it in two hands and the deep, rich browns of the birch bark are still marked with the mottling of the original tree. Shanawdithit's tiny, neat stiches tell of how she carefully worked over this symbol of her people's home, a still, safe refuge in the waves of the Atlantic Ocean, while a 'guest' in another culture's house, now that her home, and her people, were gone.

In 1828, and now seriously ill with tuberculosis, Shanawdithit was removed to St John's and the home of William Epps Cormack, an amateur ethnographer who was writing a *History of the Red Indians of Newfoundland*. Cormack, who called himself president of the 'Beothick Institution', had sent out search parties to hunt for signs of Beothuk habitation over the previous years and while none was found alive, he recorded: 'old marks of them abound everywhere from White Bay to Notre Dame Bay'. Realising that Shanawdithit was probably the last surviving Beothuk, he asked her to make drawings, for posterity, of Beothuk dress, weapons, living quarters and other cultural artefacts, as well as to draw maps of the locations where they lived. Cormack noted that Shanawdithit 'never narrated without tears' the stories of her family's recent history.

Shanawdithit's maps of Red Indian Lake are remarkable for their many-layered meanings. On the surface, they are a precise geographical representation of parts of the lake and the Exploits River where the last of her people lived until around 1823. They also tell stories, over a number of years, of attacks by English soldiers and the tribe's steadily diminishing numbers. Her map is thus a memorial to her people and her home, their last sanctuary in the woods that was finally violated. Small triangles denote wigwams; dotted lines mark her people's last journeys across frozen rivers, lakes and snowy riverbanks, inscribing their footprints forever on their land. Small rounded shapes with pennants flying atop mark the steady progress of the English soldiers up the river and to the lake where violent encounters took place and where her aunt was abducted by an English raiding party. An English tent planted right at the centre of a Beothuk camp shows how deeply and carelessly the English invaded the Beothuks' most personal spaces. While the topographical features and the small figures of the English soldiers are marked in black, her people are marked in red, highlighting their presence and memorialising their association with the red ochre of the land. Around the Beothuk encampments, clusters of dashes show how many of them are still left alive, each time frame showing a decreasing number. She marked, standing high and out of all scale with the rest of the drawing, a marine's head stuck on a pole, decapitated by her people, surely a gesture of defiance. She also recorded other, personally important sites: the place where her aunt's body was buried, and where her infant child died two days after her capture. Shanawdithit's maps not only record her people's presence but tell their story when history, as they say, is usually only ever recorded by the victor.

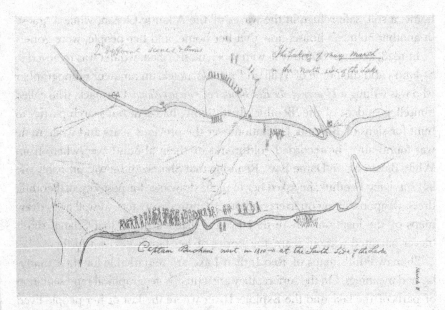

6.3 Shanawdithit's map, 'Sketch II' with Cormack's annotations, '2 different scenes and times' depicting the English abducting Demasduit, Shanawdithit's aunt, whom the English named Mary March

While it would be wrong to draw any parallel between maps made by indigenous women and those of a settler, Shanawdithit and Iligliuk's maps do shine a light on Mina's choices of what she chose to record on her map. Mina was no trained army surveyor or cartographer, and her mapping was not influenced by either ordnance survey tradition or learned society culture. Like Shanawdithit and Iligliuk, she recorded what was important to her. Mina used her map to create not just topography but a record of her relationship with her dead husband and with the landscape. This helps us understand just why she made this long journey in the face of so much ridicule and opposition. She understood that by making the map and recording Leonidas's presence in it, both in the naming of landmarks and the telling of his last days, she could honour him even though his journey ended ultimately in failure.

The 'still small voice'

In London, 1907, Mina was putting the finishing touches to her manuscript of *A Woman's Way*. Sitting in Alice Stopford Green's townhouse, she relived those days of summer 1905 when she came closer to the land than she ever would again. There, in a fierce and apparently barren country, she had learned from her indigenous guides of the so-briefly thawed soil's bounty. She saw how to brew tea from the small, pink *Ledum* flower, a kind of heather; she had watched Job Chapies fashion a pipe for her, out of a tree root; found 'bake apple berries' (cloudberries), rosy, sharp, as big as her thumb, hidden beneath their foliage; had picked and eaten, for the first time, the crow-black moss berries: tannic and dry on bright green stems, which she pronounced 'quite palatable'. She discovered how moss and balsam boughs can make a bed softer than a department store mattress. She also began a process of self-censorship and self-erasure, erecting for her book a distance between herself and her guides that had not existed in the wilds. She did not admit to smoking a tree-root pipe in those long, light evenings, nor to learning Cree. And although the book is more reserved than the diary, it still carries resonances of the yearning to stay, for the quiet reflection and for the inner peace she found in Labrador:

> This was the wilderness indeed with only the crystal river and the beautiful skies to make it glad. Only? Or was there more? Or was it glad? Perhaps yes surely, somewhere within it there was gladness; but everywhere it was beautiful with the beauty which alone, to some hearts can carry the 'still small voice' … one must wish to stay and listen to it always. Through the stillness came the sounds of the rapids below our camp. Above, fish jumped in the quiet waters where the after-glow in the sky was given back enriched and deepened. Then came night and the stars – bright northern lights – bright moon – shadows on the tent – dreams.

This image of her, suspended in time and space within the river's changing nature, somewhere between roaring rapid and quiet waters where fish jumped for flies, gives, this time in a public document, expression to her response to the wilderness of Labrador. She presents herself as shimmering somewhere between the real and the spirit world, between dream and reality. She hears both the roar of the rapids and the soft plop of the fish in the still waters above and also that 'still small voice' – of God, or Leonidas, or perhaps even, herself.

A Woman's Way Through Unknown Labrador was published in May 1908, with an introduction by William Cabot, and was widely and warmly – although not triumphantly – reviewed, in newspapers from *The Scotsman* in Edinburgh to *The Observer* in London. After its publication in North America in September 1908, the *Toronto Saturday Night*, which covered her home town in Ontario, called her book 'brilliant'. The *New York Times*, which had reported, prematurely, on her giving up and coming to grief, did not review it, although it announced the book's forthcoming publication in a small item, calling it a story of 'rare courage and perseverance'. Other reviews called it 'interesting', 'affecting', 'sprightly' and of course, many times over, 'plucky'. It was even reviewed – somewhat sniffily and cautiously – in the grand journal *Nature*; the reviewer disagreed with Mina's warning, gathered from the evidence of her own eyes and through her consultations with the First Nation Americans she met, that the caribou populations were dangerously low and that this was threatening the indigenous way of life. The reviewer in *The Queen* was perhaps most perceptive, praising Mina's courage but also describing the writing as lacking something, some heart or unguarded honesty.

It is true. Reading the published book and comparing it with her private diary one sees how much of herself she held back in the public account. The book lacks the open-hearted wonder of her diary. Perhaps, having been disbelieved, belittled and disparaged for her audacity to take on a man's work, she was wary of exposing her emotions the way she had in her diary. Because the book was first and foremost a vehicle with which to resurrect her husband's name, she effaced herself too much from it and, as a result, it has lost its heart; in the book there is a distancing that the reviewers picked up on. It wasn't a bestseller – in 12 months it sold just under 1,500 copies, although it did earn back her advance. But for a while the name of Leonidas Hubbard was everywhere (with the small prefix 'Mrs'), in newspapers, book shops, lecture halls and libraries across Britain and North America. Leonidas Hubbard finally achieved the immortality, the 'bully story' he had so craved, completed for him by his wife, and in such a different way from how he had envisaged. Which is why it was so strange, although perhaps, on reflection, not strange at all, that in September 1908, just four months after *A Woman's Way* was published, Mina chose to obliterate her own association with the name. She married again, henceforth being known as Mina Benson Ellis. It was a wildly unsuitable match – Harold Ellis was a wealthy playboy, the son of a British parliamentarian and former Under-Secretary of State for India, and the marriage was unhappy and short-lived. But maybe it did what she required of it: Mrs Leonidas Hubbard, having given her husband immortality and a place in northern Labrador maps, then disappeared herself.

7

Dorothy: the Alps, the Himalayas and China, 1926–31

'The storm still rages and I am like streaked lightning'

She was wearing the wrong boots. Dressing by candlelight in the dark Alpine hut, she had mistakenly put on an old one with worn nails, and the other wasn't even hers and several sizes too big. It made her right foot an ounce or two heavier than her left, giving her a slightly ungainly gait as she crossed the glacier. When she realised her mistake, she didn't dare suggest they return to change, it would have caused too much delay. And this was supposed to be her greatest day, the climb of her life. It was also the most perilous. The Dent Blanche is one of the most difficult and dangerous mountains in the Alps and although at times, in her heartbroken years in Canada, she had deliberately courted oblivion on those summits, it would be losing too much to slide off the face of the earth now. Too late to go back: they were already five hours into the day, which had begun cold and black at one o'clock in the morning.

It was July 1928, and down in the valleys the gentians and violas were a blazing, bee-humming sea of blue and indigo but up here at over 11,500 feet, it was another world: freezing, quiet, monochrome. At first the snow above the Bricola Hut had been granular and dry and the old nails gripped as the boots creaked over it, just enough. But as the party of four: three men and one woman rose, slowly, across the Dent Blanche Glacier, Dorothy's feet slipped over the ice. They were now roped together and every time a foot shot out, she was aware of tugging, either at the man behind her, or the man in front, testing his balance and patience. The glaciers were in a rotten state that hot summer, 'swampy', she called them, thawing and refreezing multiple times as the sun's rays strafed the high passes. Crevasses suddenly opened like blue cathedrals beneath apparently solid snow. Climbers would disappear into the mountain, like offerings to the deity, sometimes never to be seen again. An unexpected tug from Dorothy could mean one, two or all of them tumbling into the void. A few days earlier she had actually fallen 15 feet into one while crossing an ice bridge: 'the bridge went, like the Crack of Doom', she wrote in her diary. She was dangling in the 'deepest darkest cavern I had ever seen'. Roped together with Ivor and their guide Joseph, she had nearly pulled them all in with her that time too. Please God it didn't happen again, she was only too well aware of Joseph's views on women climbers.

Abandoned pitons or straggles of rope from previous, unsuccessful expeditions were sometimes helpful but also a reminder that nobody, yet, had ever achieved what they were trying to do: climb the Dent Blanche by its overhanging north ridge. Mountaineers had been trying to do it for the past 30 years, and had always failed. At some point they would have to defy gravity and traverse the underside of a stone eave, suspended above 3,000 feet of nothing. She wasn't even sure anymore why they were trying to do it. For eight years, the mountain had bewitched her. She had watched it, from all angles, sometimes clear and sharp against the bright blue sky, sometimes only dimly discernible beneath the shawl of clouds around its shoulders. She had wanted to climb it since she had first seen its sweeping bulk across the valleys but always something: bad weather, poor timing, ill health or a broken heart, had muddled the plans. Perhaps the wrong boots were just another omen, a warning sign to leave well alone. Latterly the mountain's charm had seemed less strong, as if she had broken its spell by finally ceasing her endless fight against happiness.

For now she was happy. She and Ivor had been married for a year and a half and all those doubts, all those obstacles they had both erected had at last come tumbling down. In her journal, there is an abrupt change in her mood from when she became Mrs I. A. Richards on Honolulu, at the end of December 1926. He was the love of her life; she had always known it, since those first tweedy scrambles in Wales but oh how she fought, for her freedom and autonomy. For a woman in 1926, getting married meant deliberately and knowingly becoming, in law and by custom, a subordinate; second class; subservient. And that simply wasn't Dorothy's style. It would have been difficult whatever occupation her husband had but Ivor was now a fêted intellectual, as close to a superstar as an academic could get. His lectures at Cambridge were so popular that at times they had to be held in the streets, something that had not happened since the Middle Ages. He gave T. S. Eliot, of all people, notes on his draft poems; his first books, *Principles of Literary Criticism*, *Science and Poetry* and, with C. K. Ogden, *The Meaning of Meaning*, were heralded as new ways of reading literature and understanding language. He was in demand for lectureships the world over; publishers wanted more volumes from him.

On her part, she recorded in her diary that she 'hated' Cambridge, the 'monastic spirit, dull, limited tea parties, the snob circles'. She was also wary of marrying a man who stated from the start that his work came above all other considerations, and who declared to her that while men were innovators and experimentalists, 'no woman had ever done any original work in any field'. Quite an attitude to swallow for a woman who had been in the first 'manless' rope party of women up an Alpine summit, and who edited the world's first feminist climbing journal. Her – as yet private – attempts to express in words how giving oneself up to the vastness of those great spines of rock brings the body as close as physically possible to a kind of immateriality, stripping away gender, social expectation, the limits of the mind: these are not the fruits of a narrow, conservative outlook. Richards's own attitude of course revealed deeply conservative views on women. He also had old-fashioned romantic notions of love and work: he believed that he could only create when he was miserable and lonely, in emotional pain so fierce it became physical, like Wordsworth, 'hurting himself with a sonnet', as his wife Mary described the poet's writing. This meant he could only write well during long periods of enforced separation from anyone he loved. He hadn't seemed to appreciate that the flip side of that was that his lover would be miserable and lonely too. They had come so close, so many times, to parting forever. Their encounters left her distraught and at one stage, 'in a suicidal frame of mind'.

In North America, though, in the spring before her marriage, Dorothy was offered a job that suited her love of the outdoors perfectly: to be a guide and publicist for the Great Northern Railway that plied the US–Canada border between Seattle and the Great Lakes, and which shuttled growing numbers of middle-class tourists to walking holidays in Glacier National Park. The 'Roaring Twenties' economy was booming and leisure tourism fuelled by modern American imaginings of the rugged north west frontier was big business. Swiss-style Alpine chalets and comfortable hotels were sprouting like the fruiting bodies of mycelium beside lakes and waterfalls. Native American Blackfoot (*Niitsitapi*), whose homeland covered much of the National Park area, were paid to look picturesque in traditional costume, welcoming visitors off the trains and guiding hikes. The motorcar and railroads drove new routes up into the mountains, disgorging wealthy Americans, whom Dorothy was paid to persuade 'to take muddy strolls and tell them … they are chamois, miracles of agility, born to be leaders of men. The more preposterous, the better they like it,' she recorded sourly in her diary.

She would be paid £600 a year plus expenses to map 'a park of one thousand peaks', design new walking trails, write enticing tourist blurb for publicity leaflets and deliver lectures. She had her picture taken multiple times, looking charming, healthy and capable halfway up a sheer rockface. At least, and refreshingly, in America a woman in breeches wasn't a figure of shame or fun and the Great Northern Railway authority was delighted to have the glamorous and beautiful English climber on its books. Her face, framed by her trademark headscarf, appeared in thousands of provincial American newspapers. The papers told their readers she was 20, which she felt slightly sheepish about but she knew the commercial value of youthfulness in women. By 32, which she now was, she was practically an old maid.

But still contentment evaded her. In her diary she described herself as a 'troubled spirit' and complained that the 'vulgar' GNR didn't know one end of a mountain from another. During her 'wander years', as she called them, 1925 and most of 1926, she was restless, unhappy and often unwell, with headaches and 'exhausted' eyes. Sometimes she would read all night, until five or six in the morning, as longed-for sleep evaded her, then she would go out alone before sunrise and climb on mist-slicked rock. She began writing in her diary her responses to the natural world, experimenting with imagery and emotion. A stream flowing through a frozen gulley is 'a dark, twisting band in the snow'; the 'blue shadows under snow banks' contrast with the intoxicating scent of the balsam: cool and dark; warm and heady. One of my favourites is her description of a ridge of low rounded foothills: 'the country was rolled in repeated humps like the backs of hippopotamuses [sic]', perfectly capturing that sense of full, tussocky heftiness.

She was constantly on the move, crossing borders, passing from west to east and back again through the great North American continent: Toronto, Seattle, Saint Paul, Vancouver, Montreal, Minneapolis, then back to Glacier National Park. Troublesome thoughts punctuated by the clackety clack and the steam engine's whistle. Relief when the flat prairies began to wrinkle, furrow and rise. All the while she was attempting, as she wrote, to 'choke' her feelings for Ivor, who had asked her to marry him again but when they met in the spring of 1926 seemed aloof and distant. 'The storm still rages', she wrote, 'and I am like streaked lightning.' There is pain and poetry in her journal at this point. She sees herself as some kind of creature of the wild, who wishes to remain hidden from the world of human statute, who desires

7.1 Dorothy climbing with friends in Glacier National Park, 1926

both freedom and possession: 'Can you fly many times round the world and find me? Can you build me a palace of warmed dewdrops painted green outside and spin a door of cobwebs that only you can enter. And I, your prisoner, will listen for your ridiculous singing, like the enchanted melody of a flute player across the mountains.' For all her talk of independence and professional success, she saw herself in and of the landscape and sought retreat there, behind an enchanted bower of dewdrops.

Ivor, visiting Harvard to discuss a book proposal, then pursued her across Canada and up new ascents of Mounts Baker and Shuksan on the Pacific edge of the continent. Together they made a promotional film on mountaineering for the Great Northern Railway, called *Crags and Crevasses* (1926). Much of it is lost but there remains a clip of 1 minute, 7 seconds. It's a silent movie but you can hear the wind howling in your ears as you watch. The clip opens with the camera panning across an empty landscape of peaks, high saddles and glaciers riven with crevasses. The camera then zooms in until two tiny figures can be seen labouring across this vast white and hostile terrain. At first, they are indistinct but as the camera moves in closer, the rear figure is unmistakably Dorothy, a woman in breeches, with her distinctive headscarf. The pair stop at a crevasse in the glacier and Dorothy carefully places the tip of her ice axe on the opposite side and, using it as a counterbalance, leaps across the void (I have shown this clip to modern mountaineers who all recoil in horror at her method). Another section shows the climbers cresting a vertical rockface to reach the pinnacle and you see her close up again, her body pressed against the rock, nothing but thin air beneath her as she pulls her weight up onto the stone platform, first with hands, then elbows, then knees and then feet. She's strong, athletic, supple. I've watched that clip many times and I still get goosebumps when I see her calmness, serenity almost, as she accomplishes terrifying physical feats. At one point there is even a smile playing across her face as she ascends a treacherous staircase cut into the ice. She loves it. For a woman, in 1926, to be so at home, outdoors, accomplishing great sporting feats, was utterly unusual and in many people's eyes, unnatural and indecent. It was only 30 years since women had been banned from the first modern Olympics of 1896 because women competing in sports would be 'inaesthetic' and 'indecent', according to founder Pierre de Coubertin. While by the 1920s women were allowed to compete in some categories, they were still limited to a small range of sports deemed acceptable, such as ice skating, tennis, croquet and equestrianism.

7.2 Still from the film *Crags and Crevasses*, 1926

Dorothy and Ivor had then travelled down to Redondo Beach, California, where they shared a 'little white and blue painted cabin with waves roaring below' and where she found him 'the dearest companion of our Alpine days'. There she wrote the script for the film: short chapter headings that appear in the film as white letters on a black background: 'Crevasses Must be Crossed', 'Steps are Cut for Safety' and 'Higher Up, the Ice Becomes Steeper'. It looked like they were, at last, finding a way to be together. But after further disagreements over how their married life might play out, she sailed, alone, for Honolulu. In preparation for the voyage, in San Francisco, she bought one beige and one rose silk dress, and a blue and claret evening dress for dinner at the captain's table; braced herself for the predictable vulgar proposals she had endured during her journey across the Atlantic. 'Men are so queer', she wrote, on hearing of the marriage of a man who only a few months earlier had written to her to ask for her hand. She had been able to save a considerable sum from her work with the GNR, and from Honolulu she would head further west across the Pacific, to China, and onto India, where her younger sister

Vi was now working as a radiologist in Delhi. The restless soul always on the move. 'It makes me glad that she took matters into her own hands', wrote Dorothy of her younger sister, whom she had advised the previous year. 'Violet has virtually escaped from futility to a position of freedom and possible development.' She was out on deck to watch the ship arrive at Hawaii, 'the lovely islands I have heard so much about', but they were covered in thick haze and she saw nothing of their soaring outline. A metaphor, perhaps, for her opaque future. But Ivor, chasing after her again and just a week behind her, arrived in Honolulu on 27 December 1926 and there, in the middle of the wide blue Pacific, on 31 December, they were married. His cable telling her he was on his way filled her with such joy, 'to think he cared for me so much', that she finally accepted it was useless denying her feelings any longer. They would have to somehow make it work. They would in fact, enjoy more than 50 years of married life together; fewer than 12 of those years would be spent in 'suffocating' Cambridge.

Himalayan honeymoon

The new Mr and Mrs Ivor Armstrong Richards were not yet ready to settle down to a quiet academic life. After a low-key wedding at which she wore the beige silk dress bought in San Francisco, they continued first to Japan, through lightning storms that made the night brighter than day, arriving in Osaka just before the shattering earthquake of 7 March 1927, which killed more than 3,000 people. From there they sailed to China, bound for Nanking (*Nanjing*) but as their ship sailed up the Yangtze River at the end of March 1927, a renegade group of Chiang Kai-Shek's nationalist forces stormed the city, killing several foreign nationals and looting the British, Japanese and US consulates, which drew fire from British and US warships on the river. Several bullets flew past the couple as they watched from the deck of the *Mellwhite*.

The ship diverted to Shanghai and from there they continued, via Peking (*Beijing*), Hong Kong and Penang to Calcutta, finally arriving in Darjeeling, northern India, at the end of May. Was it Dorothy who cabled the *Evening News* to relay the article that appeared in that paper on 2 July 1927 headlined: 'Romance of London Girl Climber … Honeymoon Amid Wars and Earthquake; Climbing 28,000 Feet'? There is much personal detail here: that the bride caught flu in Osaka and was still recovering when the earthquake struck; that the voyage to Japan was through a series of violent storms and that the former Miss Pilley was well known for her feats in the Alps and Rockies. Her plan to climb Kanchenjunga in the Himalayas, if successful, would make her easily the highest woman on the planet. Rather like the publicity she generated both at home and for the Great Northern Railway, she nurtured her public image. The cutting is carefully kept in a folder in Dorothy's papers in the Pilley–Richards archive, marked, in her handwriting 'Clippings from Newspapers' along with several of the publicity photographs taken of her at Glacier. It was as if she was clinging on to that part of her that wasn't a simple appendage to her husband. More than Mrs I. A. Richards, she was the glamorous 'Girl Climber'.

On board the R. M. S. *Takliwa*, which took them from Hong Kong down the South China Sea and across the Bay of Bengal to India, in preparation for the Himalayas, she read Kipling's *Kim* cover to cover. Their favourite literary phrase, even when they were well into their 70s, like other couples' 'our song', would be: 'the high hills as soon as may be'. She also read E. M. Forster's *Howards End* and, a loyal wife, I. A. R.'s *Principles of Literary Criticism*. In Darjeeling they met with Violet to a symphony of metallic buzzing of the treefrogs nearby and, far off, the distant booming of avalanches ploughing the mountains. Their plan was to spend several weeks walking in the Himalayas, culminating in an ascent of Kanchenjunga (28,156 feet). They slowly rose, for days, up through the forested lower slopes, besieged by 'ants with nips like lobster' and 'swaying piles of leeches' which collected thickly on and above boots 'until one couldn't see one's legs'. Their only thoughts were to get above the leech line. This was forest that Evelyn Cheesman would have been right at home in: in her journal Dorothy described the 'masses of pale green moss festooned from bough to bough', the aerial vegetation linking all the trees, the creepers, orchids and parasitic ferns, the dense smell of myriad tiny lives multiplying, and sucking, rotting and decomposing on the forest floor. Then, through thousands of feet of dim bamboo tunnels until finally they emerged in the 'blazing light and heat' of the high ridges, above the rhododendrons blooming in every colour. They refreshed themselves with handfuls of yellow raspberries and yak milk. Here, however, Dorothy met with an implacable foe she would never best: the sun.

At first, she simply reported heartburn and headaches, but was determined to continue: on and on, and up and up: Dzongri on 6 June (14,000 feet), Goecha La on 10 June (16,400 feet), Bokta on 14 June (13,350 feet). They talked of climbing Changla (18,000 feet) but Dorothy was already weakening fast, and her headaches hammered her into the ground. 'Ivor had already a sense of the urgency of getting out of the wild', she wrote, as yaks grunted outside their tents like large hairy pigs. They abandoned their plans to climb

Kanchenjunga, which they saw, drilling into the clear blue sky, the clouds of snow blowing off its peak like the steam from a smokestack in a gale. Next time. They would plan properly and take three months over it. They had both, it seems, lost their desire to dance with death. Dorothy was later diagnosed with suffering from a duodenal ulcer; she also mentions in her diary a possible pregnancy, and that may have added to her sickness. For the last 50 miles of walking, they covered ten miles a day, with Dorothy only able to eat Ovaltine – nothing else would stay down. They reached the first 'dak' bungalow, the extreme outpost of the British colonial administration, at below 11,000 feet and there she took to bed, and stayed for weeks. From the Himalayas on, the sun would stalk every summer climb, forcing her to hide in the shadow of rocks and peaks, climb after dark or wear wide-brimmed hats stuffed with ice and snow to keep her head cool.

And so they returned to England, via a spot of peak scrambling in the Alps, in the summer of 1927. They glanced up at the Dent Blanche, a jagged tooth in the panorama of peaks. But they were content, that summer, to 'trudge quietly on through juniper plantations', admire the bright emerald green valleys and, in early September, lie on their backs at the top of La Luette (11,600 feet), gazing up at the high red cirrus portending the end of summer.

Back in England, Dorothy made efforts to be wifely. She learned how to make sardines on toast, which they ate a lot, and braised mutton, but her heart wasn't really in it. In their later years, Ivor would do all the cooking. She bought a coal scuttle and spirit lamp at the old Cambridge department store Eaden Lilley and the couple installed themselves in a flat in a tall townhouse above a shop, overlooking King's College. They hired a cook, Mrs Balcomb, and Ivor had his study fitted with an electric light; Dorothy read a book on cabinet making. She spent one afternoon 'sorting periodicals in the corner of the room' and then berated herself for 'getting hideously domestic'. A crisis at home in Camberwell forced Dorothy to leave Ivor to his books and return to London, where her youngest brother Will was still living. He suffered from severe asthma, and spent much of his time in bed, struggling for breath. Their mother, who had always seemed to be erratic and unpredictable, had, it seemed, sunk into mental illness. 'Poor mother', she wrote to Vi, 'I'm filled with pity for her. I believe her to be very seriously ill.'

In the top attic room at Crescent Lodge Dorothy found evidence of her mother's obsessive shopping and collecting: 'Nothing that has ever come into the house seems to have left it', she wrote. She found trunks full of velvets, serge, crêpe de chines bought before 1920 in bags that had never been opened; fur coats 'full of eggs and not a hair left on them'; boxes still wrapped with strings and ribbon. Dorothy had left Cambridge on 30 October and a month later she was still in Camberwell, sorting through the detritus and keeping her parents company. In late November 1927, just as a newly divorced Mina Hubbard was, somewhat belatedly, elected Fellow of the Royal Geographical Society (women were allowed to become fellows after 1913) for her contribution to mapping Labrador, Dorothy was engaged in mapping her own mother's unnavigable mind in her parents' attic. She was frightened, repelled and full of pity in equal measure. For the next five years she would often spend extended periods back in the family home during her mother's more severe bouts of illness. A pattern of her new life began to form: winters climbing in Wales or the Lake District, and summers in the Alps; term time in Cambridge where Ivor 'paced up and down the lawn discussing T. S. Eliot's agonising new poems and the place of religion in the Universe'; worrying about her parents, and now Vi, who also seemed to be increasingly mentally fragile.

Like Ethel Gallimore across the country in the Peak District, she started to worry about the erosion of Britain's wild places: the cars that now roared along the road past Tryfan in the Ogwen valley; the blasting operations to construct new pipelines; the cutting down of trees to improve the roads for motorists. She wrote to the authorities to protest and ask for there to be some kind of statutory protection for the most dramatic landscapes in Snowdonia, prefiguring the National Parks movement. 'The beauty of the [Ogwen] valley is over for some centuries', she wrote somewhat cryptically in her diary. She kept working, writing articles for newspapers and occasionally still helping out at the British Women's Patriotic League, which mainly involved soothing the ruffled feathers of aristocratic women.

The Great Year

And here she was, Mrs I. A. Richards, as dawn was breaking over the Alps in July 1928, roped together with her husband and their two guides, Joseph and Antoine Georges. As well as odd boots, she also had to deal with the knowledge that Joseph, who had been their guide for several years, didn't approve of women climbers. In earlier diaries she had recorded how 'he couldn't bear me to be treated like a man' and was always in a bad mood whenever Dorothy led a climb. 'J is hopelessly assertive in the most objectionable masculine way to anything which he considers female', she wrote. Would being a woman in the mountains always be such a battle? Still, today, their lives were in each other's hands. Up, up they went, sometimes over frozen gravel, sometimes smooth slabs, dancing across wafers of stone ledges, and up very steep, almost vertical pitches over rocks shining under their film of *verglas*. Dorothy removed the almost useless boots and changed into her rubbers (gym shoes); Ivor found it easier in socks. By 10.00 am they were under the overhang and beneath the almost sheer 200-foot rock slab above it before the angle of the ridge finally sloped to a less fatal gradient. They were shaking all over, from terror as well as cold; the sun had yet to move round the line of the ridge and their numbed hands found it difficult to grasp the rock. Joseph had scouted ways round the overhang, first to the left, and then to the right, but both were impossible. The only way, they realised despairingly, would be right over the 'nose' and up the almost vertical bridge, climbing on sheer rocks with few handholds for more than 150 feet. One false move and the climber would be pitched into the void, quite possibly taking the other three, all roped together, with them. Ivor, more afraid than Dorothy, from what they wrote in their joint diary entries of the day, recorded later that he did not see how Dorothy could survive. It meant launching oneself around the edge of the overhang from the whisp-thin handle of an ice axe, its head buried in a tiny crack of rock and then rounding the edge above thousands of feet of nothing. Joseph, then Ivor went up first and now it was Dorothy's turn. Antoine gave her a shot of brandy from his flask and helped her onto the axe handle. Her last sensible thought was 'Now I'm for it.' After that, the next nearly 200 feet were up to her.

She later described the climb as 'unreal', making her series of moves, balancing on the tip of a rubberised shoe or holding her entire weight with an elbow and knee, as if in a dream. Once a toe and a fingertip were all that were keeping her attached to those smooth, cold slabs. Five months later the climb would still haunt her: she was in 'real terror' and she never wanted to do anything like that again. It took the party three and a half hours to reach a gradient of relative safety, and they still had a long climb along the arête and up to the summit to go: two more hours of scrambling over the golden rocks, mottled in thawing snow under the sun that had now reached the ridge. As the snow melted, dislodged stones and boulders would 'slide down a snow patch, hop, whir and vanish into the great couloir', intimations of their own challenge to gravity. Once at the summit, the sun was already sinking. It was 5 pm and they had been climbing for 16 hours. Ivor announced he was going to take up croquet instead. But they knew that they had achieved something magnificent that day. Another two hours of descent of rocks glowing in the setting sun, by now Dorothy's foot, in the wrong size boot, really sore. It was a race against distance, time and fatigue, which descended upon her 'like a black bonnet'. The climb was later described as 'perhaps the most difficult British expedition of this period [1919–1939]'. It was even reported in *The Times* newspaper. They spent the rest of the summer on gentler, lower climbs, Ivor particularly determined to play it safe. Dorothy, while agreeing with him, couldn't help 'look[ing] rather longingly' still at the higher peaks around them, as they wandered through valleys and passes.

She would call 1928 'The Great Year' and for a while she was something of a celebrity. She was the 'Englishwoman Climber' in the popular *Daily Mail* newspaper, the three men in the party conveniently overlooked in the 1920s vogue for anything done by women to be of immense interest. Women magistrates, women doctors, women aviators, explorers, racing car drivers: whatever women did, they were *news*. The Ladies Alpine Club, with whom she had had so many battles not four years earlier, asked her to be a candidate to become their President (she refused) and the publisher Alan Harris approached her to write a book about climbing, with her husband as co-author. One might think that this invitation would bring Dorothy great joy. She had after all for many years, in her private diaries, been trying to work out in words her own emotional responses to being in the mountains. It was her life's work, as she put it later, to explore, when alone on some jagged peak, 'the queerness of the feelings that had pushed you up there … a summit clear or clouded is for every sort of reason, whatever sick souls may invent, the place of musings'. Her desire to ponder how 'the modern self is haunted by mountains', as writer Peter H. Hansen recently put it, was, in 1928, unusual. This was a time when technique and equipment were evolving fast, as higher and higher summits were 'conquered', in the *Alpine Journal*'s rugged language. The western, competitive urge to bag as many high peaks as possible, driven not a little by nationalism and colonialism, was at its height. Dorothy, however, didn't enjoy the kind of book that favoured discussions of technique over emotion. She might have leapt at the chance to craft a different kind of mountaineering narrative. However, as with many aspects of her life, the book had a difficult, slow and painful birth.

Most of these difficulties stemmed from the publisher's desire to include Ivor as her co-author. While wanting to cash in on Dorothy's fame, they were unwilling to offer her sole authorship. Ivor Richards, with several books under his belt already and a Cambridge man, was, they perceived, a reliable co-author.

And besides, as they wrote to Dorothy during the book's many years of gestation, while they wanted the fame and glamour of her name, they didn't think 'too much attention should be drawn to the woman business in the book', not specifying what 'the woman business' might be. When Alan Harris first invited a proposal in December 1928, she wrote back emphasising her interest in writing a book, but it was very much a solo project she had in mind: '*I* am distinctly interested by your suggestion of *my* writing a mountain book', she wrote. She was also quite clear about the kind of book she wanted to write: 'There are many types of climbing chat I detest.' However, both Ivor and Dorothy had lunch with Alan Harris on 25 June 1929, where they agreed 'to write a joint mountaineering book to be published in 1930'. Neither of these happened.

Another barrier was her own lack of self-confidence, which battled with her strong will to do things her way. This lack of confidence had dogged her all her life: she never thought she was a good enough climber or writer. During her first years in the Welsh hills, she would reveal some 40 years later, she climbed peaks alone with a map and compass, to memorise the names of all the summits and valleys so she wouldn't appear an idiot in front of those confident young men who would make fun of her if she got things wrong. On her first visit to Arthur Beale's chandlery in Shaftesbury Avenue to buy climbing rope, she steeled herself 'to put on as much air of an expert as I could' to avoid being found out as an impostor.

She often sought Ivor's help in editing and redrafting her writing. Words seemed to come so much more easily for him. But they had fundamental differences of approach. The first major difference came during their joint writing up of the Dent Blanche climb for the *Alpine Journal*, and which also forms the climax of *Climbing Days*. While the achievement was made in 1928, and a short, technical account appeared in the next edition of the journal, it wasn't until 1931 that the full, detailed narrative of that day was published in the *Alpine Journal*. In her diaries, one can see immediately why. While Ivor wanted to gloss over what he saw as their weaknesses: their trembling with fear, and the fact that Joseph Georges, their Swiss guide, had made that first, and thus most dangerous manoeuvre up and over the nose of the overhang, she wanted to write the complete, whole truth of the day. In her diary of 7 October 1928, she writes: 'Ivor doesn't feel he can tell the truth in the *Alpine Journal* ... I know JG [Joseph Georges] took the risk and that we were definitely frightened but I think these are accepted facts on most big expeditions.' Ivor's refusal to help her write up the account leaves her 'bitterly disappointed.

I feel I can't begin to write an adequate account alone.' When their account finally appeared, it was by-lined 'D. E. Pilley and I. A. Richards', and it conveyed much of their fear as Joseph, having tried every possible route, turned to the most dangerous, over the nose itself: 'At one moment he seemed almost to be emulating a lizard on a ceiling.' Joseph's star role as lead climber was fully celebrated in the published account. It was up to them, as Dorothy wrote in her diary, to bring their stunning achievement to life by writing it up for readers of the *Alpine Journal*. She saw no shame in admitting either to being afraid or that their paid guide was the first over the overhang.

Climbing Days

This honesty is a hallmark of *Climbing Days*, and one of the reasons it is still seen as a classic of its kind: every weakness, from her serial succumbing to heat stroke to her fear of disturbing the gentians or indeed the perfect snow of the glaciers as she walks on them, is laid bare to readers. Indeed, one critic would comment that the memoir was full of 'silly accidents'. *Climbing Days* is also a uniquely feminine mountain memoir, of which there were vanishingly few in 1935. Dorothy's strong sense of being out of place and also of being unwanted in those wild places by the assertively masculine men of the Alpine Club is graven in every page. Why else would the veteran mountaineer Godfrey Solly greet her at the Refuge du Couvercle (nearly 9,000 feet), at what should be a commonwealth of serious climbers, with the demeaning and gendered demand for her hairpin? 'He had a big pipe and it was unconquerably blocked. What he most needed in life was a hairpin, and what use was woman on the mountains unless she could instantly provide one?' That this anecdote made it into her book shows the incident bit and rankled (and you don't need to be an expert in Freudian analysis to understand what Solly's 'big pipe' represented). She was only tolerated in this place, above the world, above the clouds, if she were, like Gertrude Bell dangling on a rope, able to carry out the feminine duty of providing for, and looking after, the men.

Climbing Days also leaves the reader in no doubt that the joys and luxuries of responding to those calls to the spirit that can only be experienced in truly wild places are not only reserved for half the human race. To give a woman this joy and sensibility was quite a revolutionary act. Most pre-twentieth-century female-authored travel and exploration memoirs lie buried in private diaries and letters, as if women were afraid to assert their presence in the lands forbidden to their kind. Dorothy Wordsworth's beautiful *Grasmere Journal*, where she recorded feeling herself 'dissolve' into the landscape as she lay 'upon the steep of Loughrigg' in the Lake District, would not be published until 1958. Nan Shepherd, now a celebrated lyricist of the wild, had yet, in 1928, to publish her poetry of the Cairngorms, rejoicing in the burns, 'with the glass-white shiver/Singing over stone'. As we have already seen, while women's tales of exploration, like Mina Hubbard's *Woman's Way*, and the many fashionable motoring memoirs were popular for illustrating modern woman's pluck and derring-do, there is a gulf of difference between what Mina put in her book for public consumption and what she left, undiscovered for nearly a century, in her private diary.

The literary mountaineering canon, from the classical period to the interwar years and beyond, presents us with, as the writer Kathleen Jamie so eloquently puts it, the gaze of the 'lone enraptured male ... quelling our harsh and lovely and sometimes difficult land with his civilised lyrical words'. We can go as far back as the ascetics of the *Mahabharata*; Jerome finding in the craggy spurs of the Syrian mountains a balm for his unhappy flesh and Petrarch's celebrated ascent of Mont Ventoux: millennia of the male point of view of how the mountains are intricately linked to the sublime. Earth may be the mother, Gaia; mountain features may be likened to the earth goddess's breasts, womb, buttocks or belly; but real, corporeal women with their messy bloody bodily functions were either unwelcome or indeed in 'holy' mountains were, and still are, forbidden completely. How to put into words, for public consumption, these feelings that in so many cultures and religions across the world, since before recorded time, women were not supposed to have?

It would take Dorothy nearly seven years to write *Climbing Days*. Not only was it the difficulty of finding the words to describe 'the bodily feeling, nameless and definite and irreplaceable, like a scent or a taste or an ache ... the reverberation of one's life among ... the purple chaos of rocks ... the spongy masses of sphagnum ... the swamps ... the oblique rain across the long-snouted rocks'. Ill health, constant travels, at one stage the loss of an almost complete manuscript as well as the slow wresting of control and authorship from the publishers, all played their part, too, in the delays. Shortly after that unsatisfactory lunch with Alan Harris in June 1929, Dorothy and Ivor boarded a train heading east. Ivor had been offered a lectureship at Tsing Hua University, on the edge of then Peking, in the shadows of the Xi Shan mountains west of the city. Dorothy packed away into storage their possessions in 10 King's Parade, bubbling with excitement at the thought of another adventure. The University paid for both of them to take the train from Berlin to Vladivostok via Moscow,

Signature du porteur

J.E. Pilley Richards

Vu pour légalisation:

..............., le .....ρ........... 19......

*Magdalene College
Cambridge England*

La perte de cette carte entraîne une amende de fr. 1.—

British Passport C.77756

7.3 Dorothy's Alpine pass, c. 1930s

and weeks of bone-shattering railway and diarrhoea couldn't stem her joy at being on the move again.

Finally, after travelling via Japan and Korea, a month after leaving Berlin, they arrived at the Hotel du Nord, Peking, where she was 'very glad to get good beds'. The University gave them a set of rooms in a former Lama temple, set in 100 acres of walled gardens of the old Summer Palace; their terrace was overhung with Chinese cinnamon trees and tiger lilies blazed in their shade. Her headaches returned but China enchanted her. She took Mandarin and flute lessons; she planted peach and pomegranate trees, and 150 snapdragons in the gardens. On her thirty-fifth birthday she ate black year-old eggs, shark's fin and 'stuffed crabs the size of pennies' at a welcome feast for the new lecturers, recruited from across the globe to educate a new generation of Chinese students. Dorothy was advisor to the female students, 30 out of a student body of 500. In the autumn she began climbing in the Xi Shan, the Western Hills, wading through soft snow between old Buddhist temples, pale pink and rose red, where she observed, like the remains of Ozymandias, 'gods in all states of decay, just wooden stumps in the mud'. She travelled long, dusty roads lined with willows. She climbed the Diamond Mountains in Korea, and in the summer of 1930 travelled to Japan and climbed Mount Fuji, its flanks still warm with lava flows; she observed wryly that women had only been permitted to climb the sacred mountain since 1912 but now neat little figures, under large parasols, were picking their way up the steep, barren slopes with glee. Between successive bouts of ill health, headaches and chest infections, she began to write her book, about to slay a few ancient gods herself.

8

Evelyn: Vanuatu, Papua New Guinea and Mount Nok, 1929–51

'Maybe it is some innate savagery in myself'

George Joy, army man and servant of Empire: moustachioed and whip thin. He was at his writing desk in the British Residency, at the highest point atop one of the farthest flung of all British Overseas Territories: Efate Island, New Hebrides (now the Republic of Vanuatu). The Residency was 179 steps up from the landing stage on a tiny outcrop, across a narrow channel from the main settlement, Port Vila. The location – an island off an island – was carefully selected to avoid disease and mixing with the natives. Joy couldn't see much going on beneath the vast green canopy below the broad veranda but he did enjoy an excellent view of the French Resident's quarters across the bay, with whom the British shared joint command of this cluster of volcanic outcrops and coral atolls. The French Residency was at similar altitude and the two incumbents took great pains to ensure their flags, raised at 8 o'clock sharp each morning, flew at exactly the same height. The canvas splashes of red, white and blue fluttered over the dense green forests of bamboo, tree ferns and tropical hardwoods. It was 1929 and on the far side of the world the New York stock market had started to slide but Joy's immediate concerns under the fan that turned the heavy air were the heat, the humidity and this damned Lady scientist who had just turned up.

His was a sleepy and mostly quiet posting, out here in the wide blue Pacific, overseeing this archipelagic fiefdom. Joy was responsible for the ten British settlers: missionaries, sandalwood traders and coconut plantation owners, scattered across 82 islands and 450 miles of ocean. Very little happened on Efate to distract him from his private experiments into psychophysics, that had preoccupied him since seeing action in Flanders during the First World War. But now Miss Cheesman had arrived, tiny, determined, insisting on travelling to the island of Malekula, 150 miles away so she could study bugs. He had some reason to be alarmed, he felt. Not only, in his opinion, were the natives extremely unpredictable, with a reputation for cannibalism, but the last two white men who went to Malekula had both died there. The colonial surveyor whom Joy had appointed and sent to measure and map the island had died of blackwater fever in 1928, and the Cambridge anthropologist, Bernard Deacon, had died, also of blackwater fever, in 1927. In fact, the last time a white man had successfully crossed the interior of Malekula was 1873 when the notorious Australian slaver Henry Ross Lewin, accompanied by an armed militia, slashed a track from north to south in five days. Lewin had spent a decade kidnapping Pacific Islanders and taking them to work as indentured labourers in the timber plantations of northern Australia. Since then the natives had been very suspicious of white men. Lewin himself was killed in 1874 by islanders on Tanna, in the southern part of the New Hebrides, a crime which the Royal Navy, convinced of Lewin's cruelty and villainy, refused to investigate. It was a bad business.

As for white women, well there simply hadn't been any on Malekula since the departure of a Seventh Day Adventist missionary's wife in the last century. And now this Miss Cheesman had turned up in Vila on 29 January, announcing her intention to spend two years on Malekula and some of the other islands, far from Joy's abilities to protect her, such as they were. He wrote to his boss, Sir Eyre Hutson, the High Commissioner for the Western Pacific, to communicate his concerns and cover himself if, or most likely, when, Miss Cheesman came to grief. 'I gave Miss Cheesman instructions *in writing* as to the necessity of exercising the greatest caution in visiting any places distant from the white settlement', he wrote. 'Nevertheless, with all deference and respect I express some doubt as to the advisability of *a Lady who is unaccompanied, engaging in scientific research.*' He wasn't the only one to worry. The Archbishop of Canterbury himself, a Principal Trustee of the Natural History Museum under whose aegis Miss Cheesman was travelling, had expressed grave doubts on the advisability of 'a lady' heading alone to an island where the natives were of 'an extremely primitive and suspicious type'.

While Joy was writing and worrying, Evelyn was already hunting for insects with her large, foldable net and moth screen in the hot, Malekulan nights. She had arrived on the steamer *Makambo* after a ten-day journey from Sydney, ten nights being tossed around in a cabin that was 'like an oven with full heat turned on'. Before dawn on the tenth day, she was as usual on deck attempting to suppress her seasickness when a cry went around the ship and there, lit up by the blazing stars, lay the pale violet low-lying shore, 'and a few broad white strokes like chalk marks which showed the edges of the reef'. Her stomach somersaulted with excitement at arriving at the place that was to be her home for the next two years. Nothing, she later wrote, could match the thrill of seeing the pale smudges of breakers, the dark shapes of the forests beyond and the promise of those millions of tiny, busy, winged, creeping, dancing beings, weaving their worlds at such a different pace from our own: a whole life, sometimes, of birth, procreation and death completed in one human day. On Malekula she endured the excessive heat and moisture, the air laden with volcanic dust from the active fissures that were everywhere spewing out gas and rock. She tolerated the humidity which meant that within days anything made of fibre would be spotted with ironmould and mildew: grey and black polka dots spreading across material, as if undergoing some strange meta-morphosis into a dappled creature of the woods. It was a world so very different from the one back in England: at night the jungle was lit up by the phospho-rescent mould that grew everywhere on the dead leaves and constellations of fireflies provided a tiny, alternative universe.

She laboured with damp matches, irregular meals, sleeping in deserted mission houses or native yam sheds. The bone-aching fevers and soaring temperatures of the malaria that would now accompany her for the rest of her life, and even the aggressive wild boars: all these were but minor nuisances, so deeply was she absorbed in her work. 'The insects are the serious part of existence', she wrote of this expedition later, 'all the rest is just a joke – a bad joke at times but not worth worrying about'. She had paid her respects to the British Resident, handed over her letter of introduction from the Museum and listened, politely, to Joy's warnings about the natives but ignored him. She was deliberately vague about her plans, later confessing to answering his questions with questions of her own, knowing that had she been explicit she would probably have been forbidden to leave Port Vila. She was a small and, at nearly 50, in Malekulan eyes, an already elderly woman. She had rapidly concluded that she, being neither a sandalwood trader, nor recruiter for the coconut plantations, nor press gang for ships' crews, nor indeed an anthropologist who took things away, posed no threat. On the contrary, with her aspirin, cold compresses, quinine and tea, which she distributed to sick Malekulans who sought her help, she became known as 'medicine woman'. For them she was a benign supernatural being that came from the wild bush that surrounded the safe spaces of their villages, wearing a strange costume of soft felt hat and long, many-pocketed tunic tied with a belt from which her small collecting jars hung. The Malekulans were fascinated by her foldable net, which could have been put to so many better uses than catching inedible moths and butterflies.

She was glad to be back in the Pacific. It was just over three years since her first expedition when she left the *St George* steamer and set up her own insect-collecting laboratories on Tahiti and Bora Bora. She had returned to dank England from the luminous tropics in October 1925 to find her mentor at London Zoo, Professor Lefroy, was dead. In October 1924, he had been experimenting with a new pesticide in his laboratory at Imperial College when one of the test tubes leaked and he was engulfed in toxic gas meant for his insect quarries. He survived a few days but never regained consciousness. Without him to speak up for her, Evelyn sensed the opposition to her position as curator growing, particularly with one highly influential male secretary with whom she had never seen 'eye to eye'.

She left the Zoo's employment in November 1925 and instead took up a freelance post at the Natural History section of the British Museum (later to be renamed the Natural History Museum). She arrived at the research laboratory in Kensington with 500 specimens from her collecting in Tahiti and Gorgona, including some never-before-seen wingless short-horned grasshoppers and a gecko that had fallen into her soup one evening, along with the monstrous, armoured centipede that had killed it. Beginning to realise that what she had found among the specimens she had collected represented something of an entomological mystery, she volunteered to become an unpaid researcher, supporting herself with writing books and articles about her travels. She found a small, unfurnished room in a secluded part of Kensington for ten shillings a week. It was a precarious and difficult time and often she went without meals, or subsisted for days on rice and potatoes. She avoided company, and invitations to dine out, fearful that she would have to repay the hospitality, which she couldn't.

She couldn't afford her own microscope either, and it was impossible to write anything on insect taxonomy that would gain respect from the scientific establishment without one. Fortunately, a relatively new member of the Museum's entomological research staff, William China, allowed her use of his microscope during his lunch break. China, who would become legendary in the department for his kindness (unlike the many eminent scientists there, he had studied at a polytechnic and was only able to go to Cambridge for his BSc after winning an Open Scholarship), was perhaps more sensitive than others to the obstacles Evelyn faced. Using the Greenough binocular microscope,

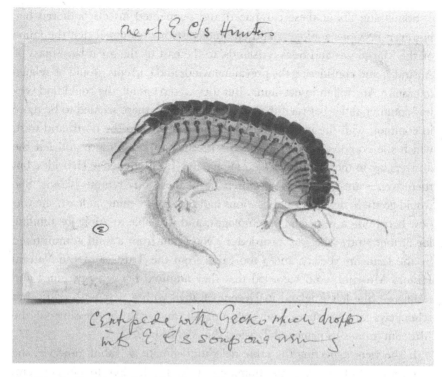

The rt E C's Hunters

Centipede with Gecko which dropped into E. C's soup one evening

8.1 'Centipede with Gecko which dropped into EC's soup one evening', water colour by Evelyn Cheesman

she was able to observe and describe a plant-dwelling bug that she had found on the Society Islands, *Eutinginotum raiteae*. It was small, brown and unremarkable, save for one thing: after extensive researches through existing learned publications, Evelyn realised that this little hairy-legged, ovoid creature, which secreted waxy flakes from its back, was '*sp. Nov*'. She wrote the truncated Latin phrase carefully in her copperplate italics: a new species, its discovery claimed by Evelyn in a scientific paper published in September 1926 in the *Entomologist*. That wasn't all: over the next two years, peering through the thick stereoscopic lenses, she identified eight more new species, including *Veliidae* (water striders), *Reduviidae* (assassin bugs), *Coreidae* (leaf-footed bugs), *Pentatomidae* (shield bugs) and *Sphegidae* (digger wasps). Her findings were published in several scientific journals and each paper at the bottom recorded: 'My thanks are due to Mr W. E. China for his very kind assistance', her way of acknowledging his loaning of his microscope while he ate his sandwiches and smoked his pipe during his lunch break.

Something about these carapaced and segmented insects bothered her, however. Previous zoologists and entomologists had assumed that the fauna of the Marquesas and Society Islands, to the east of the great land mass of Australia, and considering the prevailing winds and currents, would be related to eastern Australian insect fauna. But they weren't at all; she could find very few commonalities between the collections. In fact, there seemed to be more in common with the insects of Papua, much further to the north and west, which she couldn't explain at all. She needed to know more and felt the answers lay in the islands between Papua and Tahiti, the New Hebrides, but there were vanishingly few specimens from these tiny remote islands. She would go there next. Her publications had meant one thing, at least: she was now becoming a respected entomologist, and was able to apply for funding for further study. She was awarded a £200 grant from a fund administered by the Linnean Society, and £100 came from the Trustees of the Natural History Museum, who recorded that they admired her 'energy, pluck and resource'. She left England in December 1928 with a new bush outfit, her schooldays lacrosse shoes, and collecting kit, and with the blessings of the Museum (minus its principal Trustee, the Archbishop).

If she were expecting the same delightful climate as Tahiti, however, she was wrong. Not only was the humidity on Malekula close to 100 per cent, but the constant spewing of volcanic ash from the nearby island of Ambrym, with its cauldrons of active vents, also meant that her food, clothes, hair and skin were permanently covered in gritty ash. It lay so thickly on the leaves of the sandalwood trees that she could write her name in it. She had to shave her head, the better to kill and retrieve the corpses of the millions of black biting flies that attacked her daily. The only way to ward them off, she discovered, was standing by a thickly smoking fire so she ended up like some kind of bristly smoked mackerel covered in painful, itchy bites. And then there were the mosquitoes, clouds of them, that arrived at sunset in a golden haze, biting, sucking and transmitting malaria. The first attack came shortly after she arrived on Malekula: temperature of 104 degrees, bone-aching chills, dizziness and headaches. Sometimes she tried to continue her journeys through the thick, almost impenetrable bush but often she would lie, prostrate, in the empty mission house on a cliff above the ocean, boiling inside with her own fevers.

She took as much quinine as she dared, 'battering the malaria germs into quiescence'. Once she was so desperate, she took 15 grammes of the bitter grains, a potentially lethal quantity and drifted, for days, in hallucinatory semi-consciousness. Often the malaria attacks coincided with the frequent violent rainstorms that deluged the island, and the combination of fever and the soaring atmospheric pressure transported her to the very edges of existence. But as the storms, and the raging fevers, ebbed away, she experienced a moment of almost divine serenity when the air returned to its fresh storm-cleaned buoyancy. Then came 'a very keen sensual awareness of quite trivial matters: bird song, the delicate coldness of a stream … the big, blue convolvulus flowers … in fact every little thing gives pleasure with an intensity that is hard to describe'. As Dorothy Pilley was wading through the knee-deep soft snow of the Xi Shan hills, trying to catch the words she was searching for, Evelyn was wading through the dense bamboo forests of Malekula, butterfly net in hand; both found it hard to grasp their quarry. While the insects may have been numerous, and, in the case of the mosquitos irritating and terrifying in the same degree, Evelyn was strangely unable to find whole groups of vertebrates: no frogs at all could she find, and an entire *genus* of venomous snake seemed to be missing from a group of islands, which was extraordinary considering their location. Had she lost her collector's touch? Or was there more to the mysteries of Pacific fauna than she had already stumbled across?

King Ringapat and the poisoned spear

Despite Joy's warnings, she also made contact with the local native tribes, particularly the dominant Big Nambas, who occupied the northern part of the island. She hired the younger boys to guide her, a useful and symbiotic relationship: they gave her local knowledge of paths up cliffs and through apparently impenetrable forest, which was crucial to the success of this, and all her collecting trips. She shared her medicines and instructed them on how to use a compass and binoculars; each showing the other how to find one's way through the wild. Here she made acquaintance with their leader, King Ringapat, who had 17 wives; six were dead but the surviving 11 were kept inside his compound. She spent several nights in his enclosure, discussing insects and white traders in a mixture of broken English and hand gestures; she taught him how to use a pocket magnifier and showed him photographs of King George V on horseback. Ringapat insisted on sending her away with a gift for King George, from his own personal belongings. She chose a shell necklace and a 14-foot-long bamboo-handled spear, which she had sent via the P and O line to the British Museum, to be presented to the Emperor.

Ringapat asked for a drum-full of oil in exchange, which two years later, on her return, Evelyn duly arranged. The spear is decorated with an ornate, and terrifying, carved wooden double-sided head, which was wrapped in leaves and lashed to the spear shaft with braided sinnet. A letter of faint thanks from the King's office at Sandringham duly arrived, requesting that the spear be thoroughly cleaned. The clearly dubious Royal official added, 'there is no hurry about this', not wishing, perhaps, to play a part in poisoning his Majesty. The cautious official, it transpired, had been wise in his request. A note from the Museum's Mineral Department dated 3 February 1931 states that the tip of the 14-foot-long spear was indeed poisoned, with deadly strychnine from the *Nux vomica* tree, and that it was boiled in water, then alcohol, then ammonia (twice), then carbon tetrachloride, then hydrochloric acid and finally oil, so as to be made safe for his Majesty. In fact, the spear, for safety's sake, was kept at the British Museum, far from his Majesty's tender flesh, and is now in an offsite storage vault in east London.

I visit the spear just days after the coronation of George V's great grandson, Charles III and this material connection with my subject resonates profoundly. The spear is very long, almost three times the height of Evelyn, who was barely five foot tall. It's a measure of her courage, and also impish sense of humour, that she chose such an outlandish gift for the King. Ringapat's gift was accompanied by something far more meaningful: a solemn oath, but an oath which went both ways. Ringapat promised that he and his people would treat all white visitors kindly as long as, in return, the white men stopped stealing his boys. It was a moment of shame for Evelyn as she surveyed the depredations her kind had made in the New Hebrides: the diseases they had imported, leaving sometimes whole villages deserted from the 'sickness belong white man'; the land they had taken and, worst of all, the boys and young men either lured away or kidnapped and the young women taken by the 'recruiters' as sex slaves. A neighbouring village was still in turmoil over a recent incident when a French recruiter had kidnapped two boys, one of whom died. The French Resident had sent a bullock in reparations. She reviewed, drily, Joy's warnings to her. In British eyes she may be far from home, in the 'wild'. But the white settlers and recruiters who stalked the bush searching for cheap, or free, labour certainly represented for the islanders something far more terrifying, a darkness, an evil that lurked outside the villages' thickly woven bamboo palisades. These were the true monsters of the wild, coming from the sea in their tall boats.

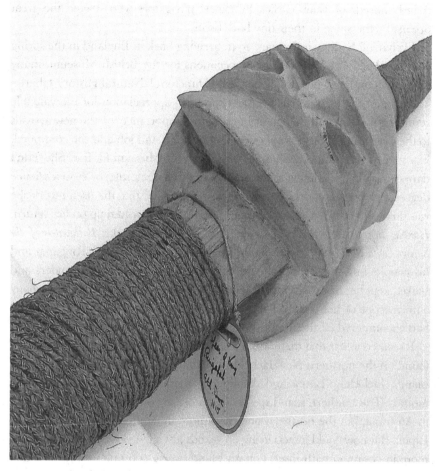

8.2 Carved head on shaft of King Ringapat's spear

When successive bouts of malaria had weakened her to such a state that she could continue with her collecting no longer, she took a steamer back to Sydney. Leaving Port Vila in darkness, she later said, she was glad the British flag wasn't flying above the Residency on Efate, for the shame she felt. But she was, for all her indignation at white rapacity, a product of her time and European worldview: she described the inhabitants of the New Hebrides, and other places she travelled, as 'primitive'. She wrote that the islands had been 'discovered' by seventeenth- and eighteenth-century European explorers, despite their having been settled, in successive waves, from Australia and southern

Asia hundreds of years earlier, by expert navigators who steered the great oceans by the stars, in their tiny bark boats.

Evelyn left Sydney in January 1931, arriving back in England in the spring with a collection of 18,000 insect specimens for the British Museum, many of them completely new to science. The Director of Natural History, Charles Tate Regan thanked her in a letter expressing appreciation for the valuable results of her trip and the 'great interest and importance' of the new arrivals to the collection. He did not, however, offer her a staff job and she continued, in a state of semi-impoverishment, working at the Museum for free. She didn't dare complain – she knew as a woman without a doctorate, or even a science degree, her position at the Museum was tenuous, despite the useful work she was doing. Two of her so-called 'pot-boilers', hastily written up on her return, *Hunting Insects in the South Seas* (1932) and the more popular *Backwaters of the Savage South Seas* (1933), with picturesque descriptions of King Ringapat and his people, and the scrapes she got into involving leeches, giant spiders and snakes, kept her from starving. At least by now, she had finally been able to buy a microscope of her own. What she discovered only deepened the mystery she had encountered earlier about the distribution of insects in the south Pacific.

It seemed to her that there was a distinct 'break' between the species she had found on the northern New Hebrides, including Malekula, and the southern islands, including Tanna and Aneityum, where she had also spent several months. The southern island species had more in common with species found in Australia, but the northern ones had more in common with the island of Papua. But how could insects living on islands just a few dozen miles apart have more in common with insects on an island over 2,000 miles away? It didn't make any sense. It could only be possible, she thought fancifully, if the islands of the northern group could somehow have been in an entirely different part of the Pacific, closer to Papua *and had moved, across the ocean, as if they were afloat,* which at the time seemed totally mad. Evelyn was working on her enigmatic insects in the days before the science of plate tectonics, the understanding that the earth's crust moved in great segments across the millennia, had been established. Ideas of 'continental drift' had been raised during the First World War, but were highly controversial and lacking in evidence. Scientists were already aware that the earth had gone through periods of heating and cooling and that land masses had undergone long periods of submersion during warm periods when sea levels were higher, but these ideas were still very limited, and evidence for the idea that the earth's crust actually moved was not fully established until the 1960s. In addition, geologists thought that Papua had

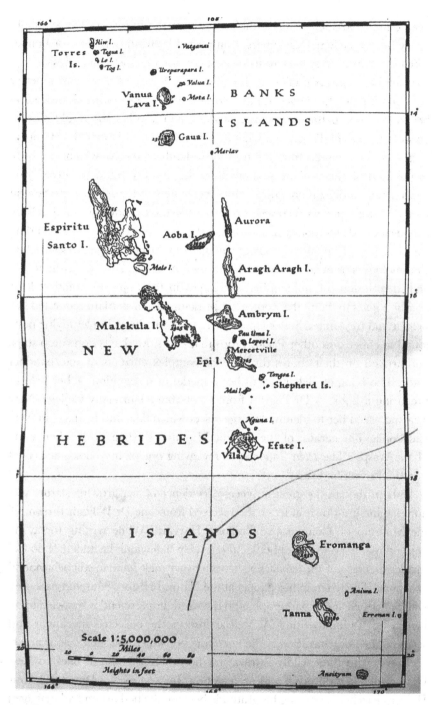

8.3 Evelyn's map of the New Hebrides (Vanuatu) showing the location of Cheesman's Line

been entirely submerged until only recently, so the insects on Papua should surely be relatively new incomers, transported by winds, or ships, or human activity, and traceable back to its nearest continents, Australia and Asia.

It felt like she was pulling at threads at the border of some vast tapestry but each thread she tugged unravelled and came loose rather than leading her to the main pattern or picture. It was obvious to her she would have to go to the island of Papua and what was then known as Dutch New Guinea, and trace these insects from the northern islands of the New Hebrides back to the land of their origin; perhaps then the mystery could be solved. She needed more money, more grants, more recognition to fund these trips. Several more scientific papers followed, each successive one showing new levels of confidence and entomological knowledge; she worked like a fury understanding the principles of taxonomy, zoology and geology. Science began to notice her. Entomologists from across the world: Sydney, Adelaide, Alberta, wrote to her with descriptions of unidentified specimens in the hope she could at least ascribe a *genus* to them; the Zoological Museum of Amsterdam requested her help, as did the United States Department of Agriculture, in identifying pests found in coffee and other Pacific crops that had stowed away on cargo ships and arrived on their shores through the complex currents of international trade. The King of Belgium sent her a medal in recognition of her help in preparing a book. A Dr Pilgrim from Canterbury University College, New Zealand asked her to identify 'a large insect which flew into my face' in New Caledonia. The curator of the Botanic Museum, Brisbane, called her 'Lady of the Wasps'. The *Daily Telegraph*, in reviewing one of her books, described her as a 'Scientific Diana'.

Perhaps though the greatest piece of evidence of her growing stature was a masculine put-down in letter she received from one Dr William Brown, of the Museum of Comparative Zoology, Harvard. While writing to say he enjoyed reading one of her books, about wasp behaviour, he added: 'I do feel that a lady, being of the female sex, needs a heavy male hand to edit behavioural accounts.' The letter, in her papers at the Natural History Museum, is scored with red pencil at this paragraph, and the word 'impertinent' is scrawled upon it, in Evelyn's handwriting. As well as insects, she collected specimens and seeds of the gorgeous flowers she encountered, which splashed colour across the forest with their wildly extravagant hues. These she sent back to Kew Gardens for identification and propagation. In 1933, Kew's Director Arthur Hill wrote to her expressing his gratitude because the herbarium had managed to propagate a *Passiflora suberosa* seed that she had sent back from New Guinea, and they raised it to produce its brilliant green star-shaped flowers. She kept Kew busy, and as recently as 2013 botanists at the orchid herbarium were still identifying flowers she had collected eight decades earlier.

Radio star

On 21 November 1932, she stood where, 24 years earlier, Mina Hubbard had spoken about her travels through Labrador, to deliver the first of what would be several lectures to the Royal Geographical Society. She spoke with detailed geological, entomological and zoological knowledge on her travels in the New Hebrides, pacing her delivery carefully, in phrases almost like musical bars, as she had taught herself to control the asthma she had suffered from since childhood. Her voice was wheezy, but also richly deep, melodious, bringing to mind the timbre of a provincial choir master with a 40-cigarettes-a-day habit. It was this voice that producers at the BBC found so engaging, as did their listeners, and between the 1930s and 1960s she was invited to speak on several programmes, for children and adults, about her travels and the creatures she had encountered, from concussed vipers to albino badgers. Only one of these programmes now survives, recorded in 1956 with a very young David Attenborough and Gerald Durrell, who sound like chirruping adolescents alongside the septuagenarian Evelyn's gravelled tenor.

Both men having enjoyed the solid backdrop of university educations and family wealth, they expressed astonished disbelief when she described how she survived her first expedition to the South Pacific on £10. They enjoyed her amusing anecdotes, laughing heartily as she described stunning a venomous snake with the handle of her butterfly net. David, now Sir David Attenborough, remembers feeling 'very flattered' to be invited to go on the same programme as a woman whom he thought of as 'truly heroic', he wrote to me recently. He has kept all her books, he said. 'For a young woman to travel by herself in the 1930s in some of the wildest parts of the Pacific catching butterflies, was an extraordinarily brave thing to do.' Hearing her disembodied voice from across the years in an airless listening booth of the British Library was an electrifying experience for me and I understood why that soothing lilt, conveying at all times mild amusement, went down so well with listeners of BBC Children's Hour and the Home Service, as well as the austere naval men of the Royal Geographical Society.

On that dark November day in 1932 she described the light and heat of the tropics, the insects she caught, the logistical difficulties of journeying through the dense bush; the paths that disappeared behind her, leaving no trace of her footsteps. She also emphasised the inaccuracy of existing Admiralty charts and offered her own sketches of the mountainous interior as corrections. She spoke of meeting King Ringapat, and of the drear reputation white men had on the island, and the reasons for it. But of the malaria that drove her back to Australia early, or the £4 she had to borrow from an elderly missionary in order to get her fare home, she said nothing. Fear of being seen as a weak and amateurish woman when she desperately needed the members of these scientific committees, dominated by military men and naturalists who had dim views of women scientists, to award her grants kept her quiet on that front. Letters in the Natural History Museum archives show her colleagues there, at least, knew of the recurring fevers she suffered from and of her endless need to economise, unsupported as she was either by salary or a well-funded university expedition.

She did however win a surprising number of admirers among the bearded and braided audience. After listening to her speak, Admiral Sir William Goodenough, then President of the Royal Geographical Society, pronounced himself a fan. Inviting her to a subsequent meeting of the Society, showing he couldn't care less if she wasn't a Captain, Doctor, Professor, or Sir, he introduced her thus: 'People sometimes arrive at an eminence where they are spoken of without any prefix, and that is why I call on Evelyn Cheesman.' They became correspondents for the next ten years as she sent back information that, as the 1930s wore on, would become increasingly interesting to even retired naval officers. Goodenough, resourceful military man that he was, passed on her details to Major Humphrey Quill, Head of Naval Intelligence, Singapore. German 'planters' cutting wide, straight roads through the forest; Japanese 'tourists' taking pictures of every cove, gently sloping beach or deep anchorage – like the insects and camouflaged forest fauna, none escaped her inquisitive eye. As she had done as a child, she drew detailed maps, sketching in mountain ranges, forests, marshes, landing strips and sheltered harbours. Only these weren't fantasies of childhood, but real islands she had visited. Her maps and photographs would be used by Naval Intelligence during the Second World War, enabling the Allies to fight the Japanese across the Pacific.

Evelyn continued winning grants and would spend the better part of ten years on Papua New Guinea and its surrounding islands. She camped deep in the uninhabited Cyclops Mountains, travelled to tiny and isolated Waigeu and Japen, climbing Mount Nok on Waigeu, thousands of feet, wearing her old school lacrosse shoes, selected as the best footwear to prevent slipping. On cloud-shrouded Mount Nok, a remnant of an extinct volcano, she picked a brilliant sky-blue orchid, which was finally named by the botanists at Kew Gardens in 2013 as *Dendrobium azureum Schuit*. In his description of the flower, botanist André Schuiteman says that, despite their reputation for outrageous chromatic brilliance, 'very few orchids possess truly blue flowers' and indeed Evelyn's orchid was the only known truly blue orchid in its *genus*. Writing more than 70 years later, in a different age, Schuiteman pays tribute to Evelyn's courageous investigations, quoting, admiringly, from her report of the expedition: 'orchids on trees with moisture continuously dripping off fringes of moss. Large clusters of a leguminous bloom like white acacia drooped from small trees. There were cream, pale lemon and brilliant blue orchids, but the colours orange and scarlet predominated, flaming out of the green.' Here she sketched, and painted the view, desperate to fix the colours and panorama in her mind.

Now approaching 60 she climbed the sheer Torricelli Mountains, hauling herself up on the plaited tree roots embedded in the rocks. Like Dorothy Pilley she watched swarms of leeches, scenting her warm blood, coming at her in waves and heard the cataclysmic storms, the *Wambrau*, threshing their way towards her, delivering tons of water a second in a solid stream, felling sometimes hundreds of trees in one night. Each time she went, she felt herself growing wilder, finding more in common with the forest than other human beings. Arriving in the Papuan jungle and gazing up at slow, purposeful giants, she and the supersized flora apprehended each other, recognised connections. 'In the first moments of initiation its grand aristocracy of trees link up with chords inside yourself and you know you have come home', she wrote. These chords, forged in her childhood among the beech-crowned Downs of Kent, now vibrated and resonated within her. The vibrations now at last were 'as complete as possible in this mortal life because here is nature in its fullest exuberance'.

Pushing through 'vegetation which closes over you and is pathless as water', she rejoiced in this 'innate savagery' awakened in her, wanted no separation between herself and the ecosystem. Like Daphne, she was becoming the trees. She noticed this deep, interlocking understanding with the natural environment that the native Papuans displayed: unlike in the so-called civilised world, there was no separation between them and their surroundings, 'human, superhuman, animate and inanimate', they understood what the trees were saying and what a simple change in the colour of the light or the sounds of the forest might mean. She grudgingly returned to her camp when night fell and intense darkness under the canopy made further exploration impossible. Sometimes even then she couldn't bear to be parted from the trees and she would creep out, climb a massive trunk on liana vines and lie on a branch among the aerial moss forests and epiphytes, watching the stars wheel through the heavens far above. 'Even to see vegetation massed in silhouette against a night sky was worth the discomfort of getting wet and dirty once more. One grudged even the necessary hours of sleep.' The native Papuans called her simply, 'the woman who walks', denoting her difference from the women of the island villages, who spent most of their days either inside the compounds, or on only short excursions to collect food or water.

Cyclopea

Contact with the west, however, had to be made from time to time, usually over the vexed issue of money. While Evelyn had been awarded £400 from the Percy Sladen Trust, administered by the Linnean Society, and the Godman Fund, set up in memory of the naturalist Frederick du Cane Godman and administered by the Natural History Museum, it fell short of the amount she had requested. On Papua she economised by walking 100 miles along the coast to reach the British Territory and a less expensive journey home but asked the museum if she could have £50 more. Her letters to Captain Norman Riley, Keeper of Entomology at the Museum, reveal the level of discomfort she endured, which she glossed over or left out of her books and public lectures. 'After a fifteen-hour thunderstorm the site of my hut was flooded and never dried again', she wrote to Riley. She lived for months with three inches of seething, breeding slime under its wooden floor. The leeches tortured her, wriggling everywhere, including into her teapot, 'but you can't imagine the incessant discomfort without respite. Always irritation and swelling from stinging plants, mosquitoes, culicoides (midges) and all that crowd. Leeches, slime, the smell of rotting herbage ... 96 degrees in the shade today; one gets to the point when it is impossible to sleep, eat or concentrate on the work.' Like an unwilling Dr Doolittle she was besieged by small fauna: frogs turned up in her drinking water bucket; an aquatic beetle shared her bath, 'a cranefly was discovered ovipositing in my salad'. And yet she stayed, and worked, and collected. In 1934 she returned briefly with 42,000 insects for the Natural History Museum, and to have her portrait taken by the *News Chronicle*, before heading back to continue her work.

Every time she went, she became more and more convinced of her theory about the distribution of insects in the Pacific and the role that taxonomists such as she could play in understanding the geological history of the earth. At that time geologists thought that during the warm late Cretaceous period, millions of years ago, when dinosaurs still walked the earth and forests covered the arctic regions, the whole of the land mass that is now New Guinea was submerged beneath shallow seas. She became convinced that, contrary to this belief, parts of New Guinea had remained above water during this important period, when flowering plants, and their captivated, symbiotic insects evolved. Although Evelyn had found a few species with origins either in Asia or Australia, the vast quantity of her collections, not just insects but reptiles and small mammals, were found nowhere else on earth. They were richly diverse, peculiar and apparently *endemic* to Papuasia, the name for New Guinea and its sur-rounding islands and archipelagos.

There was a little auburn-haired tree kangaroo and cream-coloured flying squirrel she had never seen recorded anywhere else; birds of paradise, the males with extravagantly showy feathers, almost hunted to extinction to fuel the western hat plumage trade. But it was the insects, hundreds of entirely new species, that she was interested in – butterflies with simply enormous wingspans, leaf-cutting bees, solitary wasps and praying mantis, forming part of a complete and harmonious fauna, as if Papua had existed, in splendid isolation, for millions of years, allowing these strange creatures, not seen elsewhere, to evolve in their own unusual and misfit way. She had read, in an obscure Australian science journal, that the Cyclops Mountains in the north of the island could be part of an 'ancient, wrecked mountain system, represented by relics, some of which have never been submerged', for no marine deposits had ever been found on them. She headed for these northern high ranges, the Cyclops Mountains as well as the mountainous islands east of Papua, and there, hidden from the world in the vast clouds that seemed to get tangled in the branches of trees, creating strange pearlescent structures, she continued her diligent collecting and observing.

These Papuan species matched up with those she had found across the Pacific, from Waigeu and Japen in the west, past the Solomon Islands, the New Hebrides, as far as Tahiti, thousands of miles away across the vast blue Pacific. She couldn't explain how they had got there but she knew they contained a key to some of the earliest mysteries of life on earth. With the chords of the trees, rocks and insects vibrating within her, she imagined an ancient land, could practically see it, its contours and coastline. She began to evolve her theory about how the endemic fauna of Papua came to be: that the high peaks of the Cyclops and other mountain ranges across that latitude –

Mount Nok and the Torricelli – formed the only surviving margins of an ancient, drowned continent and that the flora and fauna survived on these isolated mountain tops, gradually repopulating the land as it rose again from the sea to form modern New Guinea. In addition, she imagined some as yet inexplicable cataclysm that had somehow sheared parts of this continent – the Solomon Islands, the Banks Islands, the New Hebrides – from the central core, and sent these broken land masses hurtling south and eastwards into the empty ocean. She named that lost continent *Cyclopea*, a sea-bound paradise, nurturing and preserving a range of bizarre species, which, for a time, was somehow connected to Asia before isolation and near-submergence. It was as if she had rediscovered the lost regions of her childhood, and the nursery table where she and her siblings had sat with tracing paper and coloured pencils, creating fantastical lands to populate with the animals, birds and insects from their encyclopaedias.

Always having had to challenge tradition and rigid thinking: from the admissions office at the Royal Veterinary College, the naysayers at London Zoo to His Majesty's representatives on their isolated dominions, Evelyn now challenged paleogeologists to reassess their assumptions on the history of how the earth was formed. Listen to the botanists and entomologists, she argued. How do you explain the extraordinary flora and fauna of New Guinea otherwise? New Guinea, or *Cyclopea*, she wrote in a brilliant and colourful paper in the respected journal *Nature*, has a different history from that assumed for it. 'But whether paleogeologists decide that the land looped, festooned, arched, buckled or streamed by New Guinea, with the Solomon Islands in pursuit, is immaterial – but they must agree that *Cyclopea* existed on a land continuous to Asia prior to the early Pliocene. Any other hypothesis will be rejected as untenable because of the testimony of botanists and entomologists.' Quite a challenge from a woman who had never been to university.

She delivered this paper to a meeting of the Royal Entomological Society on 15 August 15 1951. It would, eventually, form part of the vast mosaic of botanical and zoological findings that would enable geographers to establish how the deep ocean trenches and the still-uplifting Himalayas, the earth's active earthquake and volcanic zones, represent a shifting, moving series of interlocking plates around the earth's crust. Evelyn was now 70; surely a fruitful decade of studying and analysing the vast collection of insects she had lodged at the Natural History Museum would cement her reputation? But she was still an unpaid volunteer and, once again, financial embarrassment came her way. At the end of 1951, she had to surrender her desk and the occupation she lived for in order to take on paid clerical work, 'to balance my budget', she wrote to an entomologist friend. Her work on her theory must, for a while, be put away, together with her microscope, into one of the store cupboards at the Museum. She had it carefully taken to pieces, cleaned, oiled and repaired, and reassembled and engraved with her name at a cost of £150, hoping that one day she would be able to return to her work.

9

Ethel: the Peak District and London, 1932–52

Overwork and bombs

It is April 1951 – the year that will end in Evelyn Cheesman's budgetary disappointment, following on so swiftly from recognition of her ground-breaking work on insects' role in revealing the earth's history. We now move from the epochs-long journeys of tropical islands wheeling across the south Pacific to the precipices of the Peak where Ethel Gallimore – now Mrs Gerald Haythornthwaite – is quietly celebrating. The British winter of 1950–51 had been miserable, the coldest since 1922. Colder even than the winter of 1946–47, when her committee had to organise sheep rescue parties across the moors, passing bales of hay in human chains to where the flocks were trapped in deep snow drifts. This year snow lay hard along the uplands well into April. Dark, peaty ice, like frozen whisky, lined the rocky gullies at the base of the tors. The sandpipers and dunlin, newly arrived from the south, hunched low on the ground, feathers buffeted by the wind. In a Britain living through post-war austerity and meteorological gloom, there seemed little to celebrate. Soap rationing had, thank goodness, just ended; tea, sugar, cheese and bacon were still on the ration books. But on 13 April 1951, in the dying days of the transformational Attlee government, the Peak District became the first official National Park in Britain. The 555 square miles of 'the Great North Roof of England', shaped roughly like a right-curled kidney, stretching from Bleaklow in the north, to Dovedale in the south, and from the outskirts of Sheffield in the east to Macclesfield in the west, would enjoy both landscape protection and wider public access for future generations to walk along its edges, cloughs, lows and limestone canyons.

That the Peak, crammed between the northern industrial towns, the steelworks, cement works, cotton mills and ship breakers, was not only the

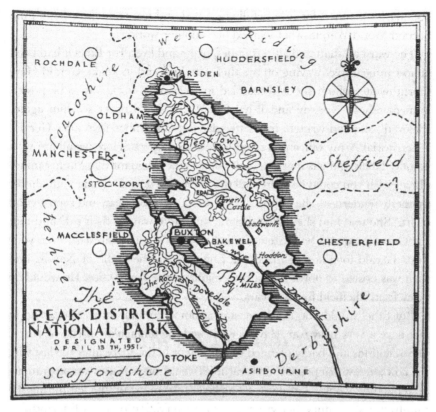

9.1 Map of the Peak District National Park, April 1951

first, but a National Park at all, was quite frankly miraculous, and a testament to one woman and her life's work. This was even acknowledged in the *Manchester Guardian*, a paper that over the years had often ignored Ethel in her battles for the Peak, favouring instead the smaller Dovedale claim for a National Park. Like so many in that part of the world, the paper had considered the Peak a lost cause. The newspaper however changed its stance and praised Ethel's committee's 'sterling' work in an editorial on 1 June 1950; within a year its deputy editor Paddy Monkhouse would be a member of the new Peak Planning Board. On 31 May 1950, Hugh Dalton, Chancellor of the Duchy of Lancaster and Minister of Town and Country Planning, announced that the Peak would be the first of what would eventually be 12 National Parks in England and Wales. The much-fancied Lake District would be second and Snowdonia in north Wales third. With the announcement came the publication of a map of the Peak park's official boundaries, following almost exactly the boundaries planned for it hopefully by Ethel and her committee before the Second World War, in what seemed like another world.

The war had shattered all certainties, plans and lives. For Ethel it had been almost unbearable, waving off another new husband in khaki. Gerald Hay-thornthwaite, whom she had married in December 1937, was to be posted immediately to Norway and Ethel feared she would never see him again. 'Beloved', she had written, in a letter dated 3 September 1939 after Gerald, a Territorial Army officer, received his call-up papers. 'Here we all are with identity labels and gas masks ... but you are the poignant thing in my mind. How I wish you could be spared all this undeserved trial.' Then, with almost motherly tenderness, she added: 'Take care of that toe, dear, and keep a good heart.' She told him she believed right, and God, was on their side and that the Germans would be beaten, signing off 'I love you, dearest ... ever, your Pup.' Gerald fought with the Royal Engineers in the battle of Narvik, and then was posted to north Africa before joining the War Office. He would be away from Sheffield for five years.

But Ethel would not, this time, stay at home knitting socks. She would in fact have a very busy war. Having witnessed the tentacular spread of roads, petrol stations and badly planned development in the 1920s after the last war, she now foresaw that pressure on rural areas would intensify as a vast programme of rebuilding would, and must, take place. Like many on the left during the mid-twentieth century, her vision for the preservation of rural England was neither conservative nor nostalgic. She never argued for the countryside to be preserved in aspic or to be some kind of museum, let alone simply a beautiful playground for the rich. Legislation like that for the National Parks was based on the understanding that conservation and preservation would have to take place within the programme of a modernising state. She always knew that to thrive, areas like the Peak needed to offer housing, jobs and productive agricultural land to local communities. If farmers were to be required to surrender their land for nature reserves, or to maintain footpaths and bridleways, stiles and fences, they should be fairly compensated.

She saw that after the years of grinding privations and violent conflict, the returning soldiers as well as the civilian population would need space to enjoy their hard-won leisure and freedoms, the 'land fit for heroes' they had been promised. Having lived through the darkest days of loss through war herself, she understood people would need 'true, *recuperative*, natural peace' that was only to be found in the wild natural places of the countryside. Having once coaxed herself back to the land of the living through her own creative responses to the moors and mountains, she believed that 'rapturous wonder at the beauty of the earth' was at the very root of human creativity, sanity and will to live.

So, in 1938 she did what she did best and formed another committee, the Joint Committee for the Peak District National Park (Hon. Sec. Mrs E. B. Haythornthwaite). When the committee first met, plans for the National Parks had been stagnating, like the water in the Kinder Scout peat bogs, for several years, and the Peak was not yet even a possibility for National Park status. Frederick, F. A. Holmes of the rival Dovedale National Park campaign, was still firing threats northwards, warning, rightly, that no government would ever accept two National Parks in Derbyshire. Nevertheless, Ethel invited John Dower, architect, rambler and drafting secretary to the Standing Committee on National Parks, the national body set up by the CPRE to keep pressure on the government, to the Peak Joint Committee's preliminary meeting. Dower, who would later be asked by the wartime government to produce a report on National Parks in preparation for legislation, came out of his meeting with Ethel's committee 'very much in favour of our going ahead', she recorded. Dower advised the committee to undertake a survey of the proposed Park's possible boundaries. The Peak was, he said, 'a prime candidate' for National Park status. This was the first scent, like early blossom in a still-cold spring, that Ethel's dream might yet come true.

Following John Dower's advice, members of the Joint Committee divided up the area and walked and surveyed the proposed boundaries of the as yet theoretical park. Ethel and Gerald, newlyweds in walking boots, tramped the eastern section, from Bradfield in the north, down Stanage Edge, past waterfalls flinging out rainbows, through picture-box pretty Hathersage and up again along breezy Froggatt Edge, then down the sheep-nibbled slopes to Matlock and Tansley, hours and hours, miles and miles, taking measurements, making notes of footpaths and bridleways, villages and railway lines. It was now 1939; the Munich agreement had left Czechoslovakia to her fate, 'only the Czechs/ Go down and without fighting', as Louis MacNeice wrote in his *Autumn Journal*; but they were digging trenches in London parks and children were performing gas mask practice in schools. Sketching the boundaries of an imagined National Park seemed like over-optimistic, even self-indulgent folly. But Ethel's passion for preserving the countryside, even in wartime burned white hot. It must be saved, even if the bombs rained down, even if she died. There would be some survivors, who would have to rebuild 'even over all our dead bodies', and the beauty of the countryside would give them a reason to live on.

The Peak Joint Committee produced statistics, arguments, photographs and expertise, all published in 1944 in a green-covered booklet, priced 6 pence, called *The Peak District: A National Park*, as if it were a foregone conclusion. At the front of the book is the map of that kidney-shaped area, drawn up by the committee's first technical assistant, Philip, P. A. Barnes, rambler and photographer, who gave up his job as an engineering draughtsman to take up the role. It's a beautiful map, with exquisite lettering; the high moors sketched in with feathery ink dashes; the towns and cities are looming black circles threatening those delicate feathered strokes. The strange kidney shape left unprotected the area around Buxton which would be folly to claim. That missing curl would forever be a scar, a reminder that when land became too much ravaged by industrialisation – in this case, the limestone quarries and cement works that nearly did for the Peak – it would lose any reason or justification for further protection. This silhouette would serve as a haunting symbol that it's never too soon to start fighting to protect the earth and its nature. The booklet would sell more than 9,000 copies in its first two years of publication – more than a quarter going to serving and returning soldiers who lived in the towns and cities around the Peak, who then sent in donations and support. An officer in Eastern Command sent a £10 postal order; a private in Normandy, having just taken part in the D-Day landings and dreaming of home, donated a book of stamps. Like so many, having given five years of their lives for their country, they felt they now, at last, had a stake in its future and ownership.

For the new Joint Committee, like all of Ethel's projects, she had, brilliantly, brought together the strangest and, on the face of it, mismatching assortment of people, from representatives of the socialist Manchester Ramblers to members of old Derbyshire farming families such as Jabez Ollerenshaw; the Labour MP for Sheffield Brightside, Fred Marshall to the recently appointed Chair of Botany at the University of Sheffield and expert on the ecology of upland bogs, Professor William Pearsall F. R. S.; and, of course, her old stalwart over so many years, and still her friend and mentor, G. H. B. Ward. Jean Smart, who worked as Ethel's secretary from the early 1960s, saw something of that genius of putting people together and getting even the most disparate of interests to collaborate: "She was polite and quietly spoken but you listened to her every word. She could get anyone to do anything for her. She was a stickler for accuracy and I learned very quickly not even to put a comma in the wrong place when writing up her notes.' Ethel's great nephew, Ben Haggarty, went to stay with his great aunts Eppy and Gag every summer from about this time. Ben remembers 'a very self-contained, kind, yet slightly remote, woman. When I say self-contained, perhaps I also mean self-controlled, which I'm sure would have made her formidable. She had very bright and lively eyes.' She would gently mock their southern accents and discuss visitors to the bird feeder, both welcome (the tits and finches) and unwelcome (the squirrels) with her great nephews, often from the sofa as in later life she suffered from a painful foot. Even in her 70s, Ben remembers, she spent most of her time in her office on CPRE work: 'She was clearly on a mission.'

The fight for the Peak, though, had started in earnest in 1931, with that bitter blow of discovering that the combined interests of grouse-shooting dukes and the cement works industrialists had persuaded the Addison Committee to leave the Peak off their list of favoured sites for National Park status. That timid, paltry, 16 square miles of Dovedale, a forelock-tugging symbol of obeisance to the dukes, still stood in prime position, if there was to be a National Park in Derbyshire. At first, the task seemed hopeless. What could she do against the massed ranks of vested interests that wanted to despoil and exploit the land? Well, Ethel didn't know precisely, but all she knew was to do what she always did: put one foot in front of the other, pay attention to the details and work hard. She formulated a three-pronged approach: the first, which she would take care of herself, would be to win over the hearts and minds of Peak District residents, through a series of exhibitions and lantern slide lectures that she would take across the moors, to far-flung villages, to deliver in church halls and schoolrooms. In the dark, casting dramatic images of Stanage Edge, Kinder Downfall and the Winnats onto whitewashed walls, she would show people what they had, and what they might lose, and what they had yet to gain. The second prong would be to gather information, all kinds, on the geography, ownership and use of every square mile of Peak District land. Information, well-kept, ordered and accurate information, was key. The third prong would be to keep an eye out for more opportunities like the Longshaw Estate: whenever a farm, or splinter of Peak District land, shaved off by a hard-up duke or the descendants of a shooting squire faced with death duties, came up for sale, she would start a campaign to raise the necessary money to buy it to hand over to the National Trust: ownership, after all, is nine-tenths of the law. A fourth and, in the mid-1930s as yet unplanned strategy, which would probably be the most important of all, would present itself during the war, but we will get to that later.

For the first prong we find Ethel, now in her 40s, on the road, usually in the dark and often in the rain, proceeding from schoolrooms to village halls with her collection of lantern slides. She gave 22 talks in 1936, from Birly Carr Methodist Hall to the Tinsley Women's Guild, and even the Young Communist League. She advertised each talk with a flier; some, like the one she gave on Friday 27 March 1936 at 7.15 pm, in the schoolroom, Wortley, beautifully illustrated with a coloured woodcut image of a cottage, a drystone wall and the rounded bulk of Mam Tor rising behind. Ideal, homely, the wild just beyond the garden gate. This she commissioned from young local artist George Hammond Steel, fresh out of art school and who would later become famous for his paintings of Derbyshire and Cornwall. Another talk she gave three days later, titled 'Need the Countryside be Destroyed?' at 8 pm at Saint Mary's School, Disley. She then, in 1937, toured with a travelling 'Save the Countryside' exhibition of 30 large photographs, mounted on card, from Sheffield, to Buxton, Stafford, Mansfield, Derby, Burton, Rotherham, Chesterfield, and the Norton and Bakewell Agricultural Shows. She stood in front of farmers, aldermen, local government officers, walkers and women's institutes, asking them to be aware of what was happening in their back garden: the piecemeal erosion of wild places, the erection of hideous advertising hoardings along country lanes, and her own pet hate, 'ugly, ill-placed petrol stations'.

At these meetings she sold copies of *Threat to the Peak*, published by her committee, with text by her and illustrated with dozens of photographs, many taken by Phil Barnes. Echoing much of the descriptions from her poem *Pride of the Peak*, she tried to fire her listeners' and readers' imaginations. Living so close to the moors, many had never seen the glories she described because they were out of bounds, forbidden to all but grouse-shooting parties, so she painted pictures for them with her words: 'The Kinder River ... plunges over the rocky edge and is flung back in clouds of spray which from a distance resemble the volume of smoke given out by a large fire. Standing in the sunshine by this fast-passing curtain of spray one may see ephemeral rainbow arcs and feel the gust of the moisture-laden air.' She described the feelings of grief that overcame people as they saw new brightlycoloured developments springing up, out of keeping with the brown, fawn and grey of the traditional gritstone buildings. She was not anti-housing: she knew the young people of the Peak needed places to live; but she was anti-ugly housing, particularly the bright pink asbestos roofs that stood out like flaming shingles sores. Membership of her branch of the CPRE rose, steadily, from 12 in 1924, to 327 in 1934, to 790 and 12 affiliated bodies in 1943.

A Domesday Book for the Peak

For the second prong, she turned to Philip Barnes. Barnes had walked, and trespassed, the moors with their mutual friend G. H. B. Ward for decades, and been part of that golden period of mountaineering in the British Isles in the early 1920s, recording several first ascents with his Box Brownie camera. He was acquainted with Dorothy Pilley's fellow Fell and Rock Club climbers, scrambling around on Stanage Edge, often in preparation for their more dangerous climbs in the Cairngorms or the Alps. On his wanderings he had taken detailed observations of landmarks, footpaths, monuments, address names and other signs of ownership. Ethel commissioned him to prepare a report on the rights of way across the Peak. She also set him the gargantuan task of discovering the ownership of every acre of land within a theoretical National Park boundary, across the high moors, the gentle river valleys and the steepling edges. Ethel, with her connections, sent him intelligence whenever she could and her handwritten 'in confidence' notes show how much she was involved with the compilation of information. 'Be careful about the waterworks people!' was one piece of advice, as was 'I understand from a [Kinder] keeper that the Crookstone Knoll property ... is on the market.' And 'Ask G. H. B. to look at maps.'

The work, completed in 1933 and presented to Ethel with the title, 'A Report on Access to Moorlands in the Peak District', is a magisterial document, a kind of twentieth-century Domesday Book for the Peak District, covering the ownership of 119 separate parcels of land, from farms and smallholdings to thousands-of-acres-wide heather and cotton-grass-clad tops. It is a snapshot of land ownership between the wars, a record of who owned what, and why, from the dukes whose property went back centuries, some as far back as the original Domesday Book, to the Victorian textile magnates, as well as the public corporations and water companies. Parcel number 18, for example, Eyam Moor and Bretton Clough (650 acres), is one of many parcels owned by the Chatsworth Estates Co., on behalf of the Duke of Devonshire, the aristocratic Cavendish family that played a blinder during the tumultuous aristocratic snakes and ladders of the Tudor period, gathering wealth and position under the reigns of Henry VIII and Elizabeth I. Barnes notes that on this moorland is Wet Withens, a ten-stone Bronze Age standing circle, a scheduled historic monument. There was a time, before the Cavendishes, when ordinary people lived and laboured on the Duke's moor. Parcel 37 (2,200 acres) is Strines Moor, owner Earl Fitzwilliam of Wentworth Woodhouse;

parcel 71 (2,900 acres) is Kinder Scout, one of many plots owned by James Watts of Abney Hall Cheadle, the son of a Victorian textile magnate. The note adds that this plot, site of the 1932 mass trespass, contains some of the most picturesque scenery of the Peak, including Kinder Downfall. The owner of parcel number 42, Langsett Moor (3,400 acres), rejoices in the name of Sir Thomas Edward Milborne-Swinnerton-Pilkington, Bart., of Chevet Hall Wakefield, scion of the Stanley family, favourites of kings across the centuries and originally gifted estates by William the Conqueror. One hundred and thirty-four towns and cities, with a combined population of 7.7 million, lived within easy reach of this mostly open land, wrote Barnes, yet there was barely a public footpath or bridleway between them. 'Bleaklow is sixteen miles in a straight line from the centres of both Manchester and Sheffield and yet surrounding this hill are 40 square miles of moorland with no access whatsoever.' The document was Ethel's masterplan, which she annotated, and added to in her own handwriting over the years. Every time her committee raised the money to buy another deceased landowner's property, the previous owner's name is unceremoniously crossed out and replaced with the words: National Trust. Parcel 59, Howden Moor (6,500 acres), was recorded by Barnes in 1933 as being owned by the Fitzalan-Howards, the dukes of Norfolk. Their name is crossed out, in pencil, and replaced with the words National Trust, in Ethel's handwriting.

This was Ethel's third prong, gradually expanding the jigsaw puzzle of pieces offering access to the public and each piece covenanted or given to the National Trust. A further 268 acres were added to Longshaw in 1936; in 1937 a 34-acre farm and 11-acre wood in the Derwent Valley; in 1941 and 1942, three farms, amounting to 400 acres, in the Edale Valley and in 1942 the piece of countryside that she first became interested in preserving back in 1924, 473 acres of land covering the wind-blown canyon of Winnats Pass and the solid, round bulk of Mam Tor. In all, Ethel was instrumental in passing ownership of nearly 2,800 acres of formerly private Peak District hillside, woodland and farms to the National Trust, to be protected in perpetuity. Most of these parcels of land were purchased through fundraising campaigns. She tapped, again and again, branch members and local businessmen and dignitaries. Almost every year, there was another request for a few thousand pounds. She always succeeded. Jean Smart saw something in the 1960s of Ethel's great ability to fundraise, while typing out her letters (Ethel never learned to type). 'She wrote the most beautiful letters', says Jean. 'When you read a letter from Ethel asking for money, you just got your cheque book out.'

Gerald Haythornthwaite, who had joined the Sheffield and Peak branch of the CPRE as technical secretary in 1936, observed his new boss with interest: 'If she wanted something urgently, she could get it. She just went along to [members of the business community] and said: "Hoy, the odd thousand pounds by next weekend please," you see, and that did happen.' Sometimes Ethel and her siblings used their own funds. An emergency acquisition, for example, in 1937, of 76 acres of Froggatt Wood, tumbling all the way down to the banks of the Derwent, was made after they were given a week to find £3,000 to prevent its being sold for executive homes. G. H. B. also put his hands in his pockets for that one. Again, this piece of land was handed over to the National Trust. There were presentation ceremonies almost annually, through the 1930s. Miraculously, there exists a flickery, black and white 40 seconds of silent film footage, the only known footage of Ethel, shot in September 1936 at a small ceremony when she handed over the deeds of yet another piece of Peak District land, 250 acres below the Surprise View above Hathersage. Philip Barnes had contributed to this one. In 1934 he published *Trespassers Will be Prosecuted*, a collection of photographs of the forbidden places of the Peak, and now considered a rambling rights of way classic work. Much of the text accompanying the images is sourced from the secret report he had compiled for Ethel the year before. In a nod of gratitude to Ethel, he donated two-thirds of the receipts from the book to the Surprise View appeal fund.

In the film the camera pans across a crowd of behatted, overcoated people showing in the background trees marching across the far horizon and why the Surprise is known as one of the best panoramas in the Peak. The camera then moves to a podium where several men, including the Mayor of Sheffield, are standing and sitting, coats drawn against what looks like a knifing wind. On the podium is a slender, neatly dressed woman wearing a smart fitted jacket and matching slim skirt suit, brimmed hat pulled down over her forehead. She looks uncomfortable in this limelight: she pulls her jacket close around her, bends down to move her handbag an inch. At one point the wind lifts an important piece of paper off the lectern in front of the main speaker and the woman stoops to pick it up and return it. Words in curled, silent movie font then appear on the screen: 'Mrs E. B. Gallimore hands over the deeds.' The woman stands and presents the papers to the speaker. She is smiling broadly, but modest and turned away from the crowd as if she feels awkward to be playing such a public role, and sits down quickly. A man silently raises his hat three times, inviting the crowd to shout three cheers. It could be G. H. B. Ward, but it isn't clear.

As part of her efforts to strengthen and professionalise the 'little local' association, and make it fit to challenge poor town-planning decisions and unsympathetic house designs, in 1933 Ethel had appointed an architect to the Executive Committee. Within a few months, for £2 local housebuilders could buy a copy of *Housing in the Peak District*, complete with architects' drawings and suggestions for materials. After the first appointee left, she advertised in the local press for a new architect and received an application, in November 1935, from a Gerald Haythornthwaite, who had recently graduated with a degree in architecture from the University of Manchester. Born in 1912 at the edge of the 'smoky cotton town' of Bolton, his fondest childhood memories were of being taken up to the moors every week by a rambling schoolmaster. There he could breathe the fresh air above the smoke stacks, and see the endless horizon. Although his previous employer had been dubious about Haythornthwaite's talent in lettering, his enthusiasm for the countryside and for rock climbing as well as his having won a prize for design, secured him the job. He started his post in January 1936 on a salary of £250 a year, paid for directly out of the pockets of Ethel and her siblings – they paid all the CPRE staff salaries out of their personal funds for the first 13 years of the branch's life.

Gerald and Ethel found complete sympathy in their love of the wild outdoors and even though there was a wide gap in age – she was 23 years older than him – in December 1937 they married. 'I wouldn't say it was the great passion that was Harry', says Jean Smart, who worked for both the Haythornthwaites in their small mews offices for 23 years, 'but there was deep, abiding tenderness and affection between them.' In an interview two years after Ethel's death, Gerald tried to articulate how their love for each other was indissoluble from their love for the Peak: 'I'm not saying that because I married her, or perhaps I married her because of that, I don't know', he said when talking about her efforts to preserve the countryside around Sheffield. That 'I don't know' speaks volumes in its very uncertainty, but it didn't matter; their partnership was for the sake of 555 square miles of land.

War, again

But another war came too soon. Gerald was called up and Ethel wrote to CPRE branch members, assuring them of the Executive's continuing work for the Peak during the war years. 'The work of this branch has not been allowed to slacken during the emergency', she wrote. 'Our Headquarters consider the importance of safeguarding the English countryside will be increased rather than diminished in time of war.' Already firing ranges crackled across Peak moorland and farmers were complaining about troop damage to the grazing meadows. By this time Ethel was sitting on both the CPRE's Standing Committee for National Parks, and the National Trust Executive Committee. She regularly took the steam train down to Marylebone, four and a half hours without a restaurant car (to make space for troops), looking at posters asking, 'Is your journey really necessary?' She stayed in a white stucco townhouse hotel in Craven Hill just off Bayswater and walked across Hyde Park, past the Dig for Victory allotments, to CPRE headquarters at Hobart Place. After 1943 she met up occasionally with Gerald, who was now at the War Office, when he was free, although, like everyone, he was dreadfully overworked. Sometimes, she thought, 'the object is to kill them with overwork as an alternative to bombs'. She had meetings with the urban planner and Chairman of the CPRE Executive Committee Professor Sir Patrick Abercrombie, and the famous Welsh architect Clough Williams-Ellis and other 'friends in high places', as Gerald described Ethel's network of allies.

What was it about this small, quietly spoken woman who was able to hold her own among great men and force quiet change? 'They liked her', said Gerald once in an interview. When, a few years later, a young history lecturer first met her at Sheffield University, he was curious to encounter the woman whose name members of the senior common room 'uttered with bated breath', and to find out why she carried such clout. Clyde Binfield's first impressions were: 'short, sharp, spare in speech and appearance, every word, every look counting, not beautiful, not exactly attractive, but unmistakable in personality'. She got her way, not through aggression, or coercion, or any kind of machismo, but because people found themselves wanting to make her happy. She also had the kind of strategic organisation that a Field Marshall would find useful. It was now she played her best hand.

In April 1942 the deputy secretary of CPRE head office was called up for war duties and shortly afterwards the secretary, Captain Herbert Griffin, was also needed. The Executive Committee was now in a terrible bind as to who would run the organisation at this crucial time – despite the war, plans for the National Parks were slowly rumbling on and much of the legwork, the surveys, selection of areas for designation, was delegated by overburdened government ministries to the CPRE. They needed an organised drafter-of-letters, an effective convenor-of-meetings, a stickler for standards and detail. Who better to turn to than the quietly efficient, 'very energetic', they called her in the minutes, Mrs Haythornthwaite? She could draft a dozen letters in the morning, brief journalists at lunchtime, make phone calls to the Ministry of Works and Planning, Royal Institute of British Architects and half a dozen water catchment boards in an afternoon, and scrutinise reports with her blue pencil in the evenings without pausing for breath.

She agreed to do it for no salary and £75 travel expenses a quarter, and from June 1942 she could be found, three days a week, at Hobart Place, pretty much single-handedly steering CPRE policy on the National Parks. In steering CPRE policy, she was also, in effect, steering government policy. These were, after all, extreme times, with Whitehall denuded of professional civil servants who had been drafted into the war effort. Temporary civil servants, friends of friends, the retired or those unable to serve due to ill health like John Dower, suffering with tuberculosis, took up sometimes quite senior positions. Unused to the ways of Whitehall, these men did things differently, often more boldly.

When E. B. H., as she initialled her letters now, arrived at Hobart Place in June 1942, the positions of Dovedale versus the Peak's claim for National Park status were still undecided but the assumption was that Dovedale, singled out for favour in the Addison Report, had the edge. F. A. Holmes, Dovedale's cheerleader, was 'implacably opposed' to combining the Peak and Dovedale claims. He refused to work with Ethel, despite her gentle warnings that a small area such as Dovedale was not what either Parliament, which was remarkably united over the need for more countryside protection, or the National Parks Standing Committee were looking for. He stood firm, firing off letters 'without any of the normal courtesies' (Ethel-speak for 'rude'), and tried to whip up support in the press, suggesting that the mighty National Trust was on his side, which was entirely wrong.

Over the summer of 1942, CPRE branches overseeing land up for National Park status had been requested to submit maps, photographs and surveys in support of their claim. In July the Dovedale papers duly arrived and with the other area claims, including the Peak, were prepared for a crunch meeting with the Parks drafting secretary John Dower in September. Dower's definition of a National Park was '*an extensive area* of beautiful and relatively wild country'. How could Dovedale's 16 square miles possibly be described as extensive? The Lake District area, by comparison, was nearly 900 square miles, and Snowdonia almost the same size. Even the smallest area for selection, the Norfolk Broads, was nearly 200 square miles. Dovedale surely wasn't serious.

The Dovedale maps weren't half as good as the carefully measured and expertly drafted Peak ones, either; they were a little rushed, a little amateurish, an air of hubris shimmering off them.

By the autumn of 1942, F. A. Holmes's Dovedale goose was well and truly cooked. Over the next few weeks, Miss Revel, the typist at Hobart Place, must have noted the subtle, insistent change in nomenclature as she typed Mrs Haythornthwaite's notes and letters, from Dovedale National Park (July), to Peak and Dovedale National Park (13 October), to Peak District National Park (22 October). Herbert Griffin wrote to Holmes with the bad news on 14 October and Ethel retired to Sheffield for a few days, writing to Miss Revel to enquire whether there had been any 'fireworks from Dovedale'. Miss Revel replied she had heard 'not a sound whatsoever'. Ethel had won that battle but still the Ministry of Works and Planning was unconvinced there was enough magnificent scenery in the Peak – compared with the 'Horseshoe' of Snowdonia or the liquid tapestry of rivers and meres of the Lake District, were the Peak's gritstone lows and boggy plateaux really of similar quality? Ethel's genius was to argue that the Peak was '*the most needed of all* because of the surrounding industrial populations'. And then, on the 1945 Hobhouse Committee, the final committee report of the many, many National Park reports, she sang her song for the Peak, the song she had been singing since first it saved her life after Harry's death. This time, not in poetry for a literary publisher, nor to be circulated for campaigns in local Sheffield publications. This song was recorded, for all time in Cmd. 7121, by order of the King and presented to Parliament, in those hopeful but hard post-war days:

> On the north and west rise the Gritstone moors with their austere, solitary plateaux, falling away abruptly in scarped edges, their grotesque groups of stones, folded valleys and broken cloughs; on the south and east are the upland limestone pastures and exquisite dales. Thus, within the space of a day or so the traveller may battle with the invigorating winds on Wessenden Head, Kinder Scout or Shutlingslow and laze under the cliffs of Dovedale or Chee Tor, refreshed by the completeness of the two-fold scene – 'the White Peak and the Dark Peak'.

She sang, as in her earlier poetry, of well-dressing ceremonies, standing stone circles, abandoned lead mines, Norman keeps and gritstone millstones, still lying where they were hewn, out on the wild moor. It was a Peak for *people*, had been for aeons, and must be forever. The other candidates for National Park – the Lake District, the Brecon Beacons, Dartmoor – all had their entries in the Hobhouse Report, but none as eloquent as the entry for the Peak. It was her aria.

A long and 'manful' fight

The Hobhouse Committee, consisting of eight men and one woman, Ethel, was appointed in July 1945, days after the landslide Labour victory in the General Election (although candidates for membership had been put forward in March 1945). If one examines the membership closely, Ethel's invisible hand is all over the selection. John Dower, an early champion and author of the idealistic Dower Report (1945), on which Hobhouse based its philosophy, was there, as was her friend Clough Williams-Ellis. Also on the committee were two of her oldest friends in conservation, both also champions of the Peak: the Quaker pacifist, Alpinist and Bradford headmaster Richard Brockbank Graham had served on her Sheffield committee for six years, from 1932–38. Theo, now Lord, Chorley was also an old friend and joined the Sheffield committee in 1946. Someone of a suspicious mind might almost think that Hobhouse was entirely rigged in the Peak District's favour. They held 80 meetings, made 17 survey tours over 85 days, and took evidence from 60 bodies and interested parties. Their report, published in July 1947, is a hymn to post-war idealism, placing access for walkers as equally important as preserving beautiful scenery and protection of wild flora and fauna. Where rights of way to popular beauty spots were inadequate, new ones would be created, through access agreements with landowners, who would be compensated. It recommended 12 areas for designation, the first four being the Lake and Peak Districts, Snowdonia and Dartmoor. After the smooth and unopposed passage of the National Parks and Access to the Countryside Act 1949, the Peak moved to the top of the list. Ethel and Gerald's maps and surveys were so thorough, so detailed, so accurate, the local authorities so unanimously on board (after a little encouragement), that the Peak presented the least amount of work for the Ministry. A quick, easy win would make everyone look good.

And so, the designation order was signed, in April 1951. Hugh Dalton, the Minister for Town and Country Planning, although a strong supporter of the National Parks and keen rambler himself, was so busy with Labour Party in-fighting that he didn't even record the event in his diary. Perhaps he had lots of documents to sign that day, and one more piece of paper was hardly worth mentioning. But it was done. And now the real work was to start. Within weeks of designation, Ethel was fighting on three fronts: with the landowners,

9.2 Ethel speaking to ramblers, 1951

who, unsurprisingly, weren't as enthusiastic as she about access agreements; with industry and developers wanting to plunder the park – she had fought 54 major threats, including new cement works, dams and reservoirs since the war already – one for every ten square miles of the Park. She lost one heart-breaking battle in, of all places, Hope, where permission for a 400-foot cement works chimney, higher than Saint Paul's Cathedral dome, had been granted. The fight, she told a rally of ramblers at Cave Dale in June 1951, was constant, and daily.

The third front, she told the ramblers, was they themselves. Having urged the government to approve access to the wild places of the Peak, reports of destroyed hedges, litter, and haystacks and shooting hides set on fire by antisocial walkers were beginning to sour the idealistic vision. The village of Eyam, she told the hundreds-strong crowd, had just repaired and restored its ancient medieval stocks. Perhaps they should be used for ramblers who treated the countryside with such disdain. 'A short period in the stocks might have a chastising effect', she declared. It was a bold suggestion to propose to a crowd of walkers, but a measure of how, in the past few years, her confidence had grown, her resolve now steely. A few days later, she was awarded an honorary MA at the University of Sheffield, described in the address as 'sleepless guardian' of the countryside around Sheffield, 'an ugly city in a beautiful frame'. She was nearly 60 now, suffering from a bad foot since a motoring accident in Ireland in 1947 left her with a limp, and would probably have welcomed a bit more sleep, but despite the National Park status, new threats to the countryside, including proposals for a motorway and opencast coal mines, kept coming.

Part of the problem was that between the initial post-war idealism of 1945, and the actual passing of the 1949 National Parks and Access to the Countryside Act, some of the more egalitarian visions for the Parks had been whittled away. John Dower's assertions in 1945 that 'whether the recreational needs of the many should, or should not, outweigh the sporting pleasures of the few – there can be little doubt of the answer: that walkers should, and sooner or later *will, be given freedom of access over grouse moors*' had seemed, in those heady days of victory, unassailable. But by the time the National Parks Bill became law, much of this vision had been watered down; as had the questions of funds and powers for the Parks. As with all politics, reality, pragmatism, commercial considerations and special interest lobbying had crept in like termites nibbling at once strong foundations. Some in the rambling and right-to-roam world called the Act 'one of the most spectacular flops of post-war legislation', allowing the dukes and other landowners to challenge and obfuscate over those Utopian ideals. The sleeping would have to wait a few more years.

Moreover, Ethel was now fighting with one hand tied behind her back. At the birth of the National Park, a main oversight management board, the Peak Park Joint Planning Board, had been created. Membership of this powerful body comprised elected county councillors from the five authorities covering the Peak's geographical range, and members nominated by the National Parks Commission with an interest in, and experience of, running a major countryside body. The new National Parks Commission asked countryside amenity groups for names to be put forward for possible nominated members of the Board. Of course, Ethel's name was right at the top: she was the outstanding choice with her wealth of experience, her quiet energy, her ability to get things done. Having steered the CPRE through the war, and having done diligent work, all those hours of meetings and report drafting, on the Hobhouse Committee, and having proved her ability on so many other boards and committees since 1924, she was such an obvious choice everyone assumed she would have a place on the Board. But when membership of the Joint Planning Board was announced, her name was not there (although Gerald, who became Vice Chairman of the Board, was selected). It was a bizarre omission. Her absence from the Board was described, in her usual understated way, in the Peak Branch of the CPRE's annual report for 1952 as 'a cause of bewilderment'. It may have been bewildering but hardly surprising that Ethel, a mere woman, was overlooked. On the final conferment of National Park status in April 1951, the new Chairman of the National Parks Commission, Sir Patrick Duff, had written to the Haythornthwaites, congratulating them on their success and for their 'long and manful fight'.

10

Wangari: Nairobi, 1980–99

'People began to fear and hate the forest'

Thirty years after the Peak became a National Park, in her little mews cottage on a steeply sloping shoulder of western Sheffield, Ethel Haythornthwaite, although nearly 80, was still writing letters and working in its defence. Dorothy Pilley broke her hip in 1958 in a motor accident, and although she could no longer dance across glossy rock faces, or balance on an ice axe handle hundreds of feet above thin air, she was still, with the help of a stick, hobbling through heather hillsides, still astonished by the beauty of snow on rock. Mina Hubbard and Evelyn Cheesman had by now departed this world, but their legacy lives on: 'Missus Hubbard's' journey has become the stuff of North American legend, in both First Nation and white Canadian storytelling. Evelyn was – and still is today – keeping the taxonomists at Kew and the Natural History Museum busy.

In 1980s Nairobi, Wangari Maathai was about to enter her most difficult two decades. Although these years would make her widely known and admired in the global women's and environmental movements, they would also take her down those dark paths she described to the nuns at Mount Saint Scholastica in her letters. She would be imprisoned several times, beaten up by the security forces, and would eventually have to go into hiding. As the government of Daniel arap Moi became ever more corrupt and authoritarian, Wangari focused her work on the problems of environmental degradation, working at the grassroots. This also meant taking on the issues of corruption and human rights violations that engendered a feeling of powerlessness among ordinary people. Much of the rapid deforestation in the country was a result of corrupt business deals between developers and the Moi administration. 'It's the silence that hurts', she would later say. 'That's how you create a dictatorship.'

Although her tree-planting project, now called the Green Belt Movement, was still in its infancy, she was becoming known in Kenya and in the international aid world. She had been Chairwoman of the National Council of Women of Kenya (NCWK) since 1980 and was head of the Department of Veterinary Anatomy and Associate Professor at the University of Nairobi. She was winning grants – in 1981 she secured US$100,000 from the then United Nations International Fund for Women, much to the irritation of Moi as it showed his government in a bad light. Aid agencies realised there was greater transparency and accountability in channelling funding through organisations like Wangari's than through Moi's sticky hands. For the moment though, she was just seen as a woman, planting trees with other women; the most technically advanced parts of her operations were donkeys employed in water carrying, and rakes and hoes; and so, for now, she was mostly ignored. Moi anyway had his hands full, dealing with opposition politicians and student activists who criticised the widespread corruption and cronyism in the country, and imprisoning or expelling dissenters. One arm of the administration gave the NCWK, and thus the fledgling GBM, a dilapidated prefab office building in Nairobi city centre.

It's somehow appropriate that the wooden building was previously a Ministry of Education book storage warehouse, near the main campus of the University. Maybe its shelves even once housed the textbooks from which Wangari first began her learning journey; it now became the seedbed from which would grow a vast and fruitful tree-planting movement with civic education and engagement at its heart. With the International Fund for Women's grant, Wangari began recruiting a small staff of young women high school leavers. These 'monitors' planned their visits and meetings with the rural women farmers, to check the health of their trees and to pay the women for every sapling that survived three months beyond planting out. By 1982, there were dozens of community nurseries across the country, most in the central Highlands, and none more than three miles from the women's villages, to reduce the burden of walking long distances. Since reforestation and environmental education were stated goals of the Kenyan government's development programme, the GBM posed no political threat. Forestry Department officials attended tree-planting ceremonies as guests of honour, and Wangari even had a seat on the National Environment Committee on which also sat the Minister for the Environment and Natural Resources.

But the world looked very different in the late twentieth century than it did in the days when Mina Hubbard stepped into her canoe in northern

10.1 Wangari Maathai in the 1980s

Labrador. For a start, the headwaters of the mighty Naskaupi were drowned beneath the Smallwood Reservoir, part of a hydroelectricity development that saw the river dammed in 1970. Lake Michikamau, the shining 'field of light', has gone. Mina's map was out of date. In the 20 years after the publication of Rachel Carson's *Silent Spring*, that warns of the catastrophic collapse of biodiversity from intensive farming, logging and development, things only got worse. Scientists and ecologists were starting to worry about the environmental destruction taking place across the globe. A new phrase, 'greenhouse effect', that would soon become 'global warming' and later 'climate change' and, today, 'global boiling' began to circulate. I remember sitting at my parents' kitchen table in 1978 reading in the *Sunday Times* an article about the 'greenhouse effect'. It warned of rising tides, and rising temperatures, and that it could extinguish human life in 100 years, wiping us out like the dinosaurs if we didn't stop cutting down forests and burning fossil fuels. But I was still a child, and was more interested in the cartoon that accompanied the article: a sweating world and a bewildered-looking Brontosaurus stuck inside a massive greenhouse floating through space. Although scientists are still arguing about timing and definition, by the 1980s the world was well into its new geological epoch, the Anthropocene. Human activity, from farming, to burning fossil fuels, to mining and nuclear warfare, transformed planetary processes through the twentieth century, and ended the stable, post-glacial Holocene Epoch, during which we emerged as the dominant species on this earth. Ecological activists across the world demanded environmental justice, not just for humans but for all living things. We share this planet with about 9 million other species, from the single-cell *Amoebae proteus* that multiplies among the rotting vegetation at the bottom of riverbeds to the *Sequoia sempervirens*, timber skyscrapers supporting their own biome of insects, plants and animals.

While in the early 1980s loggers, farmers, charcoal burners and developers were busily destroying these aerial ecosystems, in one corner of Africa Wangari and her movement were busily replanting. In fact, they were about to celebrate the planting of their one millionth tree, of which about 850,000 have survived into maturity. Through several years now of trial and error, Wangari had worked out which species complemented the local environment best. She abandoned early trials with eucalyptus, the blue gums that suck up moisture like a kid with a straw in a glass of pop; she discovered how to encourage communities to nurture the young trees until their roots became developed enough to seek out underground water sources themselves. In the semi-arid areas of Kenya, it takes four years to grow a tree from seed to a size it can be confidently left to its own ingenious devices. The network of community-run nurseries, dozens of them across the country, was vital for the project that still survives, despite a few bumps over the decades, today.

First the women collect the seeds from mature trees in the area: a mix of fruiting, shade-giving and hardy herbivore repellents work best. They prepare seedbeds, plant the seeds and water daily as, below the ground, the cells are dividing rapidly: first the root, to anchor it in the soil and search for moisture; then the stem, leaf and flower; it is tender and delicious. Now they must be protected from predation by the women's goats, and the wild herbivores, deer and antelope. Gradually the seedling's smooth upright exterior changes from green to rough brown as it protects its inner core. Sometimes it produces poison, or bitter oil; others sprout hard scales or sharp thorns. Then, when it's about six months old, the women gently lift and replant the seedling into a tough plastic bag ready for collection by local farmers, schools and church leaders, or to be taken to the edges of public forests, for planting during the long rainy season, between April and June. The recipients are given the seedlings free of charge: in the 1980s the women were paid the equivalent of 4 US cents for every tree that survived three months after replanting. Some early Green Belt woodlands were becoming established, with small thickets returning to degraded parts of the Aberdare Forest. By 1982 some of the earlier trees were already higher than the women's heads.

Wangari toured the country, speaking at schools, churches and to community leaders; she organised discussion forums where debates were held in the local tribal language so everyone could understand. Often these meetings would start with singing: joyful, spiritual, uplifting, that would bring the rural women and Wangari and her project workers together. Then she spoke to the women farmers, the ones who, without formal education, knew exactly which seeds were healthy and which were not; how much to water and when to water, which part of their farm or compound was most in need of shade or a windbreak, where small streams, that would become the great rivers, first emerged, the all-important catchment zones that should be densely wooded, and which part of their land was the most fertile. They could farm maize, sorghum and millet: why could they not also farm trees?

Wangari's most important philosophy was that the women take ownership and control of their tree-planting projects. After visiting an area to mobilise support or deliver an education session, the GBM would wait to be invited back with a formal request from the community to start a tree nursery. The women would be responsible for keeping records and ensuring the saplings reached a stage where they could survive on their own. Wangari had seen how top-down authoritarian policies tended to end in failure. Indeed, hers was not the first civic tree-planting project in Kenya. Back in the colonial era, former Assistant Conservator of Forests Richard St Barbe Baker had formed an organisation he called Men of the Trees. It was about as different from Wangari's Green Belt Movement as it is possible to imagine. For a start, subscribing to the colonial idea that indigenous women were 'backward', St Barbe Baker trained only men and boys, many of whom did not stick around long enough to tend the seedlings into maturity. Secondly, on Men of the Trees inauguration day, Baker sat on a raised dais in the middle of a clearing and told the Kikuyu recruits that they had got into bad habits and their sworn enemies, the Masai, called them 'destroyers of trees', which did not go down very well, he himself admitted. Lastly, he bade the men present themselves decked out in full 'war' dress, complete with spears tipped with rolled up balls of ostrich feathers, and told them to perform a tree-planting dance. It was never realistic and dissipated shortly after Baker left Africa at the close of the 1920s (although latterly the project, now called the International Tree Foundation and organised on very different lines, has had considerable successes across the globe, including Kenya).

In her meetings with the women, Wangari used religious imagery to try to get them to see what they were facing. She told them the world was created by God, that it was created perfect. 'He gave it to us, and asked us to care for it, but we have plundered it', she told them. The women, mostly in the Kikuyu areas of Kenya, responded enthusiastically. Later, she said, 'They work[ed] quietly and often without recognition to protect the environment, promote democracy, defend human rights and ensure equality between women and men. In so doing, they plant the seeds of peace.' She told them that if an invading army came and stole millions of tonnes of their rich red soil, they would probably respond with weapons to protect their land. But that was exactly what was happening, during every rainy season when the eroding soil washed off the land and the rivers ran red with it, eventually forming great red clots in the Indian Ocean. She showed them how to preserve the soil by leaving crop residues: stalks, leaves and roots on the fields rather than burning them, and digging trenches from the streams to their fields. She took seedlings – broad-leaved corda, East African yellow wood, the sacred fig – to Naivasha, northwest of Nairobi, to Nyanza near Lake Victoria, to Kitui in the east. But she needed more help and more funds – at the start she was paying for the seedlings herself, and trying to grow them in her compound at a safe distance from her two goats.

The chief official at the Kenya Forestry Service, Arthur Gakunga, was initially incredulous when Wangari approached him and told him she planned to plant 15 million trees. The idea was so far-fetched and ludicrous that without hesitation he insisted on donating seedlings for free, suspecting he would not be giving many out. How could poor rural women, with no formal education, possibly sustain a reforestation project on such a grand scale? The Forestry Service, then under the auspices of the Ministry of Natural Resources, was established in 1902 during the colonial era, and controlled a network of nurseries and reserves employing Kenyans mostly to farm new plantations of non-indigenous cypress and eucalyptus. But these plantations were 'dead forests', says Professor Karanja Njoroge, who worked with Wangari at the Green Belt Movement and later to save Karura Forest near Nairobi: lifeless monocultures where very little wildlife can thrive, abandoned by the Colobus monkey, the duikers, bushbucks, the Crowned Eagle and all the other radiant birds that make the living forests such wildly, joyously cacophonous places.

Wangari had no interest in this kind of forestry. Her plan to plant slow-growing indigenous trees was surely doomed to fail, Gakunga concluded. Within the year, he had to revoke his promise to offer seedlings free of charge as he was distributing so many to Wangari that it was costing the Forestry Service too much. Now the women in the rural areas, once their trees were producing seeds, were encouraged to create their own nurseries, to grow seedlings they would be paid for, and provide another stream of income. Wangari and her team kept scrupulous records of every tree planted, every seedling that survived, every payment made. Relying as she did on donations for the 2.2 million Kenyan shillings (US$34,000) annual operating costs in those early years, she needed to be as transparent as the water in the Aberdare mountain streams: she could not charge the farmers and planters to buy the saplings; she could not ask the already over-burdened women to work the nurseries for free. The Green Belt Movement paid for their water tanks, hoes and rakes. The farmers provided the manure. Wangari and her staff would tour the nurseries, check that the young trees were being looked after, and take part in the work of weeding and planting; often she would join the women farmers, knees on the ground, hands in the dirt.

But despite this apparently simple pastime, the Moi government was taking notice of Maathai, and didn't like what it saw. She was winning valuable international grants and was Chair of a powerful women's organisation – an appointment that the government had initially opposed because she was, since 1979, a divorcée, and at the headline-making divorce trial had been branded a 'disobedient' woman in some of the newspapers. She had also been sentenced to six months in jail for criticising the divorce trial judge, although she only served a few days of her sentence. She wasn't considered the right sort of person to lead such a high-profile, relatively well-funded and powerful organisation. The National Council of Women of Kenya should be supporting the government's agenda, too, whereas it was dangerously independent and non-partisan. The Moi government was also increasingly concerned about the burgeoning non-governmental organisation (NGO) movement in Kenya, *vis à vis* his own precarious position with foreign donors. There were hundreds of groups, often with international staff, engaged in education, health, local finance and ecology. These unelected civil society groups were making friends with international governments who were trying to influence Kenyan domestic policy, threatening even to withhold aid if Moi didn't stop human rights abuses. Only in power for four years, he had already set up torture units for political opponents: this was Moi's 'decade of extreme political repression'. The Green Belt Movement had to navigate these uncertain political waters.

Wangari wasn't, her daughter Wanjira says, without fear. 'I often asked her if she was scared and she said she was, but the conviction that she knew what

10.2 *Newtoniae* seedling, Karura Forest

was to be done at that time was overwhelming.' Her children were certainly scared for her. 'It was frightening', says Wanjira. 'My brothers and I were afraid she would be attacked and we would lose her.' Wanjira says it was only as she grew older that she understood what her mother was trying to do. 'When she saw injustice, she had to challenge it.' Wangari didn't go looking for confrontation but that's increasingly what she found. Mia MacDonald, an American fellow environmental activist and longtime friend, who with her partner, the author and editor Martin Rowe, collaborated with Wangari on researching and writing her memoir *Unbowed*, explains this apparent contradiction: 'She never sought conflict, but she couldn't sit by and watch things get gradually worse for the people and environment of Kenya. She also saw, that because she had been so privileged in receiving an education to PhD level, she absolutely had to put her skills and talents to good use. Once when we were together in a rural district, we passed a group of women with huge piles of firewood on their back, and she said, without any scorn or superiority, just as a simple fact: "If I hadn't gone to school, I would be one of those women." And so she did what she knew to be right, to be just even if that meant, as she said so herself, "treading on toes".'

When in 1982 a by-election in South Tetu, in her home district of Nyeri, was announced, Wangari set out to register as a candidate in order to provide a woman's voice in the campaign and, says Mia MacDonald, 'because she thought she would be good at it, and would act with the probity she viewed as required of public officials'. There were only five women MPs sitting in Parliament at the time, and Kenya had always had a terrible record on women's representation. It was, however, a disastrous move that resulted in her losing her job at the University, which meant she lost her home as well as her income, pension and status.

Whether it was through naivety or over-optimism, she simply hadn't realised the sheer scale of the forces ranged against her. She did not win the seat; she did not even stand: she wasn't allowed to register as a candidate, due to a spurious technicality. Worse, in order to run for election, she had to resign her post at the University. Although she applied to withdraw her resignation less than a day after she had submitted it, the post had strangely already been filled. There was no returning to her relatively comfortable life of academia. She wasn't the first 'difficult' academic targeted by the University. In 1978 the playwright, lecturer and outspoken government critic Ngugi wa Thiong'o had been released from a short spell in detention, but the University refused to reinstate him. In 1979 the University had been closed for a month (one of dozens of such closures) to prevent student demonstrations, and in 1979 and 1980 many student activists were either expelled or left of their own accord. The University administration, along with all other major public bodies had, under Moi, become subsumed to the government's direction and the Vice-Chancellor began to operate as a political appointee. Wangari realised that there was no going back. 'I was forty-one years old and for the first time in decades I had nothing to do', she wrote in her memoir. 'I was down to zero.' Her fellow academic Vert Mbaya simply says to me: 'I will never forgive the University for what they did to her.'

This setback provided the impetus that transformed the Green Belt Movement from a fairly modest and small-scale operation into a nationwide and, eventually, continent-wide tree-planting programme. By 1986, the GBM had planted more than 1 million trees and was tending 670 community tree nurseries, employing ten full-time staff; by 1996 it would have planted 10 million indigenous trees with a survival rate of 75 per cent, with 1,000 active tree nurseries, and 800 field workers, nursery attendants and area advisors. Some of the tree belts, like the one in Navaisha, were now 1,000 trees wide. Partnership with the Norwegian Forestry Society, and with the Norwegian International Aid agency NORAD, kept the movement well funded through the difficult 1980s and even provided for Wangari, now operating as the movement's co-ordinator with an income of US$600 a year. Six months after losing her job and University house, she moved into a bungalow she had, cannily, it turned out, bought as new in 1975, in an area called South C, close to Wilson airport and Nairobi National Park. Dr Stephen Ndegwa, who visited her in the three-bedroom bungalow as part of his research into civil society organisations in Africa, described the living room as 'an unassuming clutter of rugs, books, memorabilia and awards', with files, monitors and papers housed in the converted garage and veranda. She grew yams and sweet potatoes in the garden, also safely away from her goats; it was the greenest house on the street, the compound bursting with trees and shrubs she planted in the early 1980s.

With a return to relative, if still somewhat precarious, security, Wangari worked on, winning accolades and deepening and expanding her network of environmental contacts. In 1983 a group of Kenyan women professionals named her Woman of the Year and in 1984 she was awarded the Right Livelihood Prize (known as the 'Alternative Nobel'). In 1986, the Green Belt Movement won Bronze Medal at the inaugural awards of the Better World Society and Wangari travelled to New York to receive the award, meet philanthropist Ted Turner and give interviews to the international press. One reporter who interviewed her in New York, Louise Sweeney of the *Christian Science Monitor*, described her in 1986 as 'a handsome woman in long intricate corn-row braids', wearing a long blue jacket and ankle-length print skirt, and 'who might pass for a college student'. Sweeney passed on Wangari's warning, issued in her softly spoken, deep, slightly husky tones, the gentleness of her enunciation belying the strength of her words: 'If we do not take care of the soil, if we do not take care of the environment, we will die.' Later she would tell another interviewer, who described her as 'statuesque and elegant' with a 'mischievous' smile, 'I was a very decent professor at the University of Nairobi. I was a good girl ... but we kept finding doors closed, so we had to force them open.'

Uhuru Park

It was this inability to look away when she saw that action was required, and her willingness to speak the truth, even if it made people feel uncomfortable, or indeed enraged them, that resulted in her highly public confrontation with the Moi government at the end of 1989. MPs in Parliament publicly cursed her and accused the Green Belt Movement of being 'bogus'. Parts of the Kenyan press, too, turned from being mildly supportive to reflecting the regime's strident vilification. In November 1989, the Kenyan papers were full of articles and letters about the government's plan to build a 60-storey office block and media centre in Uhuru Park, a large expanse of natural and semi-wild garden, lakes and wooded areas in the heart of Nairobi. The Kenya Times Media Trust (KTMT) building was to be the tallest skyscraper in Africa, and adorned, in the tradition of all good dictators, with a 30-foot statue of Daniel arap Moi.

Wangari had heard of the plans in the late summer and began writing letters and galvanising opposition to the project. The skyscraper attracted widespread criticism throughout Kenya: one letter writer to the press, who lived in Nairobi, said the Park with its 'forest of trees and grass' was the only way he could 'get lost' from the noise of the city. Another correspondent warned that Nairobi would lose its epithet, the 'Green City in the Sun'. A third said the Park was the only place in Nairobi where, at ground level, it was still possible to see Kenya's famous 'big sky' that at night shone with the light of millions of distant worlds. Another wrote that it was one of the last parts of the city that had an unbroken connection with land that was once marsh and tropical forest, that contained a memory of the wild place it once was. Wangari Maathai called for a public consultation before the works went ahead. Meeting indifference from MPs, on 7 November she wrote a letter to the KTMT, copying in the British High Commissioner to Kenya, Sir John Johnson in her efforts to track down British media magnate Robert Maxwell, who had a stake in the development. MPs in Parliament turned on her – how dare she, a woman and a *divorcée* to boot, criticise the government, they asked. She had 'gone round the world collecting money' for a 'bogus' organisation; she had 'repudiated' her husband in public. She had 'no respect for men'. Ali Bidu, the MP for Kinangop, called on MPs to issue a *tumupige salala*, to curse her. If she didn't like how things were done in Kenya, she was free to leave the country, another said. Go and live in Europe, if you like it so much there, one taunted. The House was full to capacity, the newspapers reported, and all the MPs laughed at her. It must have been terrifying to read about.

Yet the very next day, she wrote a public letter in reply, and this is where we learn something of that inner core that kept her going, that she told the nuns in Kansas she had learned from them. Where others might have slunk away to lick their wounds, or perhaps have asked someone else to enter the fray on their behalf, she braced for action. Like the good professor she was, she wrote a long and reasoned letter to the men who were literally baying for her blood. She wrote that she had contacted the British High Commissioner to try to locate Robert Maxwell, that there was nothing wrong in encouraging people to raise their voice, if they didn't like the Uhuru Park complex; she admonished the MPs for referring to her marital status. 'The debate should not be distracted by the anatomy below the line. The debate requires anatomy of whatever lies above the neck.' She would use this tactic again and again: reasoned, pedagogical, witty and bound to infuriate her antagonists.

Professor Karanja Njoroge saw her method at another protest, ten years later, when private security guards armed with bows and arrows and whips tried to prevent her from planting trees in Karura Forest. The forest, public land, had been divided into lots and sold cheaply to Moi's political allies so they could build luxury homes. Njoroge watched as, rather than flee, or yell, or throw things, Wangari approached the guards and asked them to explain to her why she should not do what she was doing. 'She had no hard words for them, even as they were tormenting her; she passionately wanted them to understand her arguments. She would tell them, "You have misunderstood me," and repeat her point. She would listen to them, she wanted to hear what they were fearful of. She sought dialogue. She was very different to the rest of us.' Her Uhuru Park letter to the MPs included an invitation to take them on a tour of some of the Green Belt projects. She would be happy to meet the MPs to explain how the Green Belt Movement worked, and she finished with a quote in Gikuyu, '*Ihiga, ona waga kwaria ni waigwa*' – 'Rock, even if you don't reply, you have heard.'

Of course, this letter was bound to stir the MPs, and Moi, into a frenzy of hatred and masculine insecurity. So now Moi waded in, and it's no small thing to be publicly derided by a head of state who tortures his political opponents. He said that Wangari and her supporters, had 'insects in their heads'. He asked the women of Kenya to discipline the woman who 'shows no respect for men as required by African traditions'. Where are all these trees she is supposed to have planted, he asked. In December 1989 the police turned up at the offices of the Green Belt Movement to give her 24 hours to vacate the building. She moved all the Green Belt Movement files and computers into the garage of her bungalow and continued her work from home along with her youngest child, Muta who was still living with her, and at times up to 80 members of staff perching on sofa arms and veranda steps.

'But we still had fun, and laughter, and pots and pots of tea', says Vert Mbaya, fellow University of Nairobi academic, longtime friend of Wangari and Treasurer to the Green Belt Movement for nearly 45 years. 'They couldn't stop our joy. We drank cups and cups of tea and ate Mandazi – sweet doughnuts. The laughter kept us going, and brightened our darkest hours.' The GBM work went on and so did the attacks, even as the letters of public support flowed into the nation's newspaper offices. The MPs called for the Green Belt Movement to be banned; Wangari responded by filing a High Court injunction seeking to stop the Times complex construction and calling for a mass demonstration in favour of preserving the Park. Then, in the midst of the fight, and wearing a bright green jacket, representing the green of the trees and grass at Uhuru Park, she attended a reception at the United Nations campus north of Nairobi centre, where she was applauded and embraced by the international environmental community. She wasn't averse to a little theatricality. Indeed, this kind of public attention would show Moi she was to some extent protected by her status. If she disappeared into one of his torture houses, the international community would notice. By now, international donors were beginning to question the need for the Uhuru Park Tower – it would cost around 4 billion Kenyan shillings, of which 3 billion (US$155 million) would be offshore loans. By the end of January, the project was being scaled back; soon the fences in Uhuru Park came down and in 1992 it was officially abandoned. Wangari and other women danced a dance of victory at the site.

From then on, she would be a marked woman, particularly as she refused to go back quietly to simply planting trees. For Wangari her environmental activism and her fight for democratic freedoms in Kenya were part of the same struggle. The Green Belt Movement may have been for Moi 'the most unpopular NGO in Kenya' but he couldn't stop her, and perhaps that is what infuriated him most. She was also attracting powerful allies. US Senators including Al Gore and Edward Kennedy wrote letters of support. Once, the former President of the USSR, Mikhail Gorbachev sent Moi an admonitory letter about his regime's treatment of her. Opposition to Moi's regime was growing within Kenya too, under the umbrella of the Forum for the Restoration of Democracy, in which Wangari played an instrumental role. In January

1992, having been arrested at a demonstration and put in a police cell where she spent nights on a damp floor, she was taken to hospital after her court appearance. The police would claim she had been 'suffering silently from rheumatism'. In June 1992 she was invited to give the keynote speech at the United Nations Earth Summit in Rio de Janeiro, on behalf of a large grouping of environmental and development NGOs. At the time, Wangari was, yet again, due in court, this time to answer charges that she was part of a coup to overthrow the government, and her lawyer had to seek permission for her to leave the country to attend the summit.

She and Moi both went to Rio: she fighting to save the natural world; he busily parcelling off tracts of forest to give away to political allies. The clip of her eight-minute speech is still on YouTube, and shows a tall woman standing on a grey podium in front of a conference hall gaping like an aircraft hangar, but which is less than a quarter full. Some of the suited delegates listen intently, others confer with neighbours, some are seen getting up and leaving the room. The Earth Summit was the first UN summit to begin in earnest discussing climate change and during the 11-day conference some 109 world leaders breezed through in their jets. Jane Fonda, the Dalai Lama and Fidel Castro put in appearances, waving stardust over proceedings. George Bush senior turned up in a helicopter and told the conference that 'the American way of life is not negotiable'. But Wangari had a message, one that she and her fellow environmental activists had been working on for the previous two years. And so, she stood there, speaking quite softly and occasionally stumbling over her words, accusing some governments of being bent on preventing progress and charging others with seeking only cosmetic change that would do nothing to address the degradation of the environment. She singled out the United States, 'that consumes so much of the earth's resources', for its failure to take a leadership role on such an important issue. Well, at least they didn't arrest her, but George Bush and other world leaders didn't listen either, even though when she finished her speech the audience clapped politely. She returned to Kenya and, shortly afterwards, went into hiding after a colleague received death threats and once again the police came to her home to arrest her.

Karura Forest

Through all their leader's persecution, the Green Belt Movement kept on planting, and at the end of the twentieth century its nursery attendants, farmers and volunteer planters had nurtured to maturity somewhere between 20 and

30 million trees throughout Kenya, mostly as belts along the edges of farms, but also within the margins of established forests. But Moi was still in power, and Kenya's forests were still vanishing: 450,000 acres (700 square miles) of forest disappeared between 1987 and 1996. Journalists investigating stories of illegal logging were often set upon by gangs protecting the lucrative trade in rare and much-prized Muhugu trees. Tourists love its rich, buttery yellow colour and fine straight grain for souvenir salad servers and figurines. A 12-tonne lorry of *Brachylaena huillensis* (Muhugu) trees that took 300 years to reach their full, dizzying 150-foot glory could be felled in one night and be on the way to the sea at Mombasa, earning the loggers around US$750. Much of this forested land was parcelled off and the titles given to supporters of the ruling party KANU in the 1990s. It was discussed, quite openly, in the press as the 'land-grabbing mania' and Ministers and their officials did very little to hide their corruption.

According to one estimate made at about the turn of the new millennium, if Kenya's forests were to continue being destroyed at the same rate, by about 2060 there would be none left. One very vulnerable forest was Karura, at the northern edge of Nairobi. So close to the burgeoning megacity's centre, it was an ideal, paradisical even, green and leafy location for millionaires grown rich on Moi's corruption to build their palaces. The 2,500 acres of Karura, and a few other remnants, are all that is left of a vast, unbroken forest that once stretched nearly 100 miles, all the way to the Aberdares and Mount Kenya. Its remains are a vital buffer of water catchment, cooling, shade and shelter at the edge of the fast-growing city. Although the colonial government had designated it a protected Crown Reserve in the 1930s, nobody, it seems: the illegal loggers and charcoal burners, the colonial railways and the admin-istration, could resist taking little nibbles out of it. Many species like the Muhugu were felled, virtually to extinction. The forest was like the doomed Dodo of Mauritius: for all that it was known to be on the brink of extinction, and European zoologists vainly begged other European hunters and ships' crews to desist, they could not resist killing the birds because, large, tasty and earth-bound, it was just *so easy*.

During Moi's presidency, Karura became an increasingly dangerous place where even the few rangers still employed by the Forest Service feared to tread. Gangs of robbers used the forest as their base from where they mounted raids on nearby suburban homes, and then, under the cover of the trees, met to divide up the spoils. There was an illegal liquor distillery there, and a bizarre freestanding chimney where the Bank of Kenya burned decommissioned currency notes. Only a few brave dog walkers still used the paths, but only with a large stick or side arm in their hands, just in case of attack. The forest was becoming the dark wood, the home of dragons and ogres of Kikuyu myth. Even the birds and animals were fleeing it: the African Crowned Eagle and Colobus monkeys could no longer sustain populations there. Only the Forest Service's popular tree nursery, right on the southern edge, closest to the city, and near the main gate, was still regularly visited. According to Professor Karanja Njoroge, the abandonment of the forest was a deliberate ploy, so people would not object when officials, under instruction from Ministers, de-gazetted the forest in order to sell it off. 'It was inhabited by gangsters, dead bodies were routinely found in it. The Government's neglect of it made it impossible for it to be safe. People began to hate and fear the forest, which is of course exactly what Moi wanted.' For at the same time that tales of the dark deeds done in the forest were circulating, developers were bulldozing trackways onto the plots of land sold to them, or given to them by the regime.

Wangari found out about these new developments in the forest in the summer of 1998, and in the September wrote a letter to the Attorney General requesting a halt to any further clearing of the forest. The *Daily Nation* newspaper sent a helicopter up to fly across the forest and take pictures of the devastation. The grainy, black and white images show great, shorn patches of land, the lush green canopy ending abruptly in a mess of mud, tree stumps and low vegetation; arrow-straight access roads have been driven straight into its heart. Clearly having learned nothing from the Uhuru Park debacle, the government's first response was to ignore both Wangari and the outcry from ordinary people. The citizens of Kenya wrote letters to the newspapers: some very sad, others very angry. One chided Kenyans for their naivety in believing the Ministry of Natural Resources was there to protect the country's last wild spaces. 'The Ministry of Natural Resources has its main job ... to hand them out to powerful politicians and their ... idle, greedy sons and daughters.' When it became clear, through its complete silence on the matter, that the government was not going to intervene, Wangari and her supporters began a campaign of guerilla tree planting on recently cleared land in the forest. Carrying watering cans and seedlings in their soil bags, they circumvented guards armed with pangas and clubs. They removed their shoes and waded across rivers and marshes, carrying the tender seedlings in their hands. Tiny year-old strands of xylem and carbon molecules: miniature *Olea Africana* and *Syzygeum cordata*, or waterberry tree, that grows along woodland rivers, and the medicinal *Warburgia ugandensis* or greenheart, pushing their roots into the damaged soil.

Often, the private security guards charged at them, and they scattered. But always they returned, 'every Wednesday', Wangari promised in October 1998. It is a bizarre, topsy turvy world where women who come to plant trees in a public forest are set upon.

Throughout October, November and December there were clashes between the private guards and protestors, which now included University students and a handful of opposition MPs. One day millions of Kenyan shillings worth of expensive equipment, including earth movers, trucks and a large works office, were burned to the ground (this action was nothing to do with the Green Belt Movement). Still the government maintained its silence even as lawyers, MPs and journalists began to join the dots between the private developers and government Ministers. Moi, who enjoyed a reputation as a President who protected the environment with his attempts at stopping elephant poaching, still said nothing. A list of companies which had been given title deeds to land in the forest was, eventually, released but none of their names were found in the records of the Registrar General. Things came to a head on 8 January 1999 when, after confronting the security guards, Wangari and her supporters who had once more come to plant trees, were set upon with shocking ferocity. In a three-hour confrontation, some journalists who were there were whipped and beaten; a BBC Isuzu Trooper had its windscreen smashed. Somone took a club and beat Wangari over the head with it: it was a deep cut and she would need four stitches. The police watched and did nothing. At the police station later, Wangari signed her statement in her own blood.

There are many clips of Wangari on YouTube and elsewhere: the gracious winner of the Nobel Peace Prize; the delighted storyteller contributing to a documentary on dirt, the precious soil; the leader of the Green Belt Movement, rotting log in hand, explaining how trees contribute to the earth's richness, and speaking to world leaders suffering varying degrees of deafness at international environmental conferences. There is one clip, however, that has particular impact, and it's a piece of film footage of her immediately after the Karura Forest attack. She is hurt, she is angry, she is bleeding. She turns to a camera and speaks passionately: 'If we are going to shed blood because of our land, we will: we are used to that. Our forefathers shed blood for our land. We will do so. This is *my* blood.' Her voice is controlled but you can hear the outrage. It was the moment perhaps of greatest jeopardy. Her children, abroad at the time, watched the footage, aghast, as young men armed with bows and arrows, clubs and pangas, ran at Wangari and the other women of the Green Belt Movement. No one considered the irony that at the time there was an ongoing campaign to challenge violence against women in Kenya.

This was, however, a pivotal moment. The then UN Secretary General, Kofi Annan, who had appointed Wangari to his advisory board on peace and disarmament, said in a statement that he expected 'the authorities to take appropriate action against those responsible for attacking Professor Maathai'. Nairobi MPs turned on the police for standing by; some accused the police of committing the violence alongside the private security guards. The government was embarrassed enough to call a halt to development in the forest and the bulldozers, what was left of them, melted away. It would be another three years, however, before the government began to revoke the title deeds to the illegal plots. Wangari Maathai, by then an MP, would be part of the government that enacted the revocations. In time, as we shall see, walkers, botanists and parties of school children on nature trips would return to the forest, as would the eagles and monkeys.

Part III

FOREST

11

Mina, Dorothy, Evelyn: 10,000 miles of stones

When Mina Hubbard first stepped into her canoe at North West River in 1905 her presence in northern Labrador was considered an afront by those rugged New York outdoors magazines and the masculine exploration fraternity. For them, she was an outrage to nature, to the social order of things, to white north American manhood. Her First Nation guides were afraid to let her out of their sight, for if any harm came to her the consequences for them would be catastrophic. The Montagnais women she encountered on the George River feared she was some kind of supernatural being emerging from the wild around *their* home, come to penetrate their camp, to either hurt them or steal their children. Although in her diary she recorded deep, peaceful delight among the willow-clotted flats, the dark lakes and the wildflowers, Mina was a woman out of her place on every level. By the time of Evelyn Cheesman's last insect-hunting expedition in 1958, women's status in many countries across the globe had changed radically, as had ideas of what they were permitted to do in the realms of power, politics and business. In most countries, by the middle of the twentieth century women had the vote. Sirimavo Bandaranaike, Indira Gandhi, Golda Meir and Isabel Peron would all, shortly, be elected as Prime Minister, or head of state in Sri Lanka, India, Israel and Argentina.

In that other realm closed to women, the kingdom of natural beauty, the high mountains, the wide seas, the dark forests beyond the bounds of human statute, beyond the city wall, garden gate or village paling, women's presence would still be problematic. To look at extremes, the first woman to climb Mount Everest was Jubo Tabei in 1975 and the first known woman to reach the north pole on foot, Ann Bancroft, did so in 1986. The first Black African woman, Saray Khumalo, would not climb mount Everest until 2019. Even today, the outdoors is a contested space for women: not just those dimly lit parks where women joggers wonder whose steps are behind them, or those suburban streets where women bunch their keys in their fists before they reach home, but also in what is left of the wild. Women's backpackers' guides written as late as 1980 suggest that society still believes there is something unnatural or odd about women in the wilderness, and women fear they will somehow lose their femininity by going there, that they will undergo some transformation and will lose the very essence of themselves. *The Backpacking Woman* guide (1980), as an example, asserts: 'Planted deep in most women's psyches is the insidious question, by going outdoors will I lose my femininity?' Another guide, *Wild, Wild Woman: A complete woman's guide to enjoying the great outdoors* (1978), is explicit about what this transformation might be: 'Outdoor woman ... will conjure up visions of large unisex females with chapped lips and heavy shoes who talk in hearty voices', the guide asserts; 'Outdoor woman' will thus become some kind of modern version of the medieval 'loathly lady', a grotesque creature with perverse sexual desires, who stalked those barren lands beyond the castle walls. Modern US studies of 'wilderness' sites show that women (and also Black and Hispanic men) feel less safe than white men in the remote outdoors, and that they prefer places where there are obvious signs of law enforcement officers, rubbish bins and orientation boards with lists of rules. And because bears can't read noticeboards, it's not the bears women are most afraid of. Even in the remotest region of the planet, at the Antarctic research stations around the south pole, women scientists and fieldworkers report sexual harassment and boorish behaviour intended to 'other' and exclude them by the men at the bases.

It is now more than a hundred years since a young Dorothy Pilley realised that the men of the Alps, even at 10,000 feet above sea level, would make her feel like an unwanted outsider, unless she had a nurturing or caring role to fulfil. It's also a century or more since Evelyn Cheesman, on her first collecting trip, was robbed of her status as expedition entomologist by an amateur male naturalist, who also appropriated her collecting screen and assistant. So, what did our outdoor pioneers do when ill health, old age and fragility became greater obstacles than gendered stereotypes? Dorothy and Evelyn would, as we will see, be drawn into the wild for the rest of their lives. Dorothy, who would live to be nearly 92, saw in her last New Year, 1986, in a climber's hut on the Isle of Skye, still marvelling at the colours of the heather and rock, still taking notes in her small A5 journal, a Camel cigarette between her fingers. Evelyn would continue her collecting in the South Pacific well into her 70s, but after that would travel in ever-decreasing circles, her last expeditions into Tarifa, southern Spain in 1958 at the age of 78, where, beneath a large shaded hat, she tried to catch frogs and giant water beetles in flooded quarries.

But we shall return first to Mina, whose remaining years of life are something of a mystery. Not that we don't know what she did, but that despite her ardent desire, recorded in her Labrador diary, that she might 'spend my summers like this always', apart from a few short canoe trips, she never set foot in the wild again. She was certainly proud of her achievement: one of the first things she did, upon receiving her *decree nisi* from her second husband, Harold Ellis, in 1927, was to apply, successfully, to become a Fellow of the Royal Geographical Society at a time when women Fellows were still a rarity. Her entry describes her as 'of independent means'. Her divorce settlement gave her an income of £2,000 a year for the rest of her life and, after the three children she had with Ellis (born 1909, 1911 and 1913), reached 21, £500 a year for her son John, and £250 a year for each of her two daughters, Mahlo and Margaret. She became a suffragist before and during the First World War, supporting the radical suffragette newspaper the *Woman's Dreadnought*.

She began to reject the Methodism of her childhood, and rejected too western medicine, despite having trained as a nurse. Instead she studied eastern religions, spiritualism, herbalism and clairvoyance. Some time before 1920, she wrote to her friend Helen Bridgman, 'begging' her to study the Indian poet and philosopher Rabindranath Tagore. While Mina may have completed her search for the headwaters of the Naskaupi, recorded Bridgman, 'she is still searching for the truth – in matters of the soul now, seeking some faith to cling to.' In a letter to her publisher John Murray in 1921, Mina explained that sorrow on earth was down to western ignorance making us concentrate on the wrong values in life and that the sages of the east had managed to find a better, and deeper, truth. She became estranged from her English husband's family (as she had become estranged from Leonidas's family too). After her children were grown up (by all accounts, while they were little, she was an attentive, if strict, mother), it was as if she was constantly seeking outsider status, never fitting in, never settling, never happy.

Up until the outbreak of the Second World War, she sailed the Atlantic almost every year, sometimes with, but increasingly often without, her three children, to visit family in Toronto and Ontario. In the summer of 1921, she spent several months near Toronto looking after her sister Annie who was dying of cancer. She could easily, from there, have mounted any number of expeditions, for she had the means and the contacts: the ethnologist and explorer William Brooks Cabot remained a firm admirer. Once she took her son John on a canoe trip and before the outbreak of the Second World War she gave lectures on her journey, in 1936 becoming the first woman ever to deliver the annual lectureship of the Ontario Agricultural College. She also, in the 1930s and now in her late 60s, met up with George Elson and together they went on at least one, and maybe two, canoe journeys to James Bay and up the Moose River in northern Ontario. She spent the winter of 1947/48 in a hotel in Victoria, British Columbia, contemplating living out her last days in Canada but returned to England again.

Photographs show a thin, wiry woman fond of eccentric hats and not particularly happy or smiling. She was described as 'difficult to live with' and had bitter rifts with two of her three children when they became adults, over their marriages and lifestyles, of which she did not approve. In some of the modern Canadian adventure stories constructed out of Mina's journey, there are hints, speculations that Mina and George Elson fell in love during the summer of 1905, or at least he fell in love with her.

Even in modern times, Mina's journey and motivations have still been circumscribed and questioned by the men who have written about her. So, in Pierre Berton's *The Wild Frontier* (1978), a collection of tales from the Canadian wilderness, he describes Mina as 'a little unhinged' and 'jealous' of Dillon Wallace because her husband spent his last six months on earth with him. Why she was never jealous of George Elson for the same offence is not explained. In another retelling of the story, *Great Heart* (2000), authors James West Davidson and John Rugge, as well as introduction author Bill McKibben, think Elson fell in love with Mina's 'sweet girlishness' while they were on the trail together but that once they reached so-called civilisation and the Fords' home on Ungava Bay 'she snaps back into her New England *primness*' – there is definite opprobrium in that word reserved just for women – thus both leading Elson on and hurting him. She of course did have to protect her reputation, as a young widow having achieved a degree of notoriety. There would be a crowd of newspapermen waiting for her at the pierhead in New York and people were bound to talk. At the end of the journey Mina asked Elson to sign a declaration stating that nothing 'unbecoming honourable Christian men and women' had happened between them and watched, from the windows of the Fords' home, her erstwhile guides singing and camping, now part of a world that had already grown strange to her.

Both George and Mina would marry other people in the years after the journey. But Mina did buy a large, finely made canoe for George, and she did also send him regular payments, for the rest of his life, in thanks and recognition for the contributions he made to that voyage. Mina encouraged George to write his own account of her husband's last days, which he did, and which was published as an addendum inside the covers of her own book. In so doing, she gave a First Nation man a voice in a European-authored text. How to unravel these apparent contradictions? Her trail diary is so happy, a love letter to the wild; there is genuine affection and respect between her and her guides and, unlike so many other early twentieth-century European explorers, there are authentic efforts to understand, and communicate with, without attempting to dominate, the First Nation people she met along her way. But after her book was published, she never returned to the wild. It could only be that she couldn't bear to.

As a divorced woman of comfortable means and particularly after her children obtained their majority, she would have been free to do and go exactly what and where she wanted. In fact she lived much of the rest of her life in central London, far away from her Canadian family, a stranger a long way from home. Her expedition had been for a sole purpose, to finish the work her husband had started. It gave her great joy but also much pain, and although her story became woven into the fabric of Canadian folklore, for her it was a journey of the heart and mind, as much as for the body. The wild had taken Leonidas, and her only real happiness. That journey, when she felt him so close all around her, was like extending, for a few sunny months, their life together as much as protecting his legacy. While there is much to be admired in her book, it is in her diary, which was only published for all to read in 2005, that we begin to perceive the real Mina, and so in those gaps and absences her thoughts and motivations were misinterpreted by others, her story mansplained over the decades. Had she been writing her book even 20, or 30 years later, perhaps she would have found the courage, as Dorothy Pilley would, to confront society's expectations of how a woman should behave outdoors, and write more openly about the enchantment of those Labrador days, the easy companionship she enjoyed with her guides, that we read in her diary.

Time and again I return to her map, where, hiding in plain sight she records in code the secrets of her broken heart. It is a map that does not seek to draw boundaries or assert ownership; it simply tells a story of love and loss. At its heart is that agonisingly small space that separates the site of her husband's death and the mark 'where George Elson found the flour' – too late! The map also shows how close Leonidas got to Lake Michikamau, and tells how, if the weather had been kinder, even having lost their way, the men might have had a chance. Leonidas might have lived. That ardent wish to 'spend

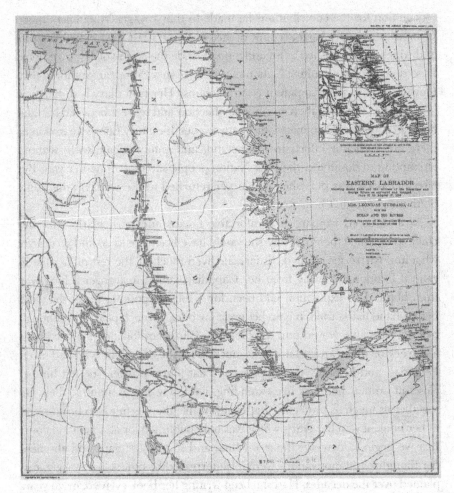

11.1 Mina's full map of her journey across northern Labrador

my summers like this always', was to live where she could still sense Leonidas; it was a journey to try to cross over to the other world, to reach him, bring him back and even though she tried, later on, through clairvoyance and spiritualism, to reach him in other ways, he was lost to her. In her later years, Mina's journeying went into herself. She became a student of Rudolf Steiner, practised a form of anthroposophy and, according to her nieces, became more tolerant and less in need of imposing her will on others. In the 1950s she stayed in a series of central London hotels, gradually becoming more erratic and forgetful. On 4 May 1956, aged 86, she walked under a train at Coulsdon station, south London and was killed instantly.

Her map lives on. While much of the Labrador that Mina crossed in 1905 is now submerged beneath the Churchill Reservoir, modern maps of the area between North West River and the reservoir still carry faint traces of her journey. Names of lakes, names little pondered by modern walkers, persist, peopling the wilderness with ghosts. Appropriately enough Lac Elson, or Elson Lake, now in modern Quebec and named for her Cree guide, is still there, as is Disappointment Lake, named for the point at which her husband realised he was never going to fulfil his dream.

Evelyn Cheesman has also left her mark on maps, although not any kind of map a traveller could navigate by. Since her last collecting expedition to the Pacific in 1955, the discipline of biogeography has rapidly developed with scientists' understanding of plate tectonics and palaeobotany. Lines of rupture in evolutionary processes have been found across the world, where great and ancient sunderings of the earth's crust have disrupted once continuous biological regions. Wallace's Line, Huxley's Line, Hedley's Line, Lydekker's Line are biogeographical, rather than cartographical boundaries, along the edges of continental shelves and deep Pacific trenches, and mark stages in the vast tearing between the ancient vanished continents of Gondwana and Laurasia. Alfred Wallace, Thomas Henry Huxley, Charles Hedley and Richard Lydekker were of course all men, and very much the archetypal bewhiskered eminent imperial naturalists of the late Victorian era. Etchings and photographs of them at their book-laden desks show them as contemplative, educated masters of all they survey.

Much more recently, in 2010, a group of biogeographers proposed another line, marking the distinctive break in flora and fauna between islands in the southern and northern groups of the Vanuatu Archipelago (formerly the New Hebrides). Working on the strange discontinuities between various reptiles and amphibians between the two groups of islands, and employing recent findings of how these volcanic islands have moved and rotated in their journeys across the Pacific, these geographers went back into the literature of the islands' natural history. Here they discovered that in 1957, and writing in the journal *Nature*, Evelyn Cheesman had first theorised that this break was similar to the Wallace Line in its significance. The contemporary scholars agreed. 'We suggest', they write, 'that this discontinuity be referred to as Cheesman's Line', to honour her contributions to our understating of evolutionary biology.

She would have been pleased, no doubt, to have received this honour had she been still alive, but would also have brushed it off as a bauble not to

Bora Bora
House on the Reef

11.2 Evelyn's home on Bora Bora, 1925, sketch by Evelyn Cheesman

interfere with her continuing research, as she did when she was awarded an OBE by Queen Elizabeth II in the New Year's honours for January 1955. She was on Aneityum, southern New Hebrides (Vanuatu) at the time, living, at the age of 74, in a leaky wood-stilt and brush hut she named Red Crest, collecting evidence to bolster her theory. In many cases her specimens literally emerged from the walls of her home: creeping, stinging, biting, sliding from out of the dark infested hollows, sucking her blood and laying eggs in her food. In her letter to Captain Riley of the Natural History Museum, who had informed her of the award, she wrote: 'I am quite overwhelmed by the honour H. M. has bestowed on me. I take it as recognition of the services rendered by our whole team of collectors,' and, barely pausing for a metaphorical breath, 'By seamail I am despatching botanical material (121 specimens of plants and ferns) … Hymenoptera, Lepidoptera, Diptera'. She devoted a far larger part of her letter to the more than 300 different species of insects she was rushing to get onto the mail steamer before she missed the sailing window to get her specimens away from the hot, damp conditions which threatened to damage them beyond useful analysis.

More helpful to her was the civil list pension she received in 1953 at the age of 72 whereby, as her *Times* obituary put it, 'her lack of means [was] somewhat eased'. On her return from that last journey to the Pacific she moved into a retirement home near Chelmsford, Essex. There she wrote her memoir, *Things Worth While* (1957), which became something of a minor publishing success, resulting in further invitations to speak on the radio about her adventures. In her memoir, and its sequel, *Time Well Spent* (1960), she tried, more than in any of her other books, to express the 'urge', as she called it, to travel and research, risking her life, and health so often, living alone, sometimes for months on a handful of small sweet potatoes a day and shaving her head to save herself from insect infestations.

The forest, she wrote, had bewitched her, put her in a trance from which it was difficult to awaken. The trees, ferns and invertebrates were more real to her than any human creation. In her small retirement flat, surrounded by the other residents of Writtle Park, she wrote despairingly of 'this noisy, bustling world of ours where so much energy is dissipated in the insignificant. Real isolation is freedom of the mind.' She also wrote passionately about the need to treat the indigenous peoples that western explorers encountered with respect and sensitivity. Westerners were, after all, blundering into somebody else's homeland and although the flora and fauna maybe marvellous and novel to the visitors, to the people who lived in these lands for centuries, they were as familiar as wasps and stinging nettles are to us, she wrote. Listen to these people, she urged, respect their customs, we might learn something.

Despite her advancing age and infirmity, those four close walls were like a prison to her. She needed to be off again. By some great stroke of serendipity, at Writtle Park there was living another elderly woman naturalist, the botanist Lettice Digby, five years older than Evelyn but like Evelyn missing her collecting expeditions. With the sales of *Things Worth While* earning her, for the first time in her life, a reasonable income, the pair hatched a plan. Not the Pacific, of course, they both knew neither was up to that kind of a journey, but they chose what was then a remote and undeveloped corner of southern Spain, a green valley outside Tarifa between Gibraltar and Cadiz. As they flew in at night, Evelyn reminisced that she had previously seen Gibraltar in 1939, arriving from New Guinea on the very last Dutch cargo boat to depart the Pacific before the Second World War erupted. It wasn't Vanuatu, or Tahiti, nor New Guinea but for three sun-filled weeks she was out in the swarmy flower meadows. There she found a new species of mason bee, and 'beetles frantic with greed' but, disappointingly, not as many varieties of grasshopper as she had hoped.

On her return she presented the Natural History Museum with a collection of 1,000 insects.

In the 1960s she could still be found, in her retirement home, examining with her microscope the thousands of species yet to be identified, named and catalogued, for the Natural History Museum. She still received remuneration for her research: for the financial year 1963/64 she was paid £50, at the rate of 5 shillings an hour, representing one thousand hours of work peering into the magnifying lenses and making notes. I would have loved to hear the conversations between the staff discussing this tiny old lady and her boxes upon boxes of dead bugs brought back from across the world. She was still as busy as those solitary wasps she had observed so closely on Tahiti but time was not on her side. A fall down stairs left her with a fractured shoulder, and a car accident with a spinal injury; her lifelong limp got worse after a hip operation in 1960 and in 1966 she lost the sight in one eye. A few months after this she suffered a severe stroke which left her paralysed and unable to study any longer. She died in April 1969, still leaving thousands of specimens to classify. Today, more than 200 species of insect and plants bear her suffix, 'Cheesmanae' (although some of the earlier ones bear the masculine 'Cheesmanii', thus named by scientists who assumed that Evelyn Cheesman was a man). Several have been named in just the past few years: a small, shiny beetle with hard corrugated wing cases, *Dicraspeda cheesmanae* in 2009, a water beetle *Exocelia evelyncheesmanae* in 2012 and *Hydraena cheesmanae*, a tiny beetle that lives under stones on river margins, classified in 2011, nearly 80 years after she found it. There will, doubtless, be many more to come as her specimens are examined.

While 1958 had been for Evelyn a miraculous year, one of planning and escape from the tedium of age and infirmity, for Dorothy Pilley it was disastrous. She and Ivor were passengers in a car heading back from a snow shoe-walking trip one November evening to their home in Cambridge, Massachusetts (Ivor was now a Professor at Harvard), when they were involved in an accident. 'A drunken driver, swinging across the traffic piled up a car wreck into which we had to ram', wrote Dorothy a year later. It meant the end of serious climbing for her. In an article for the *Pinnacle Club Journal*, she told its readers: 'There is a limit to what a ruined hip joint can be made to do. One therefore makes the most of it. And each of us, for herself, must work out what that most may be.' Up until then, the lists of climbs and walks she submitted annually to the Ladies Alpine Club had recorded at least a dozen Alpine peaks each summer. In the 1930s she recorded several first ascents, in Canada and China. In 1938, she walked, alone, 200 miles from Dali in Yunnan, China, to Bhao in Burma (now Myanmar), crossing the Mekong and Salween rivers on high bamboo suspension bridges, the forest paths festooned with orchids. Tantalisingly, her diary for that year is missing. In 1954, at the age of 60, she again reached the summit of the Matterhorn. No climbs are recorded for the years 1959, 1960 and 1961, as doctors in the United States and England tried to pin together her shattered bones. Just before she went into surgery for one of a series of operations, Ivor, who after years of being a critic was now writing his own poetry, wrote 'Hope' for her, capturing their heady youthful days:

> And that stiff-frozen dawn
> When Time near ceased to flow;
> The glacier's chin our unmade bed,
> I heard you through your yawn
> (All cramps from tossing so)
> 'Leaping crevasses in the dark;
> That's how to live!' you said.

The poem is a perfect summation of her resourcefulness, her glee in the face of danger and also her stoicism, which she needed to call on greatly after 1958.

The walks, and modest climbs, begin again in 1962 with a ride on horseback up the 12,300-foot Mount Agua in Guatemala. Writing about this trek later, for readers of *Fell and Rock*, she revealed the countless different ways she had already tried to overcome her injury: 'Once despised wire ropeways of all varieties now find me a *connoisseuse*. Carrying chairs too, as in ancient China would appeal ... I even read a bit enviously ... of the way Cortez' Indian *cargadores* could bundle you up in a hammock and porter you off thirty miles or so in a night.' Arriving at the summit and gazing down on the ruins of the once-great Mayan city of Tikal, she asked herself why she still did it. She was, after all, now 68 and had a lifetime of climbing behind her; yet here she was at dawn, sitting atop a horse, having ascended a volcanic scree for hours in the darkness, her hip aching and she searching for the two oceans this thin isthmus divided. She had no answer, either for herself, or her readers, except it was the only thing she knew to do that made her truly happy.

Among the climbers of the Pinnacle, and Fell and Rock clubs, her words and observations were always sought after. *Climbing Days*, which was finally published in 1935, spoke to the soul of those who ached, like Dorothy, simply to be up on high, with nothing but air between them and the infinite. In June 1935 she wrote in her diary, '*Climbing Days* is going very well, though not, of

11.3 Dorothy and I. A. R., 1966 at the Cabane Rossier, Dent Blanche on the centenary of the first ascent

course, as well as the author fondly dreamed.' And then, on another line: 'I am very proud of it.' The summer after its publication, she noted that there were more women than ever before in the Alps, and surely Dorothy and those other women who put up with the jibes and male 'mockery and waggery' in earlier years had helped blaze a trail. Since then, *Climbing Days* has gone into three further editions, the latest published only recently, in 2024.

After years of peripatations, mostly in Harvard and New England but also in China, which they had fallen in love with, the Richards finally returned to Cambridge in 1974. By this time they were 80 and 81 years old and they moved into Wentworth House, a handsome if higgledy piggledy eighteenth-century building with lawns flowing, unfenced, down to the River Cam at the back. It is owned by, and stands next to, Magdalene College, their gardens divided by an old brick wall. Ivor died in 1979 but Dorothy lived on, her sight gradually failing, 'learn[ing] to live with the void'. She was now completely alone, having lost all three of her younger siblings. Vi had died tragically young in 1936 – her death certificate cites 'tetany and tumour of the suprarenal gland'; and Will, the youngest, in 1953, of a chronic asthma attack. John died in 1968 but his two sons, Chris and Anthony, kept in touch with their aunt who had, truth be told, somewhat over-awed them when they were boys.

She kept in close touch with them too, sending letters and presents to Chris's two children, of whom she was very fond. Anthony, in his 30s and a musician and artist, visited her several times in Cambridge, where he observed her still playing 'the great lady' in college society, 'but that wasn't her at all', he says. To find the real Dorothy you had to go into her kitchen, where despite being surrounded by the mod cons of the 1980s, she preferred to cook and prepare food using camping equipment, as if she were still on a great mountain flank: still restless, and unwilling to settle down, even as an octogenarian. The life of the town and city, he suspected, was completely alien to her: 'the spectacle of her own life as lived amongst woods and mountains had left far behind the sophistication of cities. I feel cities were for her, *virtual reality*, turn off the current and life goes dead. In the mountains, humans are challenged and enhanced by the power of nature and seen for who they really are. I think that must have been one of the great attractions for her.'

Anthony took her on a spur-of-the-moment day trip from Edinburgh to Fort William after Christmas 1984, where they nearly had a disaster racing to the top of a snow-covered hill in Anthony's little white Renault van. His aunt had encouraged him to have a go at getting to the top of a very icy track and, as ever, her spirit infected him. 'It was a magical, sunlit, blue, white and green day', he recalls. They nearly didn't make it, the Renault's tyres spinning in the ice, but they both had a whale of a time. After a hernia operation in 1985, she wrote to Anthony telling him that now she was 'weak and miserable', and confined to Wentworth House, she felt like a 'caged bird'. So, after Christmas that year, Anthony sprang her and drove her up to Mallaig on the west coast of Scotland. Knowing they could be stranded for several days, they caught the ferry across to Skye. 'As always when I was out and about with my aunt a feeling of adventure took over', he wrote later. On Skye they stayed at the Glen Brittle Mountain hut, 91-year-old Dorothy sleeping in a hostel bunk bed, a wine bottle filled with hot water to keep her warm, after an evening of climbing tales, whisky and Scottish folk tunes. While on Skye Anthony would take her to picturesque vantage points where she could look at the white-capped mountains far away or, close up, a layer of snow crystals on the branch of a pine tree. Wearing a beret, and smoking a Camel cigarette, she would sit on a rock, or in the car, and take notes, still trying to work out what made a view or a concoction of wood and frozen water, beautiful. 'It was as if the experience was made complete by writing about it', Anthony says.

Dorothy died in September 1986, just before her ninety-second birthday. At that time, I was living in Cambridge in a student house on Jesus Green, just opposite the part of the Cam where the green lawn of Wentworth House slopes down to the green river. I must have seen her, an elderly woman hobbling about her garden, and no doubt, with that arrogance of youth, did not give her a second's thought. Had I only known her story, the questions I would have asked and the stories she could have told me. On a drizzly autumn morning in 1987, 70 years after she first put hand to rock to reach the summit of Tryfan, Dorothy's nephews Chris and Anthony Pilley clambered, with Chuck Evans, the son of one of Dorothy's climbing friends, up the mountain's old and broken slabs. In a backpack they carried a cardboard box containing her ashes. Nine years earlier Ivor's ashes had been scattered there and it was Dorothy's wish her remains be returned to the rocks that she had loved for so long.

When they opened the box, a sharp breeze caught its contents and cast Dorothy, so eager to be free, across a wide arc around the mountain's flanks. 'It seemed appropriate', Chris tells me, 'the way she made her bid for freedom.' I think of another poem Ivor wrote for Dorothy in 1972, when they both realised they should probably accept that old age and infirmity were gaining the upper hand. They had, after all, a lifetime of mountains so embedded in their bodies you could probably find rhyolite and granite in their DNA:

> We have them in our bones
> Ten thousand miles of stones,
> Moraine, debris and scree.

Now the mountain has them back.

12

Ethel and Wangari: rise up and walk!

On 8 October 2004 Wanjira Mathai, Wangari's daughter, was sitting in a packed restaurant in Nairobi, eating lunch. Her mother, no longer vilified or the target of police brutality, was now a Member of Parliament for the Tetu constituency in Nyeri District, near the place of her birth. Wangari won the seat with 98 per cent of the vote in the election at the end of 2002. Her slogan, from the New Testament of the Bible, was 'Rise up and walk!', to urge the poor and dispossessed, and grumbling, of her constituency, to take control of their lives, to grasp what help is offered. Twenty years after her first failed attempt to stand as an MP, she faced the electorate again, convinced that while civil society groups could make important, grassroots changes, real change across the whole of Kenya could only come through a new government free from Moi's corruption and cynicism.

This was a watershed moment for Kenya and a time of great hope. The elections marked the end of arap Moi's regime and the new President, Mwai Kibaki of the National Rainbow Coalition, appointed Wangari Deputy Minister for the environment and natural resources, with special responsibility for forests and conservation. It should have been her dream job. Now in power, she no longer had to go guerilla planting, dodging security guards and spears, but could organise reforestation widescale across Kenya. In government, however, and effectively in a sinecure job with little actual power, Wangari was deeply frustrated with the lack of progress on halting illegal logging and clearance for cannabis plantations to make *bhang*, which was still continuing apace throughout the major forests in Kenya. Ever the energetic optimist, she was contributing ideas to a new Forests Bill that would halt the piecemeal selling off of parcels of forest and hand over more control to local people under Community Forest Associations. The new regime was also weeding out corruption and nearly 1,000 forestry officers had been fired since the election, although this move was widely seen as part of a turf war between the new Environment Minister, Dr Newton Kulundu, and the head of the civil service, Dr Richard Leakey. But all this was taking precious time, and Kenya's forests were running out of it. Karura was still a dangerous, no-go area; Moi's cronies still had their land titles and the eucalyptus monocultures were squeezing out what remained of its vibrant, diverse wildlife. Wangari came close to resigning her position on a number of occasions.

Back to October 2004: nobody in the restaurant knew that the young, elegant woman in her mid-30s quietly eating her lunch and watching the television news was their famous Deputy Environment Minister's daughter. The broadcast switched to the live announcement of the winner of that year's Nobel Peace Prize. There were rumours that in 2004 the coveted award might be won by someone from Africa, most likely HIV campaigners in South Africa, so there was considerable interest across the continent. Since the Nobel Prize's inception in 1901, you could count on the fingers of one hand the numbers of Nobel Peace laureates from sub-Saharan Africa: anti-apartheid campaigner Albert Luthuli (1960), Archbishop Desmond Tutu (1984), Nelson Mandela (with F. W. de Clerk, 1993) and Kofi Annan (2001), so this was a big moment. Suddenly the restaurant erupted in cheering and clapping. Not only had an African won, but a Kenyan, and it was Wanjira's own mother, Wangari Maathai, for her contribution to 'sustainable development, democracy and peace', particularly her linking the twin causes of environmental protection and social justice. She was the first African woman ever to win the famous prize.

'I froze in place', says Wanjira. 'I remember looking around this wildly cheering restaurant and knowing that nobody there knew who I was and yet this extraordinary announcement had just been made.' Wanjira tried to call her mother but the line was busy. 'So I finished my lunch, and I paid and I left, and I went to find my mother.'

Her mother, meanwhile, was in a van heading for her Tetu constituency. It was a Friday, a day normally reserved by MPs to leave Nairobi to go to listen to their constituents' problems. Mia MacDonald, who was in Kenya helping Wangari with research on her memoir, was in the van with her, as was Wangari's assistant and two police protection officers. The road outside Nairobi was bumpy and rutted and reception wasn't good but suddenly both Wangari and her assistant's phones started ringing. One was a local journalist asking a far-fetched-sounding question about the Nobel Peace Prize. The other was the Norwegian ambassador sounding not so far-fetched. 'There were some "Wows", some gesticulating and some tears', says Mia. 'Then Wangari simply and softly said: "I didn't know anyone was listening."'

Shortly after, Wangari's van pulled into the lushly beautiful grounds of the colonial-era Outspan Hotel in the Aberdare National Park for a break and a quick photo opportunity for the journalists who had raced after her out of Nairobi (and a Norwegian journalist who had been tipped off in advance). The hotel's enterprising manager had rustled up an indigenous Nandi Flame Tree seedling for the cameras and Wangari kneeled on the grass, 'put my hands in the red soil, warm from the sun, settled the tree seedling in the ground … at that moment I felt I [was] on sacred ground'. The symbolism of Wangari kneeling and 'facing Mount Kenya' was not lost on those who knew something of Kenya's history and struggles, the words echoing those of the country's founding father, Jomo Kenyatta. Wangari then continued to the meeting, where she had arranged to see her constituents in a field outside a rural school. 'The Norwegian journalist had advised her to go back to Nairobi, to be available for television interviews', says Mia, 'but Wangari said, "I can't cancel my meeting – I can't phone them and they will have travelled by *matatu* or walked several miles to come and see me."' And so, she continued to her constituency, although in fact the meeting was cut short after about an hour when a presidential helicopter arrived with orders for her to head back to the capital. Mia, her assistant and police officer climbed in with her. 'I rode along', says Mia. 'The ground below looked very green.'

Meanwhile, back in Nairobi, the news had reached the offices of the Green Belt Movement, where Professor Vert Mbaya was still working, still Treasurer, nearly 30 years on. 'I had been at the University [of Nairobi], they got on the phone to me and I shot over. We were so happy, we sang and clapped and put the tea on to celebrate,' says Vert. Money then came pouring in from environmental organisations across the world, all wanting to be associated with what the papers called 'the green goddess'. 'We had been going through a bit of a slow patch; the movement had its ups and downs, it flowed and slowed, a bit like a river. Donations and planting picked up after that,' says Vert. As a reward for showering Kenya with stardust, President Kibaki ordered an upgrade of Wangari's official car, from a Toyota saloon to a Mitsubishi Pajero 4 × 4, a somewhat bizarre gift for a woman focused on saving the environment. A joke made the rounds of the Cabinet that she was the only Assistant Minister who became more famous than the Minister himself. That may have been part of the problem.

The award of the Nobel Peace Prize was, Kenyan writer Egara Kabaji wrote later in the *Daily Nation* newspaper, a moment when Kenya really woke up to 'the fact that Professor Wangari Maathai lived in our midst', something the country, often 'suffering from collective amnesia' failed to appreciate. 'Rarely do we celebrate our own heroes.' For despite her more than 30 years' work for the Kenyan environment, the country, even in 2004, hadn't recognised what Wangari was to the nation. Gongs and awards are of course useful to we humans, who care for these things, but the trees and the rains and the southward-marching Sahara don't give them a second's thought. Wangari knew this, and as soon as she could, she was back at her desk working on the new Forests Bill. She knew without – and, sadly, even with – legal frameworks underpinning her plans, when she left office any progress she had made might be lost. As it was, when the Forests Bill finally became law at the end of 2005 Wangari distanced herself from large parts of it, as it still allowed smallholder cultivation (*shambas*) at the edges of forest reserves. Although ostensibly giving local farmers and landless people the means to a living, the *shamba* system was widely abused and resulted in illegal forest clearance, which Wangari adamantly opposed.

By now the fragile alliances of the Rainbow Coalition were beginning to fracture. Wangari for a while had tried to play peacemaker but there were too many egos, clashing like bull elephants in musth. In December 2005 she declined her reappointment as Deputy Environment Minister (the natural resources part of her brief had already been removed during an earlier round of politicking) after a government reorganisation, and continued the rest of her time as MP from the backbenches. While government meant power, it also meant endless political games, jockeying for position and compromise. She saw that the final iteration of the Forests Bill, although providing something better than before, in implementation was nowhere near how she had dreamed of it. So she concentrated on helping her constituents access development funds for schools, water pipes and medical centres through a new government grant system. By now, too, her work had expanded beyond Kenya's borders. In 2005 she became Goodwill Ambassador for the Congo Basin rainforest and was advising the ten heads of state from the region who had appointed her. She also was given a senior role at the African Union, convening the Economic, Social and Cultural Council to advise the governments, with a strong focus on civil society. She would shortly be speaking in Angola, Cameroon and the Democratic Republic of the Congo, as well as to UN conferences and at universities all around the world.

Like Wangari and the forests of Kenya, Ethel Haythornthwaite, half a world away and half a century earlier, feared that the Peak District's National Park status would not be enough to protect the moorlands she loved so much. Ironically, after 1951, for the next 20 years at least until ill health and frailty began to take their toll, Ethel was busier than ever. Ethel's mother died in 1955 and Ethel, her sister Gertrude and Gerald, all three getting on and beginning to rattle around, held their last executive committee meeting at Endcliffe Vale House in late November 1956. They sold the great villa to the University of Sheffield for student accommodation and moved their offices into the former stable mews, up the hill at Endcliffe Crescent.

It's quite an unassuming red-brick and plaster terrace but for the two massive dressed and carved stone gate posts either side of its rear driveway, evidence of its former life as a stable block to the now long-gone big house. There, as the 1950s rolled into the 1960s and 1970s, Ethel could still be found, writing letters in long-hand, nursing her bad foot, and gently terrifying Sheffield councillors, university lecturers and her great nephews with equal gusto. She wrote letters every day, still conjuring cheques out of the great and good to fund London barristers to represent the CPRE at the latest planning inquiry. Her secretary, Jean Smart, enjoyed observing her somewhat reserved boss's technique. 'She wrote all her letters with pen and ink and then put them in front of me to type. I used to sit there typing with a great big grin on my face, they were such beautiful works of persuasion. Even though her feet and ankles were now so bad she could no longer walk the moorlands she had fought so hard for others to enjoy, she always dressed for dinner.'

Although she had been snubbed by the National Parks Commission in her bid to be a member of the Joint Planning Board, she was still the energetic and vastly experienced Honorary Secretary of the Sheffield and Peak CPRE, and would remain so until 1980. In the late 1940s and early 1950s, Ethel's committee resisted proposals for several opencast coal mines in the countryside around Sheffield. Then Sheffield City Council proposed a 50-acre open-air refuse tip in an old shallow slate mine 1,300 feet above sea level at Ringinglow, within the National Park Boundary. At the public inquiry, held in 1960, Ethel's committee was able to provide documentary evidence of the council's previous efforts to protect the area from development and that the tip plans, which would involve 80 lorries winding up the lanes through Porter Clough every day, would make those efforts a nonsense. One of the worst threats was, in 1955, a plan put forward by Derbyshire County Council to build a 12-mile-long 200 mph Grand Prix racing circuit, with car parking for 25,000 cars, grandstands, pits and associated amenities in Dovedale, of all places. Amazingly, the planners envisaged turbo-charged rocket cars roaring through two quiet limestone gorges, Long Dale and Hand Dale. After successfully joining the fight to resist the threat, along with local farmers, churches and walking groups, Ethel was able to write, with some satisfaction: 'In the course of our many fights we have rarely stirred such a volume of national controversy.' In January 1956 the project was formally postponed indefinitely. Another plan by the Electricity Board to build pylons across open moorland was also headed off; the cables were laid instead in a disused railway tunnel.

Of course, the Peak Park Planning Board was often the final authority in many of these fights, although ably supported by Ethel's committee and other amenity groups. The Board had genuine powers, enjoyed uniquely by the Peak National Park and not the others, because of Ethel. Her genius and far-sightedness in making sure the Peak District was the first National Park meant that from the start its planning powers trumped those of the county councils; it also had more financial clout, through its ability to charge the county councils in its area a precept, again, Ethel's legacy. The Peak employed its own staff, the only park to do so for over 20 years. As successive National Parks came into being now under a new Conservative government, the powers they were given decreased. While the Lake District did have a board, it had to rely on sharing staff with the county councils. None of the other eight parks created in the 1950s was given a board with executive powers; many from the start struggled financially.

Meanwhile in the Peak, the first access agreement came to fruition in 1953, between the Park and the Duke of Devonshire, over 5,624 acres of moorland on Southern Kinder. The following year, access over Jaggers Clough, Win Hill, Mam Tor and Lose Hill was agreed: land that Ethel, G. H. B. and so many others had trespassed across now open to walkers. In 1958, agreement was reached on access across the Kinder Plateau: all 15 different owners fell into line after the Peak Park Planning Board had threatened to serve access orders on the owners. In 1957 the Duke of Devonshire came to an agreement over access to another much-yearned-for walkers' target, the second highest peak after Kinder, Bleaklow. In 1965, the country's first national trail, the Pennine Way, was opened: 268 miles from Edale in the Peak to the Cheviots in Scotland, along the rooftop of northern England. In September 1982, when Ethel was 88, the National Trust bought 3,800 acres of Kinder Scout for £600,000, declaring it 'open for access in perpetuity'. On a winter's evening, if you tread quietly, it's possible to surprise the pale smudges of grazing snow

12.1 Jacob's Ladder and Kinder Scout, Peak District

hares, ironically introduced in the 1840s by the grouse-shooting dukes to make their game bags more interesting. The hares have done better, numerically, in the intervening years, although inherited aristocracy still owns about a third of Britain.

On the whole, though, access arrangements between landowners and the National Parks were largely judged a failure in the early days. The 1949 Act had left too much to the county councils' discretion, and many of the authorities, whose elected members had close ties with the landed gentry, saw no reason to push for a right to roam over uncultivated land. When, in 1970, nearly 20 years after the first National Parks were created, an assessment of access was made, only 46 agreements covering 29,133 hectares had been made. Almost all of these were in the Peak District thanks to the extra powers the Peak Planning Board had been gifted, through Ethel's efficiency. It would however take a new Labour government and the Countryside and Rights of Way Act 2000 before the larger part of the Peak District's mountain, moor and heathland became open to walkers. When Ethel and her friends began their campaign to fight for the Peak in 1924, as Phil Barnes pointed out, there were just 12 footpaths longer than two miles across Peak District moorland. Today there are more than 1,600 miles of footpaths and other public rights of way.

Those of us who now, with joyful heart, can go up, take a stone stile at the far edge of the sheep pasture into the birch, beech, oller and larch brakes and then up past the sentry crab apples, to feel the wind on our faces, may have very little thought for those endless hours of committee meetings, the carefully written, and later typed, notes of minutes, the headachy evenings poring over maps and deeds. The well-signposted footpaths, and the sturdy hebbles spanning the grifts and groughs, keeping our feet dry as we cross them, are all her children. Ethel died peacefully at home in Endcliffe Crescent after a long period of ill health, on 11 April 1986, almost exactly 35 years since the Peak became the country's first National Park. For a while she passed into oblivion; it was often her husband, Gerald, who outlived her by nearly a decade and who was the public face of the Peak Planning Board for years, that people remembered. Memories have a way of recovering, however. In 2022, a 'Blue Plaque' to Ethel was unveiled at the site in Sheffield where Endcliffe Vale House once stood and the Peak District now has its 'Ethels' as the Highlands of Scotland have their Munroes: hills in the Peak District over 400 metres high. There are 95 of them and I've been up a few, rejoicing in their names: Slitherstone, Chinley Churn and Neb. As I walk, I think of Ethel, especially when I reach a particularly isolated spot, and more so if the rain starts to lash, better still if it's hailing, and I thank her for these great gifts she left to us.

Like Ethel's, Wangari's is a long and still-blossoming legacy. There's a story in Kenya, published in the *Daily Nation* in the years after Wangari's death and state funeral (usually reserved for heads of state). The story goes that as Wangari was dying of ovarian cancer in 2011, her beloved elder brother Nderitu, 82, was also dying. Wangari had been treated in the United States but came home to Nairobi several weeks before her death. But for him, she may never have gone to school in the 1940s – and her and Kenya's paths may have been very different. When Nderitu passed away in August 2011 Wangari, now very unwell, left her bed in Nairobi Hospital to attend his burial. She died just four weeks later on 25 September. At the time of her death fewer than one-third of the trees in Karura Forest were indigenous. Now, nearly 60 per cent are, thanks to the work of the Green Belt Movement and the Friends of Karura Community Forest Association, formed in 2009 under the auspices of Wangari's Forests Act. The monocultures of eucalyptus have been selectively removed, and in their place now grow Silver Oak (one of these planted, in 2022, by Florence Conrad Salisbury at a memorial to her friend), the towering *Warburgia*, the densely bushy *Syzigium* and African Olive. Wangari was the first

12.2 Karura Forest

patron of the Karura Community Forest Association and saw its first steps of transformation.

With the return of indigenous forest, so have returned the invertebrates, the birds and small mammals: the cream and black Mocker Swallowtail ('flying handkerchief') flits silently through sunny clearings; bush pigs, crested porcupines and pouched rats rootle for grubs by the river banks. The shouts, songs and calls of the birds and animals are like a symphony, punctuated by the shrill cry of the apex predator, the African Crowned Eagle, which has now returned after many decades of absence to this ecosystem wildly different from what it was in the 1980s and 1990s. Professor Karanja Njoroge, who spent many years with Wangari working on restoring Karura, says that trees they planted together in 2010 are already over 30 foot high, starting to cast shade, bear fruit and give home to insects. 'When we are long gone, our kids will say at least in Karura we tried', he says. Every year now, Kenya holds an annual tree-planting day and forest cover across the country currently stands at 12.3 per cent, a full 10 per cent more than at its lowest point, when Wangari began her work; the government's ambition is to increase this cover to 30 per cent, nearly one-third of the country's land mass.

'When I think of my mother I think of the beauty and splendour of the trees ... she was so alert to their beauty and majesty and the role they play', her daughter Wanjira tells me. 'I worked with mother for 12 of her last years and so I had the chance to reflect on what she had done and how clearly she saw it two decades ago and more. She was a gift to us.'

Acknowledgements

So many people have helped me in the writing of this book in so many ways. I would like to thank everyone for their generosity, and enthusiasm for this project. First, I would like to thank the family members who have helped me: Wanjira Mathai, Wangari's daughter; Chris and Anthony Pilley, Dorothy's nephews; Dan Richards, Dorothy's great, great nephew; and Ben Haggarty, Ethel's great nephew. Thank you all for your help with reminiscences, finding material and granting permission for use of material and images.

Thank you so much to Lucy Farrington, current owner of Evelyn Chees-man's childhood home Court Lodge, in Westwell, Kent, who, despite it being in the middle of the pandemic, allowed me to wander around the amazing garden and go down to the chalk stream where Evelyn spent so many happy hours. My subjects' friends and acquaintances too have been incredibly generous with their time and memories. My deepest thanks to Sir David Attenborough for his reminiscences of meeting Evelyn Cheesman in 1956. Jean Smart, Ethel Haythornthwaite's secretary for 23 years, has been absolutely wonderful. Professor Clyde Binfield, who also knew Ethel, was very generous in sending me a lecture he gave on her years ago. Thanks too to Dave Sissons, hugely knowledgeable rambler and writer, who so generously sent me information about the great access fights of the twentieth century, and let me see his copies of the *Clarion Ramblers Handbooks* from the 1920s. Many too of Wangari's friends: her best friend from college, Florence Conrad Salisbury; her colleague at the University of Nairobi and Treasurer of the Green Belt Movement for nearly half a century, Professor Vert Mbaya; her fellow activist and forest lover Professor Karanja Njoroge and her co-author Mia MacDonald: thank you Mia and Florence not just for your time, but for your careful reading of early drafts of my chapters on Wangari, and for putting me right several times!

For the use of images particular thanks to Harvey Croze and his amazing photographs of Karura Forest, and to David Blumekrantz for his beautiful portrait of Wangari in chapter 10. Thanks so much too to the Sisters at Mount Saint Scholastica, Atchison, Kansas, and especially to archivist Elaine Nadeau, who found me images of Wangari while she was there, her contributions to the *Mount Mirror* and letters she wrote to the sisters after she had left. All image copyright holders are referenced in the list on pages 233–234; while every effort has been made to trace these, there may be some inadvertent loopholes, for which do please get in touch.

Thank you to the amazing team at Manchester University Press, to Emma Brennan, who steered my proposal through early choppy waters with some wonderful ideas for improving it, and for your unstinting support. Thank you to the two anonymous readers of my proposal, whose constructive comments and enthusiasm helped me shape a better book. Also to Kim Walker, whose comments and suggestions have helped me hone and polish this manuscript and Alun Richards, who took over editing this book and who has been unfailingly supportive and enthusiastic. Very special thanks to my brilliant copy-editor Diane Wardle, whose miraculous eyes spotted many errors and omissions. Any remaining errors are mine alone.

I owe an enormous debt to the archivists and librarians who have helped me find material. All sources of archive material are listed in the bibliography. Special thanks goes to Anya Hesel, from Glacier National Park, who tracked down the one minute seven seconds of footage of Dorothy leaping crevasses in 1926 and to Emma McDonald of the Alpine Club Library, who produced for me Dorothy's two beautiful ice axes: seeing their slender strength, and imagining the times she lent on them never fails to move me. Special shout out to Tim Knebel at the Sheffield Archives for helping me find all sorts of material on Ethel, including the original iconic image of her speaking in 1951, at the height of her success, in chapter 9. Thanks also to the many staff at the British Museum and Natural History Museum for finally, after much searching, tracking down and then granting me access to see the spear of King Ringapat that Evelyn Cheesman sent to King George V. Quite a moment! Thank you to the estate of Ivor and Dorothea Richards for permission to quote from Dorothy Pilley's unpublished diaries, and to the Pepys Library, Magdalene College, Cambridge for facilitating so many visits. Finally, a world of thanks to the reading room staff at the British Library, without whom none of this book would have been possible. Much of the research for this book was undertaken as we were gradually opening up after lockdown: difficult days of negotiating access and contact, all of which was achieved with patience, skill and gentle humour. It was so good to get back to the books and the historical newspapers and magazines after those quiet, remote days of Covid.

Thanks to my wonderful family, my husband John, and son and daughter Tom and Livvy, who all helpfully read and commented on draft material, and to my parents, John and Moya, who did the same, with so much love.

List of figures

Notes and references

Notes to prologue

viii   'East of the Sun and West of the Moon' is a Norwegian folk tale first collected in the mid-nineteenth century by Peter Christen Asbjornsen and Jorgen Moe. It was first published in English in Andrew Lang's *The Blue Fairy Book* (1889)

ix   '94 per cent' of climbing memoirs in Moraldo (2013)

Notes to introduction

1   The *Gilgamesh* and *Mahabharata* stories and their meaning in Abusch (2015); for interpretations of Shamhat, and other female characters' roles, Sonik (2021)

1   Sources for the Gawain tale: Arner (2006); Salisbury (2014)

1   Source for the *Kalevala*: Friberg (2021)

2   Source for the development of city states in ancient Greece: Cole (2004)

2   **'Histories of slavery...'**: Lerner (1986)

3   Hesiod, **'the woolly sheep are heavy with fleeces...'**: Cole (2004)

3   **'patriarchal belt'**: Zaman (1995); Littrell and Bertsch (2013)

3   **'the geometric line...'**: Mernissi (1994), p. 3

3   **'A family's status is undermined...'**: Zaman (2011), p. 114

3   **'In Mesoamerican tradition...'**: Pennock (2011)

3   Chinese foot binding: Fan and Wu (2020)

3   **'Early medical superstition'**: see for example Cole (2004); Pennock (2018); Tan et al. (2017)

4   **'Backpacking guides...'**: Nichols (1978)

4   **'By going outdoors...'**: Glotfelty (1996), p. 449

4   **'early hominins ...'**: Halliday (2022), p. 35

4   Women in big game hunting: Haas et al. (2020)

5   Sources for hunter-gathering: Bird (1999); Grund (2017)

6   **'Pre-industrial rural...'**: Gray (2000)

6   **'In modern day Cambodian...'**: Park and Maffii (2017), p. 1239

6   **'in modern-day pastoral societies...'**: Kaua and Gitonga (2023)

7   **'Mohammed received his first revelation...'**: in Ireton and Schaumann (2020)

8   **'And before she came down...'**: Lujan (1994), p. 255

8	**'Nanda Devi tops the scene...'**: Aitken (1994), pp. 7–8
8	**'Studies of nineteenth- and early twentieth-century Finnish...'**: Ridanpää (2010)
9	**'western myth of mobility...'**: Hubbard and Wilkinson (2019), p. 258
9	Thoreau's **'knight errant'**: Heddon and Turner (2012)
9	**'If you are ready to leave father...'**: Thoreau (1951), p. 57
9	**'We contest *in toto*...'**: cited in Bell and McEwan (1996), p. 298
9	**'Monarch-of-all-I-survey'**: Pratt (1992), p. 197
10	**'As the eye dilates...'**: Burton (1961), p. 43
11	Critical views of Mary Kingsley's writings in Pratt (1992) and Bekler (2023)

Notes to chapter 1

17	Descriptions of the height of land from Mina Hubbard's diary (henceforth MH diary), entry 10 August 1905; the Naskaupi River is normally spelled this way; sometimes Naskapi. In Mina's day it was spelled Nascaupee
17	'*Metsheshu Shipu*' means 'Eagle River' in Innu, a sub-dialect of the macro-Algonkian language; it was also called *Mushuau Shipu*, or 'River of the barren land'. I am conscious that European names such as George River obliterated the original Innu names for landmarks. In her work on the Innu struggle to reclaim their land, Marie Wadden (1991) writes: 'They named every lake, river and mountain' (p. 4)
17	Length of the Naskaupi as it was then (part of it is now flooded in the Smallwood Reservoir) in Hubbard (1906b), p. 531
17	**'Far from the world...'**: MH diary, 10 August 1905
17	**'All so grand...'**: MH diary, 16 July and 3 July 1905
18	*Namaycush* is a species of Labrador lake trout; the name is from the Cree word for fish, *namekus*
18	Bacon starting to smell: MH diary, 1 August 1905: 'Sugar is done all but about a lb. Bacon getting pretty strong'
18	'busted' from Leonidas Hubbard's diary (henceforth LH diary), 18 October 1903
18	**'weak and starving...'**: Hubbard (1908c), p. 558
18	**'softer than a mattress'**: this description of the balsam fir camping bed is from *Little Rivers* (Van Dyke, 1903, p. 301). The book was a gift from Leonidas to Mina, one of the last things he gave her before he died
18	**'just for a minute or so'**: MH diary, 7 July 1905
18	**'News of Leonidas's death...'**: Hart (2005), p. 85
18	**'This work keeps me...'**: MH diary, 5 July 1905
19	**'lonely death'**: reported in *Forest and Stream*, 9 April 1904, p. 1
19	**'No Tidings'**: *Manchester Evening News*, 14 November 1903, p. 2
19	**'First Nation Innu'**: the Innu Nation is the group of First Nation Americans who settled in what they call Nitassinan (eastern Quebec and Labrador) over 2,000 years ago. European settlers called one group Montagnais (because they hunt in the mountains) and another group the Naskapi, an old Innu word meaning 'beyond the horizon'. The Innu belong to the macro-Algonkian linguistic group which dominates Atlantic coastal north America down to New York; Innu culture and language are similar to that of the Cree, MicMac and the Beothuk (Wadden (1991), Savard (1969), Lipman (2015))

19 Innu folk tales in Desbarats (1969)

19 **'Many scoffed...'**: see for example letter to *Forest and Stream*, 2 April 1904, p. 270, 'Mr Hubbard's Death in Labrador' and editorial in the following week's issue

19 Biographical details of Leonidas Hubbard and his ancestors in Hubbard (1908a), pp. 3–18

20 **'American Geographical Society...'**: for details on the AGS and its attitude to exploration and mapping during Mina Hubbard's time, see LaFramboise (2001)

20 **'Powerful brokers in the lucrative fur trade'**: see Pennock (2020)

20 Innu navigation techniques from Fitzhugh (1977); tree 'blazing' is where landmark trees are marked for navigation, such as bark peeled away (Scott, 2015)

20 **'A region where no footsteps...'**: Wallace (1905), p. x

20 **'Archaeologists had already found...'**: Fitzhugh (1977), pp. 35–37

20 **'Nasty place...'**: LH diary, 8 July 1903

20 **'bully story'**: LH diary, 17 September 1903; he records seeing all kinds of evidence for indigenous Innu (although never meets one), but it doesn't seem to occur to him that this means he is not in fact the first to explore the area

21 **'Too hard for Mina'**: LH diary, 18 September 1903

21 **'A man's game'**: Wallace (1905), p. 294

21 **'At home in the lovely amplitude of time'**: I have taken this lovely phrase from John Moss's 'Gender Notes: Wilderness Unfinished' (1998), p. 168

21 **'In a way that I could hardly...'**: Hubbard (1906), p. 539

21 **'Northern exploration...'**: Ross (2004)

21 **'They will scarcely...'**: MH diary, 8 July 1905

22 **'And what would we do...'**: MH diary, 28 July 1905

22 **'Because I was seeing things...'**: MH diary, 28 July 1905

22 **'I could feel my ears...'**: Hubbard (1908a), p. 95

22 **'Mrs Hubbard's strange visit'**: 'Mrs Hubbard Suspicious', *New York Tribune*, 13 June 1905, p. 1

24 **'We cannot blame...'**: 'Explorer's Widow Follows his Trail', *New York World*, 13 June 1905, p. 3

24 **'to feel the necessity...'**: Whitney (1905), p. 643

24 **'Mina Benson was born...'**: details of Mina's family and early life in Hart (2005)

24 **'Lot 29...'**: Milne and McGillis (1990)

24 **'settlers fleeing...'**: White (1985)

25 Details of First Nation maize-growing culture and treaties in White (1985), Lipman (2015)

25 **'Delicate'**: description quoted in Grace (2004), p. xx

26 **'Madam...'**: in Hubbard (1903a), p. 721

26 **'No white woman...'**: Hubbard (1903a), p. 721

26 **'With them on the last part of the journey...'**: William Cabot's observations of the Hubbard/Wallce party are recorded in Cabot (1912), pp. 16–24

27 **'On the night ....'**: MH diary, 10 August 1905

27 **'sense of littleness grew upon me'**: Hubbard (1908c), p. 559

27 **'well-worn portage routes...'**: MH diary, 10 August 1905; she was in fact slightly further south than this but her measurements were affected by her inability to take readings for longitude

29 **'These included two...'**: journey inventory from Hubbard (1908a), pp. 23–24

29   **'1,000 pounds'**: in Hubbard (1906), p. 531

29   **'One newspaper estimated…'**: Hart (2005), p. 97

29   **'sensational adventure story'**: Dillon Wallace: *The Lure of the Labrador Wild* (1905)

29   **'I…wished…'**: 'Why I Go to Labrador: Mrs Hubbard's Own Story', *New York World*, 2 July 1905, p. 2

29   **'I suppose…'**: Hubbard (1908b), p. 82

30   **'three crucial weeks…'**: she makes this earlier date of departure and her reasons for it explicit in her article for *Windsor Magazine* (1908c), p. 555

30   **'Newsprint industry…'**: although Canada's newsprint production didn't fully take off until after the First World War it still produced around 400 million tons per year, double that of the United States. Canada exported 95 per cent of its production (Dick, 1982, p. 659)

30   **'spring green'** etc.: MH diary, 17 June 1905

30   **'The most recent official map of the region'**: history of mapping in Canada in Greene (2005), pp. 6–8

30   **'Her artificial horizon relied on water…'**: Hubbard (1907), p. 172

30   **'She briefly re-enrolled…'**: Hart (2005), p. 91

31   **'While by 1905 women…'**: see LaFramboise (2001); Bell and McEwan (1996)

31   **'There must be a way…'**: MH diary, 16 August 1905

32   **'Woman Explorer Gives Up'**: *New York Times*, 15 August 1905, p. 1

32   **'*Outing* claimed …'**: Whitney (1905), p. 619

Notes to chapter 2

33   The spider incident on Gorgona is recorded in her memoir *Things Worth While* (Cheesman, 1958); see also *Reynolds News*, 12 May 1957: 'Woman Trapped in a Giant Spider's Web. Saved by her Nail File'. Descriptions of Gorgona taken from contemporary travel accounts, notably Collenette (1926) and Douglas and Johnson (1926)

34   The snake incident is recorded in Cheesman (1960), p. 61; also in a BBC recording, 'The Travellers', Evelyn made in 1956

34   **'monarch-of-all-I-survey'**: Pratt (1992), particularly pp. 197–223

34   **'More prey than predator'**: here, I think, Cheesman is consciously echoing Victorian explorer and entomologist Mary Kingsley whose *Travels in West Africa* (1897) challenged the male narrative of domination; she, too, nearly came to grief in a swamp: 'those awful slime lagoons, one of which, before we reached Ndorke, had so very nearly collected me' (Kingsley, 1982, p. 338)

34   **'Second Voyage of the Beagle'**: various *Daily Mail* stories including 'Off to the South Seas', *Daily Mail*, 10 April 1924, p. 7 and 'Wonders of the South Seas', *Daily Mail*, 19 March 1925, p. 3; other records of the St George expedition are in Collenette (1926) and Douglas and Johnson (1926)

35   **'carefree happy days…'**: Smith (1969), p. 217

35   **'wrapped up in one another'**: Cheesman (1958), p. 28

35   Notes for an obituary, Cheesman Collection, NHM Box B 1:1

35   Descriptions of Court Lodge, with thanks to the current owners for allowing me to visit and contemporary sales particulars in the keeping of the owner

36   **'The reason of the name...'**: from Wood (1876c), pp. 361–363
36   Roman snails etc.: Cheesman (1958), p. 13
37   Brothers' qualifications: Cheesman (1958), p. 30; see also Cheesman (1933); Cheesman (1926)
37   Details on women's veterinary training: Hipperson (2017)
37   **'grey forms...'**: Cheesman (1958), p. 32
37   **'During quiet moments of leisure...'**: Evelyn recommends young entomologists read this novel by Gene Stratton-Porter, first published in 1909 in her first book, *Everyday Doings of Insects* (1924). She wrote that it inspired her when she first read it
38   Women's science education, Bedford College etc. from Crook (2001)
38   **'missing five ounces'**: in Gates (1998), p. 19
38   Incapacity through menstruation: Gates (1998), p. 20
38   Queen Charlotte, Sarah Sophia Banks etc.: in Fara (2004)
38   Gulielma Lister in DeCesare (2005), p. 94; information on slime moulds in Sheldrake (2020)
39   Women botanists, naturalists etc.: Pardoe and Lazarus (2018) and Gates (1998)
39   **'Thanks to her fluency...'**: Cheesman spent nearly a year in Germany 1904–5 in between governessing jobs; Cheesman (1958), p. 38
41   Grace Lefroy information in Smith (1969), p. 217
41   **'white ants'**: Deb Roy (2020)
41   Maxwell Lefroy: 'Gas Masks in Westminster' *Times*. 8 August 1917, p. 3; 'Professor Maxwell Lefroy' (obituary), *Times*, 15 October 1925, p. 16
42   **'On 4 May 1917...'**: Evelyn Cheesman's employment card, ZSL Library
42   **'Most of the glass-fronted cages were empty...'**: Cheesman (1958), p. 72
42   **'sugar ... shortages'**: although official rationing did not begin until early 1918, sugar had come under government control at the very start of the war, diverting much of the supply to the troops; voluntary rationing began in 1917 (Oddy, 2003)
42   **'wood wasps...'**: 'Scorpions and Wood Wasps', *Times*, 31 July 1920, p. 9
42   **'fruiterers of Covent Garden...'**: Touzel and Garner (2018), p. 419
44   Peacock butterflies etc.: 'New Insect House and the "Zoo"', *Times*, 6 October 1913, p. 4
44   'policemen had to control...': 'Popularity of the "Zoo"', *Times*, 14 April 1914, p. 4
44   Royal Entomological Society records: via email from the RES archivist Rosemary Pearson
44   RES's admission of women in 1833 in Bell and McEwan (1996), p. 296
44   Appointment to curator: employment card, ZSL Library
44   **'"erratic" but "unusually interesting"...'**: Cheesman (1958), p. 73
44   Land crabs in Cheesman (1923), p. 173
45   **'Always careful and meticulous'** : Cheesman (1960), p. 62
45   Older brother and sister etc. from Cheesman (1926) and Cheesman (1922)
46   Details of the *St George* trip, and its personnel are in Douglas and Johnson (1926) and Collenette (1926); a *Times* review of the latter book describes Collenette as 'the entomologist of the expedition', which no doubt irritated Evelyn ('Voyaging in the South Seas', *Times*, 8 June 1926, p. 10)
46   Sponsorship and funding of the trip: 'The Scientific Research Association', *Daily Mail*, 20 October 1923, p. 4

46 **'the "official" entomologist…'**: Cheesman (1950)

46 **'Miss Longfield and Mr Collenette collected ardently'**: Cheesman (1958), p. 86

46 **'One large (6′ × 8′) insect-catching screen'**: Collenette (1926), p. 123

47 Longfield's role as assistant entomologist is described in Douglas and Johnson (1926), p. 279 and Collenette (1926), p. 48

47 **'*Euglossa gorgonensis Cheesmanae*'**: Evelyn described it in a paper published by the Entomological Society of London (1929); it was named in 2013 (Hinojosa-Diaz and Brosi (2013))

47 Frank Carels letters, 3 February 1935 and 7 March 1935; Cheesman Collection, NHM Box B 1:1

48 **'by the merest chance….'**: Cheesman (1958), p. 92

48 **'200 species…'**: there is a useful appendix of all the insects and plants which have so far taken her name in Touzel and Garner (2018), although more are being added every year, including a rare blue orchid very recently (see chapter 7)

48 Incident on Nuku Hiva in Cheesman (1932), pp. 220–237

48 **'at one with all nature…'**: Cheesman (1932), p. 223

49 **'more than three quarters over a shining wall…'**: Cheesman (1932), p. 235

49 Descriptions of the lagoon and her hut in Cheesman (1927), pp. 19–36

49 **'no longer cramped'**: Cheesman (1958), p. 130

49 **'She caught several…'**: Craig (2006), p. 16

50 Toadstools etc. Cheesman (1932), p. 18

Notes to chapter 3

51 **'sleepless with excitement'**: Pilley (1965), p. 3

51 **'how well the body fits the rocks'**: Pilley (1965), p. 4

51 **'For a young woman…'**: DEP, recording 13 March 1940 (Chris Pilley private collection)

51 **'choice of bedtime reading…'**: records in DEP's diary (these particular ones for 1921)

51 **'In Gribble…'**: details in Gribble (1899)

52 **'Henriette d'Angeville…'**: while another woman, Maria Paradis, is known to have got to the top of Mont Blanc in 1808, she freely admitted that she was carried and hauled up the last section (Williams (1973), pp. 19–20)

52 **'to be up there, on it'**: DEP, recording 13 March 1940 (Chris Pilley private collection)

52 Records of her going to 'wife school' where she learned to launder and cook appear in her diary for January–May 1914

52 **'Blinding snow…'**: DEP diary; this record is for 24 December 1918 although it is recorded in a 1901 diary that she clearly cannibalised for later use

52 **'grey soft mist'**: DEP diary, 24 September 1914

52 **'black clouds rolling up'**: DEP diary, 26 September 1914

52 **'feel like a caged bird'**: DEP diary, 3 February 1912

52 **'feeling of unity'**: DEP diary, 25 December 1918

52 **'I'm afraid I was hauled'**: Winnifred Ellerman ('Bryher') (1963), p. 171; Winnifred Ellerman, who changed her name to 'Bryher', would later become an avant-garde

filmmaker and patron of the arts, funding the literary magazine *Life and Letters Today* and the modernist film magazine *Close-Up*

52   **'Something had happened...'**: Pilley (1959), p. 9
52   **'The cottage has...'**: DEP diary, 12 September 1914 and 19 September 1914
53   **'all those black creatures...'**: DEP diary, 1 March 1922
53   **'stuck in a dark...'**: letter DEP to IAR, 8 December 1925
53   **'grey village street'**: Pilley (1965), p. 1
54   **'Wales and particularly Snowdonia...'**: Turner (2018)
54   **'quickest and most comfortable route...'**: *Daily Mail* display advertisement, 5 July 1904, p. 8
54   **'intrepid *Daily Mail* journalist'**: from 'The Coming Play-ground of England', *Daily Mail*, 10 May 1909, p. 4
54   **'A spring day...'**: DEP diary entries, 24 and 25 January 1915
54   **'attacks of ill health...'**: DEP various diary entries; 'recurrence of pleurisy in left lung', diary, 22 January 1922; also letter to IAR, 1 December 1925: 'My eyes which I hoped were stronger, are in no ways fit ... my schoolgirl headaches have returned ... I rarely do more than an hour or two of close work at a stretch'
55   School report is among her papers in the Papers of Mrs I A Richards (henceforth IAR)
55   **'Clapham High School'**: Dorothy records sitting the exam in her diary, 22 September 1908; she records Violet attending the school in January 1910
56   Details of Queenwood from Bryher (1963), pp. 128–147
56   **'highly strung, nervous woman'**: interview with Chris Pilley, 14 December 2023
57   **'Rather dreading...'**: DEP diary, 13 September 1912, IAR
57   **'Swanley Horticultural College...'**: Optiz (2013)
57   **'surplus women problem...'**: Moore (2021)
58   Viscountess Wolseley's Appeal: 'Need of Women Gardeners' *Daily Mail*, 2 January 1915, p. 4
58   Pilley and Ellerman's fathers' refusal in Bryher (1963), p. 185
58   **'Argument with father...'**: DEP diary, 10 July 1921
58   BWPL details from BWPL Archive, Women's Library, LSE
59   **'mine certainly is'**: DEP diary, 8 January 1921
59   **'Do has left us...'**: John Pilley diary (aged 16), 10 October 1915, Chris Pilley private collection
59   **'fully alive'**: DEP diary, 24 January 1915
59   **'after endless fighting'**: DEP diary, 18 December 1926
59   **'Her mother sewed...'**: Pilley (1959), p. 9
59   **'This is life, adventure, joy'**: DEP diary, 31 December 1918
59   **'Her picture appeared in the *Daily Graphic*'**: no date, but probably 1919
59   **'Wouldn't supply a penny...'**: DEP diary, 3 March 1922
59   **'A knickerbocker suit...'**: Dorothy Pilley, 'Holiday Climbing: English heights a training ground for women mountaineers', *Daily Express*, 21 December 1920
60   **'In 1910'**: report in *Alpine Journal* 25/187 (February 1910), p. 246
60   **'*never* alone...'**: Williams (1973), p. 17
60   **'the first party....'**: Roche (2013), p. 246
60   **'the skirt was decently worn...'**: Daniell (2009), pp. 28–29. Emily Hilda Daniell was the 'real' name of the novelist E. H. Young. The article, 'Reminiscences' was

originally published in the *Pinnacle Club Journal*, no. 4, 1929–31. E. H. Young wrote
several novels between 1910 and 1947, her better-known ones being *Miss Mole*
(1930), *The Vicar's Daughter* (1928) and her last, *Chatterton Square* (1947)

61   **'The educationist Mabel Barker...'**: Mabel Barker, 'The Way of Neophyte,'
     Pinnacle Club Journal No. 5, 1932 – 34.

61   **'green corduroy...'**: Pilley (1965), p. 22

61   **'You were the first original thinker...'**: DEP to IAR, 8 December 1925 (IAR
     Archive)

61   **'A. C. Benson...'**: quoted in Russo (1989), pp. 18–19

62   **'Dear Miss Pilley...'**: letter from IAR to DEP, 19 January 1917 (IAR Archive)

62   **'Moel Hebog...'**: Pilley (1965), p. 11

62   **'tramp all day ...'**: DEP diary, 23 December 1918

63   **'She joined the crowds...'**: DEP diary, 11 November 1918

63   **'spontaneous joy'**: 'Spontaneous Joy at Palace', *Daily Mail*, 12 November 1918,
     p. 3

63   **'so great as to seem implausible'**: Luckett (1990), p. xiv

63   **'the excitement...'**: Pilley (1965), pp. 106 and 109

63   **'A. C. dotards...'**: DEP diary, 6 August 1921

63   **'the Ladies Alpine Club...'**: *Alpine Journal*, 24/179 (February 1908), p. 275

64   **'Virginia Woolf's father...'**: Roche (2013), p. 253

64   **'In a tribute'**: R. P. H. (1926), pp. 296–298

65   **'announced in the *Manchester Guardian***': 2 April 1921, p. 8

65   **'a dead secret...'**: Pilley (1965), p. 131

65   **'strewing the whole...'**: Bray (1924).

65   **'Up 4.am...'**: DEP diary, 25 July 1921

66   **'those fatuous mandarins'**: DEP diary, 6 August 1921

66   **'seems to lean over...'**: Pilley (1965), pp. 149–150.

67   **'disappear into the void'**: DEP diary, 15 July 1925

67   **'little wooden cabins...'**: DEP diary, 26 July 1925

67   **'record-breaking 25 peaks...'**: *Zanesville Signal*, 21 November 1926; *Billings
     Gazette*, 16 June 1926; DEP diary, July–September 1925

67   **'rotten rocks...'**: DEP diary, 24 August 1925

67   **'climbing among'**: DEP diary, 27 July 1925

Notes to chapter 4

69   **'red cloth-bound minute book...'** CPRE/2000 Sheffield Archives

69   Description of Ethel by Professor Clyde Binfield, who knew and met her on several
     occasions (telephone interview, September 2022)

69   **'over-decorated'**: from photographs and inventory of the house; various newspapers

69   G. H. B. Ward's fine for trespassing – issued in March 1924; recorded in the
     Sheffield Clarion Ramblers' minute book (henceforth SCRMB); 2015/32 Sheffield
     Archives; Ward's restrictions on women's ramblings also here and in various *Clarion
     Handbooks*

69   **'inclined to the left ... fugged-up smoky tearooms'**: Gaze (1988), pp. 69
     and 67

70   **'sloming...'** means to wander around aimlessly; 'sanky' means boggy; 'brays'
     means hillside; see Gallimore (1926), pp. 94–95

70	**'Indomitable'**: in Binfield (2018), p. 1
70	**'called her Dear Boss'**: email exchange with Jean Smart, 6 August 2022
70	**'small local committee…'**: *Sheffield Daily Telegraph*, 29 November 1924, p. 8
71	**'hideous…ceaseless pain….'**: Gallimore (1926), p. 7
71	**'under a cloud…'**: Gallimore (1932), p. 9
71	**'Notice boards…'**: Barnes (1934), p. 3
71	**'only 12 footpaths…'**: Barnes (1934), p. 5
72	**'a few score…'**: Barnes (1934), p. 3
72	**'Unfortunately over certain moors…'**: Brown (1938), p. 364
72	**'noisy with the din…hordes….'**: Morris (1914), pp. 5 and 9
72	**'Dore and Chinley railway…'**: Meadowcroft (1994), p. 4
73	**'As a child…'**: Gallimore (1926), p. 7
74	**'three Weslyan ministers…'**: family history from Binfield (2018)
74	**'1,000 tons of scrap metal a day'**: Binfield (2018)
75	**'stables, harness room'** etc.: from sales particulars of Endcliffe Vale House, *Sheffield Independent*, 27 February 1897, p. 4
75	**'At West Heath she studied…'**: details from West Heath Old Girls Association, www.whoga.org.uk/History.html (accessed 21 November 2022)
75	**'She passed her final examinations…'**: Westfield College student records (WFD), QMUL
75	**'Written in a thundering hurry…'**: EMBW, France journal (1913)
77	**'many young women immediately left'**: see for example Vera Brittain's *Testament of Youth* (1933); *Hermes* magazine for this time contains lists of the names of students who left to volunteer as nurses
77	**'zeppelin drills'**: Sondheimer (1983), p. 77
77	**'midnight alarms…'**: *Hermes* magazine, October 1915, p. 3
78	**'One woman who attended'**: cited in Sondheimer (1983), p. 78
78	**'spartan conditions'**: Marian Delf's reminiscences of her days at Westfield, Westfield College Archives WFD 27/5/4
78	**'Sheffield Prisoners of War…'**: *Sheffield Daily Telegraph*, 27 April 1918, p. 3
78	**'There could not have been…'**: Binfield (2018), p. 14
78	Biographical details of Henry Burrows Gallimore from obituary, 'A Gallant Gentleman: How Captain H. B. Gallimore met his death', *Sheffield Daily Independent*, 1 June 1917, p. 5
79	**'I can't see why…'**: etc.: Gaze (1988), p. 67
79	**'mid the greenery…'**: Gallimore (1926), p. 8
80	**'her faith in God…'**: Binfield (2018), p. 15
80	**'like the nests of birds…'**: Gallimore (1926), p. 42
80	Various addresses – letters to Arnold Freeman, Sheffield Educational Settlement (SES), University of Sheffield Archives (MS 91/3/2/1)
80	**'London Missionary Society'** etc.: *Sheffield Independent*, 28 June 1924; 22 November 1937; 6 July 1931; *Sheffield Daily Telegraph*, 19 June 1916
81	**'Good old England!…'**: Leonard Ward to his father, 19 January 1919 from Paris; Sheffield Archives X304
81	**'schools that would win…'**: SES MS 91
81	**'with pleasure…'**: letter to Arnold Freeman, June 1921, SES, MS 91/3/6/15
81	**'undeserved honour'** etc: SES MS 91/4/34/2
81	**'friendly haven…'**: SES MS 91/17/5/6

82 **'organising midnight...'** and details of help paying walkers' trespass fines, Sheffield Clarion Ramblers committee minutes (SCR), 20 October 1921; Sheffield Archives 2015/32

82 **'They had great admiration...'**: email exchange with Jean Smart, 6 August 2022

82 George Willis Marshall's walking journal is reproduced in Beedham (2011)

82 **'With all the strength...'**: Gallimore (1926), p. 67

82 **'*Sheffield Clarion Ramblers' Handbooks*'**: 1927 (p. 33) and 1928 (p. 18)

83 **'The packhorse path ... hallowed rings...'**: Gallimore (1926), pp. 11 and 40

83 *Westminster Gazette*, 22 July 1926, p. 6

83 *Sheffield Daily Telegraph*, 15 October 1926, p. 2

83 **'Daring little Sheffield committee...'**: letter from G. H. B. Ward to the editor of the *Derbyshire Times*, 30 June 1930; Sheffield Archives 2020/13

83 **'It examined...'** etc.: CPRE/2000 minutes for meetings held 28 July 1925, 12 May 1926, 2 December 1926; 'Derwent Footbridge', *Sheffield Daily Telegraph*, 4 December 1924, p. 9

83 An account of the Ward family's financial support to the committee is in the archives of the CPRE, Reading (SR2SHPK SP4/1 85/88)

84 CPRE inaugural meeting: 'Rural England', *Times*, 8 December 1926

84 Ethel's attendance at the inaugural CPRE meeting is recorded in CPRE/2000 (Sheffield Archives), 17 February 1927

84 List of first CPRE affiliates, 'Conference of Representative Societies interested in the preservation of Rural England convened by the President of the Royal Institute of British Architects 2 March 1926.' Conference notes p. 11; SR/CPRE (Museum of English Rural Life, Reading)

84 **'She could charm the birds off the trees'**: interview with Jean Smart, 26 May 2022

84 **'A survey of trees...'**: Ward (1939), p. 147

84 **'Looking back at the committee's early years in 1951'**: 'Twentieth Annual Report of the Executive, 1951', CPRE SHPK CI/5

85 **'*Manchester Guardian*...'**: 'Beautiful Tract of Moorland', 17 September 1927, p. 9

85 **'Testy letters...'**: Sheffield Archive, G. H. B. Ward correspondence 2020/13

85 **'I do not want it spread broadcast... '**: letter from Duke of Rutland's Estate office to G. H. B. Ward, 23 October 1907; G H B Ward Papers, Sheffield City Archives 2020/13

85 **'afford[ed] several...'**: SR SHPK C II 9 CPRE Archives, Reading

86 Longshaw purchase details from CPRE/2000 and Longshaw Deed of Conveyance between Henry Monagu, Duke of Rutland and the Citizens of the City of Sheffield 16/1/1928; CA 629 (39) (both Sheffield Archives)

86 **'hatless, yellow-jerseyed ...'**: 'Access to Mountains', *Times* 7 March 1939, p. 15

86 **'*Bolsheviks*'** etc.: Gaze (1988), p. 69

87 Access to Mountains Bill: Barnes (1934), p. 31; Smith (2020)

87 **'rickety, pigeon-chested...'**: Lowerson (1980), p. 270

87 **'brave but badly planned'**: etc.: unpublished notes G H B Ward Papers, Sheffield

88   **'National Park Committee'**: Report of the National Park Committee (1931) Cmd 3851

88   **'asked for Ethel's help...'**: Jones (2001)

89   **'Ethel could barely open a paper...'**: see for example 'Dovedale as a National Park', *Manchester Guardian*, 7 February 1930; F. A. Holmes, 'Make Dovedale a National Park', *Ashton Under Lyme Reporter*, 28 May 1932; F. A. Holmes, 'In Praise of Dovedale: Playground and Scenic Wonderland', *Nottingham Guardian*, 10 May 1932; 'Dovedale for the Nation', *Manchester Guardian*, 6 September 1936; 'Beauties of Dovedale', F. A. Holmes, letter to *Manchester Despatch*, 7 October 1939

Notes to chapter 5

90   **'a young Kikuyu...'**: Maathai (2008), p. 38.

90   Details of colonial government clearing, planting, resource extraction etc. in McClanahan and Young (1996), Atieno-Odhiambo (1995), Ofcansky (1984)

90   **'European farmers...'**: Shanguhiya (2015), pp. 141–142

90   **'The first species of *Homo* appeared...'**: Halliday (2022), pp. 34–35

90   **'a European visitor in 1893...'**: *Blue Book Africa* quoted in Kenyatta (1965), p. 47

91   **'By the end of the first decade...'**: Ofcansky (1984): by 1908, Europeans occupied 264,400 acres of forested land (pp. 137–138)

91   **'blue gums...'**: Maathai (2008); Ofcansky (1984)

91   **'It was a standing joke...'**: Day (1964); Ramaer (1974)

92   **'Recent studies ...'**: Muiruri et al. (2022)

92   **'stretched as far...'**: Maathai (2008), p. 16

92   **'Kikuyu folk stories...'**: these have been recorded and collected in Routledge and Routledge (1968). Also Brinkman (1996) and Namulundah (2013)

93   Descriptions of Ihithe and the forest in Maathai (2008), pp. 32–43

93   **'exploding with stars'**: Maathai (2008), p. 47

93   **'narrow, fast-moving...'**: Maathai (2010), p. 3

94   **'This is a tree of God'**: interview with Wangari Maathai conducted by Krista Tippett, 24 April 2008, American Public Media

94   **'passed her primary school exams...'**: many details of her early life and education from University of Nairobi citation for her honorary doctorate, conferred 11 March 2005, http://erepository.uonbi.ac.ke/bitstream/handle/11295/780/mathai%20final.pdf (accessed 17 July 2023)

94   **'the Mau Mau insurgency...'**: Nicholls (2010), p. 63

95   **'Of the 630 students...'**: Harper (2017), pp. 97–98

96   **'On 15 September...'**: Kennedy Airlift details in Stephens (2013); the journey across the Sahara in Maathai (2008), p. 75

96   **'Thousands of people...'**: descriptions of the scenes at the airport in Maathai (1962)

96   **'Several thousand Kenyan students...'**: Burton (2020). Mboya insisted that young women should also have the chance of education and so just under a quarter of the nearly 800 places offered for the four Airlift years were awarded to young women like Wangari

96   **'soon the hardy Tamarisk…'**: Saharan flora and fauna and expansion in Le Houerou (1997) and Thomas and Nigam (2018)

97   **'In an article…'**: 'Mountie Citizens of British Colony View Progress, Independence of African home', *Mount Mirror*, 19 January 1962

99   **'I will never forget…'**: interview with her best friend from college, Florence Conrad Salisbury, 25 July 2023

99   **'In a letter she wrote…'**: I am indebted to the nuns at Mount Saint Scholastica, Atchison, Kansas for finding and sending me copies of letters that Wangari sent to them over the years

100   **'Sister Thomasita'**: email interview with Sister Thomasita conducted June 2023

100   **'Florence Conrad Salisbury remembers'**: interview, 25 July 2023

101   **'What you are observing…'**: interview with Wangari Maathai conducted by Krista Tippett, 24 April 2008, American Public Media

101   **'the sky is the limit…'**: Maathai (2008), p. 96

102   **'largely a matter of showing up'** and details of post-independence Nairobi in Jacobs (2011), p. 166

102   **'perhaps acknowledging its own role…'**: the University had insisted she resign in order to fight a by-election in 1982. When the government disqualified her due to a technicality, the University did not reinstate her (Michaelson, 1994, p. 281)

103   **'Wangari joined…'**: interview with Wangari Maathai conducted by Krista Tippett, 24 April 2008, American Public Media

103   **'did not translate…'** and details of Kenyan women's groups post-independence in Riria Ouko (1985)

103   **'They were asking for water'**: interview with Wangari Maathai conducted by Krista Tippett, 24 April 2008, American Public Media

103   **'were not "turned off…"'**: Cooper (2002), p. 4

103   **'Many Europeans kept the top jobs…'**: Ochieng (1995), pp. 91–98

104   The new government's agricultural policies in Ching Saeturn (2017)

104   **'Kenyatta's priority was growth'**: Jacobs (2011), p. 178

104   **'an extra row of maize…'**: Kenya Government, *Kenya Development Plan 1965/66 to 1969/70*

104   **'just 2 per cent of Kenya's land…'**: Presbey (2013), p. 282; Ngigi and Tateishi (2004)

104   **'Levees which used to run…'**: Maathai (1988), p. 10

104   **'that social, political and religious conditioning…'**: Maathai's philosophy on community and self-empowerment in Maathai (2010)

105   **'Vert would shortly be "digging…"'**: interview with Vert Mbaya, 9 November 2023

105   Karura Forest details in Croze and Boy (2019)

105   **'Her daughter, Wanjira Mathai…'**: voice notes interview with Wanjira Mathai via WhatsApp, 4 October 2023

105   **'for the first time the idea of human rights…'**: Ebbesson (2022)

106   **'a melting pot of ideas'**: email interview with Oscar Mann, 25 July 2023

106   **'The city grew rapidly after *uhuru*…'**: details of Nairobi, and Kenyan society and culture post-independence, in Maxon (1995), pp. 110–147

106   **'The *New York Times*…'**: Lawrence Fellows, quoted in Maxton (1995), p. 97

107   Stories in the *Daily Nation*: various articles 1970–77, for example 'Now Protected Forests Have Come under the Axe', 28 May 1977, p. 5; 'Act to Save our Trees', 16 June 1977, p. 7

107   Nderitu and his school project (begun 1970): 'The Quiet Force Behind Wangari Maathai', *Daily Nation*, 15 October 2013

107   **'[He] literally drafted me...'**: Maathai (2008), p. xiii

108   **'just the tonic I needed'**: Maathai (2008), p. 130

108   **'The Kenyatta government had become...'**: Ochieng (1995), pp. 103–106

108   **'And so, at first, Wangari did not criticise...'**: analysis of Wangari's initially consensual and non-confrontational approach in Michaelson (1994)

108   **'Nobody warned me...'**: Maathai (2008), p. 140

Notes to chapter 6

113   **'Just around the corner...'**: DEP diary, 6 January 1908

113   **'Into this chamber swept...'**: Betty Cawkill Ellis quoted in Hart (2005), p. 365; *Daily Telegraph* report, 7 January 1908, p. 4

113   Description of the Royal Geographical Society's lecture theatre and Mina's lecture from 'Lonely Labrador: A Lady's Plucky Journey', *Daily Telegraph*, 7 January 1908,

113   **'elocution classes...'**: Hart (2005), p. 365

114   **'forcibly and entertainingly...'**: *North Adams Evening Transcript*, 21 December 1905, p. 5

114   **'one of the horrors'**: cited in Bell and McEwan (1996), p. 298

114   **'very helpless and sad...'**: Hubbard (1908b), p. 82

115   **'Just a few years later...'**: DEP diary, 'Up to lecture at the Geographical Society...', 2 January 1914

115   Details of Julia Henshaw's talk the day Dorothy Pilley was in the audience are contained in an RGS flier for the event, RGS/CB8/Children's Lectures 1911–1920

115   **'successful penetration'**: *Outing* December 1906, p. 396

115   **'Mrs Hubbard Returns...'**: *New York Times*, 23 November 1908, p. 5

115   Cabot's meeting with the Innu, who also met Mina, and also his use of her map, are recorded in Cabot (1912), pp. 173 and p. 10

115   **'she described how the fragrance...'**: Hubbard (1906b), p. 538

116   Details of *Harper's Monthly Magazine* in Epp (2014)

116   **'Herbert Lawrence Bridgman...'**: *Century Magazine* letter to Gilder from Bridgman, 24 November 1905, at https://digitalcollections.nypl.org/items/b120b530–1f9 b-0134–569a-00505686a51c#/?uuid=b10d9300–1f9b-0134–2341–00505686a51c (accessed 16 February 2023)

116   **'My Explorations in Unknown Labrador'**: Hubbard (1906a), pp. 813–823

117   **'that remarkable wife and widow'**: Bridgman (1920), p. 80

117   £100 advance from John Murray Archives, National Library of Scotland MS.40377

117   **'Murray took Mina on...'**: details of dinners etc. in various newspapers including *Westminster Gazette*, 3 February 1908, p. 7 and *Rochester, Chatham and Gillingham Journal*, 4 March 1908, p. 3

117   **'New Vagabonds Club'**: Goodwin (2013)

117   **'Alice Stopford Green...'**: Green (1901); Paseta (2004)

117   Descriptions of Alice Stopford Green's home, patronage etc. in McDowell (1967)

117   **'overlooking the Thames at Pimlico'**: Green's address in 1907/08 was 36, Grosvenor Road, Westminster

118   **'Green had written her obituary'**: Green (1901)

118   **'at railroad speed'**: MH diary, 22 August 1905

118   **'sleep only five times'**: MH was told this by the Innu she met on 20 August (MH diary)

120   **'Mina's guides, particularly...'**: MH diary, 14 August 1905. In this context George Elson was referring to a shaman when he said 'conjurer'; as it was, the Montagnais women and children were on their own

120   **'In 1967...'**: these stories are collected in Desbarats (1969); 'Missus Hubbard', p. 78

120   **'Much screaming and shouting...'**: MH diary, 17 August 1905

120   **'Go away, go away'**: Hubbard (1908a), p. 156

121   **'Studies of other nomadic hunting communities...'**: see for example Bird (1999); Waguespack (2005); Grund (2017)

121   **'I mean to try...'**: MH diary, 25 August 1905

123   **'She also continued to take observations...'**: diary records of taking observations, fretting over their accuracy and working on her maps on 25, 26, 29 and 30 August; and 11, 16, 17, 18 and 20 September; she also took charting lessons off one of the other passengers on the *Pelican*, Henry O'Sullivan, who was a Quebec government surveyor, on her long journey back around the Labrador coast

125   **'colonial administrators had relied...'**: Cole and Hart (2021)

125   **'All Indian maps...'**: in Cabot (1912), p. vii

125   Iligliuk's map is available to see digitally here: https://jcb.lunaimaging.com/luna/servlet/detail/JCB~1~1~4058~6400004:Eskimaux-Chart-No-1-Drawn-by-Ilig?qvq=q:iligliuk&mi=0&trs=2 (accessed 30 June 2022); the original is at John Carter Brown Library, Brown University

126   **'Shanawdithit was the last...'**: most information on the Beothuk is found in Howley (1915); also Chare (2020), Polack (2018) and Sparke (1995)

126   **'two hundred years of haphazard genocide'**: Sparke (1995), p. 6

126   **'at times she fell into...'**: Marshall (1996), p. 181

127   **'old marks of them...'**: Cormack quoted in Howley (1915), p. 220

127   **'never narrated without tears...'**: Cormack quoted in Howley (1915), p. 229

129   Details of Mina's berry collecting etc.: tea: MH diary, 24 July 1905; pipe making: MH diary, 14 July 1905; bake apple berries: MH diary, 4 August 1905; moss berries: MH diary, 24 August 1905; balsam boughs and moss bed: MH diary, 5 August 1905

129   **'This was the wilderness indeed...'**: Hubbard (1908a), p. 164

130   Reviews/notices of *A Woman's Way*: *Toronto Saturday Night*, 19 September 1908; *The Queen*, 16 January 1909; *New York Times*, 20 June 1908; *The Scotsman*, 18 May 1908; *The Observer*, 7 June 1908

130   **'in the grand journal *Nature*...'**: *Nature*, 79/2049, 4 February 1909, pp. 401–403

Notes to chapter 7

131   **'She was wearing...'**: this, and much of the Dent Blanche section, from DEP diary, 20 July 1928; also Pilley (1965), pp. 310–319; Pilley and Richards (1931), pp.

276–283; she refers to the boot incident again on 10 December 1928 diary entry, this time calling it 'comical'

131 **'one of the most difficult and dangerous...'**: W. B. Coolidge, quoted in Huxley (1962), p. 129

132 **'His lectures at Cambridge...'**: Russo (1989), *passim*

133 **'monastic spirit...'**: DEP diary, 5 October 1926

133 **'no woman had ever...'**: DEP diary, 20 August 1926

133 **'he believed that he could only create...'**: draft of letter to Violet, in DEP diary, December 1926

133 **'Wordsworth...'**: cited in Wilson (2021), p. 107

133 **'in a suicidal frame of mind'**: DEP diary, 11 February 1926

133 **'American imaginings of the rugged north west...'**: Wyckoff and Dilsaver (1997)

133 **'to take muddy strolls'**: DEP diary, 15 April 1926

134 **'During her "wander years"'...**: all from DEP diary, 1925 and 1926

134 **'the country was rolled...'**: DEP diary, 28 August 1928

134 **'The storm still rages...'**: DEP diary 2 May 1926

136 **'Can you fly...'**: DEP diary, 21 June 1926

136 *Crags and Crevasses* (1926). The short clip can be seen here: www.alpenglow.org/mountaineers-history/notes/movie/dw-16mm-extras.html (accessed 5 October 2023)

137 **'little white and blue painted cabin'**: DEP diary, 1 November 1926

137 **'Men are so queer'**: DEP diary, 25 October 1926

138 **'It makes me glad'**: DEP diary, 18 December 1926

138 **'the lovely islands...'**: DEP diary, 17 December 1926

138 **'fewer than 12...'**: Luckett (1990), p. xv

138 Osaka earthquake: Davison (1928), p. 456

138 **'Chiang Kai-Shek's nationalist...'**: the raid on Nanking was the subject of a statement by Austen Chamberlain, Foreign Secretary, and reported in *Hansard*, 28 March 1927

138 **'Their favourite literary phrase...'**: Luckett (1990), p. xxii

138 Details of the Himalayas, the Alps summer of 1927 and early married life in DEP diary 1927

141 **'she started to worry about the erosion...'**: Dorothy records her observations of the destruction of nature in her diary, 6–13 April 1929

141 **'treated like a man'**: DEP diary, 5 August 1922

141 **'J is hopelessly assertive...'**: DEP diary, 7 August 1922

142 **'Ivor ... recorded later...'**: Ivor wrote three pages of the account of the climb in DEP's diary for 21–23 July 1928

142 **'slide down a snow patch...'**: Pilley and Richards (1931), p. 282; other details of the climb in Pilley (1965)

143 **'like a black bonnet'**: Pilley (1965), p. 318

143 **'perhaps the most difficult British expedition'**: Lunn (1957), p. 177

143 Report in the *Times*, 'The Northern Arete of the Dent Blanche', 24 July 1928, p. 16; 'one of the few great unclimbed ridges of the Alps'

143 **'Englishwoman Climber'**: 'First to perform Alpine feat', *Daily Mail*, 25 July 1928, p. 13

143 **'the queerness of the feelings...'**: Pilley (1959), pp. 13–14

143 **'the modern self is haunted'**: Hansen (2013), p. 148

144 **'the woman business…'**: letter sent from Alan Harris to Dorothy, 1929. Cited in Richards (2016), p. 177

144 **'*I am distinctly interested…*'**: draft of letter to Alan Harris, back of DEP 1929 diary; lunch, DEP diary

144 **'During her first years…'**: Pilley (1959), p. 10

144 **'a short, technical account'**: the 'short technical account' appears in the regular section 'New Expeditions' of the *Alpine Journal* for 1928 (40, no. 237, pp. 376–377; no author named)

145 **'Lizard on a ceiling'**: Pilley (1965), p. 215

145 **'it was up to them'**: DEP diary, 7 October 1928

145 **'Indeed, one critic would comment'**: DEP diary, 2 June 1935

145 **'He had a big pipe…'**: Pilley (1965), p. 112

145 **'Most pre-twentieth century…'**: see Mills (1993)

146 Dorothy Wordsworth's *Grasmere Journal* cited in Wilson (2021), p. 113

146 **'with the glass-white shiver…'**: Shepherd (2014), p. 1

146 **'lone enraptured male…'**: Jamie (2008), p. 25

146 **'the bodily feeling, nameless…'**: Pilley (1965), p. 56

147 Records of China, Korea and Japan in DEP diaries 1929, 1930 and 1931. Also Pilley (1931) and Pilley (1932)

Notes to chapter 8

149 British Residency, Port Vila described in Rodman (2001), pp. 51–56

149 **'ten British settlers'**: details of the conditions and populations etc. in the then New Hebrides from Cheesman (1933b)

149 **'Lady scientist…'**: letter G. A. Joy to the High Commissioner, 22 March 1929 (Papers of Evelyn Cheesman, Natural History Museum)

149 **'Psychophysics'**: Joy was a co-founder of the Institute for Psychophysical Research, www.celiagreen.com/founders.html (accessed 3 March 2023)

150 **'the notorious Australian slaver Henry Ross Lewin…'**: Hunt (2007)

150 Archbishop of Canterbury etc. in *Nature*, 123 (1929), pp. 401–403;

150 **'an extremely primitive and suspicious type'**: letter from E. E. Chester, Natural History Museum, to the Trustees (Cheesman Papers)

150 **'like an oven with full heat turned on'**: Cheesman (1933a), p. 26

151 **'and a few broad white strokes…'**: details of her arrival in the New Hebrides in Cheesman (1933a), pp. 26–29

151 **'ironmould and mildew…'** etc.: Cheesman (1933b), pp. 27–44

151 **'phosphorescent mould…'** etc.: Cheesman (1932), p. 112

151 **'The insects are…'**: Cheesman (1932), p. vii

151 **'later confessing to answering…'**: Cheesman (1958), p. 319

151 **'She had rapidly concluded that…'**: Cheesman (1950), p. 63

152 Details of Professor Lefroy's fatal experiment in 'Professor Maxwell Lefroy' (obituary), *Times*, 15 October 1925, p. 16

152 **'She left the Zoo's employment…'**: ZSL employment card for Evelyn Cheesman

152 Ten shillings a week, rice and potatoes etc. in Cheesman (1958), p. 147

152 **'China, who would become legendary…'**: Knight (1980), p. 165

153   New species in Cheesman (1926); details of all her new species papers in Smith (1969)

154   Details of her grants to go to the New Hebrides contained in letters from E. E. Chester, 16 March 1931 (this letter also refers to her 'energy, pluck and resource') and Charles Tate Regan, 7 April 1931 (Cheesman Papers, Natural History Museum)

154   **'She had to shave her head...'**: Cheesman (1960), pp. 136–137

154   **'took 15 grammes...'**: Cheesman (1933b), p. 111

155   **'a very keen sensual awareness...'**: Cheesman (1933b), pp. 47–48

155   **'no frogs at all ...'**: this surprising finding has been confirmed by modern-day biologists and geographers; see Hamilton et al. (2010), p. 150

155   **'14-foot long bamboo-handled spear...'**: ethnographic descriptions of the spear in Braunholtz (1931)

156   **'Letter from Sandringham...'**: 30 December 1930 (Cheesman Papers, Natural History Museum)

156   **'A note from the Museum's Mineral Department...'**: Natural History Museum, Keeper of Entomology's Expedition Files, DF ENT/305

156   Ringapat's gift and oath in Cheesman (1932), pp. 200–204

156   Evelyn spoke of her shame, and gladness of leaving the New Hebrides in darkness, when the British flag would not have been flying, in a discussion at the Royal Geographical Society held 22 March 1937 and published in the *Geographical Journal* June 1937, pp. 504–505

158   **'18,000 insect specimens...'**: letter, 4 April 1931, from Charles Tate Regan, Cheesman Papers, Natural History Museum, Box B 1:1

160   **'Entomologists from across the world...'**: letters in the Cheesman Papers, Natural History Museum, Box B 1:1

160   **'The King of Belgium...'**: letter dated 7 October 1938, Natural History Museum, Box B 1: 1

160   **'Scientific Diana'**: headline of a review of *The Land of the Red Bird*, *Daily Telegraph*, 1936, p. 6

160   **'Kew's Director Arthur Hill...'**: letter to Evelyn Cheesman, 24 November 1933, Cheesman Papers, Natural History Museum, Box B 1:1

161   **'Her voice was wheezy...'**: ascertained by listening to 'The Travellers', BBC Home Service, first broadcast 26 December 1956

161   Details of Evelyn's BBC appearances can be found here: https://genome.ch.bbc.co.uk/ search/40/20?q=Evelyn+Cheesman#top (accessed 14 April 2023)

161   **'very flattered'**: letter from Sir David Attenborough to the author dated 8 June 2023

162   **'People sometimes arrive...'**: 'Northern New Guinea 1936: Discussion', *Geographical Journal* 89/6 (1937), pp. 504–506

162   German 'planters' and Japanese 'tourists' in Cheesman (1941)

162   **'Her maps and photographs would be used by Naval Intelligence...'**: letters between Evelyn and Humphrey Quill, Naval Intelligence, Singapore, Cheesman Papers, Natural History Museum

162   **'Evelyn continued winning grants ...'**: letter from EC to Captain Riley, Natural History Museum 8/4/36, Cheesman Papers

163   **'very few orchids possess truly blue flowers'**: Schuiteman (2013), p. 19

163   **'orchids on trees with moisture continuously...'**: Cheesman, cited in Schuiteman (2013), p. 21

163   **'Large clusters of...'**: Cheesman (1949), p. 72

163   **'swarms of leeches'**: described in Cheesman (1943), p. 104

163   Descriptions of the *Wambrau* in Cheesman (1943), p. 43

163   **'moments of initiation its grand aristocracy of trees...'**: Cheesman (1958), p. 234

164   **'the woman who walks'**: Laracy (2013), p. 187

164   **'After a fifteen-hour thunderstorm...'**: letter to Captain Riley, 8 April 1936, Cheesman Papers

164   **'A cranefly...'**: Cheesman (1940), p. 216

165   **'She had read, in an obscure Australian science journal'**: Cheesman (1951), p. 597

166   **'New Guinea, or *Cyclopea*, she wrote**...': Cheesman (1951), p. 597

167   **'to balance my budget'**: letter to Dr Van der Vecht, 26 December 1951, Cheesman Papers, Natural History Museum, Box B 1:1

167   **'She had it carefully taken to pieces...'**: invoice from Charles Perry, instrument maker, 19 December 1950; Cheesman Papers, Natural History Museum

Notes to chapter 9

168   **'The British winter of 1950–51...'**: Hawke and Champion (1952)

168   **'But on 13 April 1951....'**: some sources put the date as 17 April 1951. This earlier date is given by Ethel, in her CPRE annual report; it is also reported in the *Yorkshire Post*, 14 April 1951: 'The Minister of Local Government and Planning Mr Hugh Dalton has decided to confirm the Designation Order for the Peak District National Park ... the ministry announced *yesterday*'

168   **'the Great North Roof of England'**: coined by *Observer* reporter Ivor Brown, 'Make the Peak a Park, Not a Parking Place', 4 June 1944, p. 5

169   **'a testament to one woman...'**: Ethel's work was singled out as the reason why the Peak was named as the first National Park in a *Manchester Guardian* editorial, 'The First National Park', 1 June 1950, p. 7

170   **'Beloved...'**: letter from Ethel to Gerald, 3 September 1939, private collection

170   **'Gerald fought with the Royal Engineers...'**: Binfield (2018), p. 21

170   **'Like many on the left...'**: see Matless (2016) and Navickas (2019)

170   **'true, *recuperative*, natural peace'**: Haythornthwaite (1944), p. 3

171   **'very much in favour of our going ahead'**: interview conducted between Gerald Haythornthwaite and Fiona Reynolds, 29 January 1988; transcript the property of Jean Smart

171   **'Ethel and Gerald ... tramped the eastern section ...'**: Jones (2001), p. 62

171   **'even over all our dead bodies'**: letter from Ethel to her friend Joan Batten, quoted in Jones (2001), p. 63

172   The 1944 boundaries are contained in a booklet written by Ethel, published in May 1944, *The Peak District: A National Park*

172   **'sell more than 9,000 copies...'**: CPRE Sheffield and Peak Annual Report 1945; CPRE Archives, University of Reading, Special Collections SR SHPK/C/I/5

172   **'An officer in Eastern Command...'**: CPRE Sheffield and Peak Annual Report 1944; CPRE Archives, University of Reading, Special Collections SR SHPK/C/I/4

172   **'She was polite and quietly spoken'**: interview with Jean Smart, 26 May 2022

172   **'Ethel's great nephew, Ben Haggarty...'**: email exchange, 16 June 2022

173   Fliers from her lantern lectures, travelling exhibitions and details of land handed over to the National Trust in CPRE Archives, University of Reading, Special Collections SR SHPK C/II/ 9 and SR SHPK D/I/1

174   **'She gave 22 talks in 1936...'**: details of her talks in CPRE Sheffield and Peak, Fifth Annual Report 1936, CPRE Archives, University of Reading, Special Collections SR SHPK/C/I/1

174   **'ugly, ill-placed petrol stations'**: text to accompany the Save the Countryside touring exhibition, CPRE Archives, University of Reading, Special Collections SR SHPK/C/VIII/1

174   **'The Kinder River ... plunges'**: Gallimore (1932), p. 8

175   **'golden period of mountaineering in the British Isles...'**: obituary of P. A. Barnes, *The Climber* 4/10 (August 1966), p. 20

175   **'Be careful about...'**: CPRE/165

175   **'The work, completed in 1933...'**: there is a copy of this report in the Sheffield Archives CPRE/165 (1933)

176   **'Bleaklow is sixteen miles ...'**: from Barnes's secret report compiled for Ethel in 1933, Sheffield Archives (2007/138 CPRE/165), p. 2

176   **'Ethel was instrumental...'**: National Trust report, 'Ethel Haythornthwaite', 7 February 1977

176   **'She wrote the most beautiful letters...'**: interview with Jean Smart, 26 May 2022

177   **'If she wanted something urgently...'**: interview conducted between Gerald Haythornthwaite and Fiona Reynolds, 29 January 1988

177   **'An emergency acquisition...'**: CPRE Sheffield and Peak annual report, CPRE Archives, University of Reading, Special Collections SR SHPK/C/I/2

177   **'In a nod of gratitude...'**: 'Demonstration by Ramblers', *Manchester Guardian*, 1 July 1935, p. 8

177   Footage of 'the Surprise View handover' is available on YouTube here: www.youtube.com/watch?v=mrjb6kuvr8o

178   **'smoky cotton town'**: interview conducted between Gerald Haythornthwaite and Fiona Reynolds, 29 January 1988

178   **'I'm not saying that...'**: interview conducted between Gerald Haythornthwaite and Fiona Reynolds, 29 January 1988; transcript the property of Jean Smart

178   **'The work of this branch...'**: letter from Ethel to CPRE Sheffield branch members, December 1939, CPRE Archives, University of Reading, Special Collections SR SHPK/E/II/1

179   **'four and a half hours without a restaurant car...'**: information from *Bradshaw's Guide to the British Railways, August 1942*; restaurant cars were removed from trains during the war, so more carriages for moving troops around could be provided

179   **'the object is to kill...'**: letter from Ethel Haythornthwaite to Herbert Griffin, 7 January 1943, CPRE Archives, Reading (SR CPRE C/1/78/6)

179   **'They liked her'**: interview conducted between Gerald Haythornthwaite and Fiona Reynolds, 29 January 1988

179 **'uttered with bated breath...'**: Binfield (2018), p. 1

179 **'much of the legwork...'**: Mennen (2023)

180 **'She could draft...'**: details of Ethel's activities as deputy secretary of national CPRE 1942–43; CPRE Archives, University of Reading, Special Collections SR CPRE C/I/78/6

180 **'Whitehall denuded of...'**: Blunden and Curry (1990), pp. 44–45

180 **'implacably opposed...'**: Jones (2001), p. 72

180 **'without any of the normal courtesies'**: Jones (2001), p. 73

180 **'definition of a National Park...'**: this and other notes on the National Parks history in Mennen (2023), Parker and Ravenscroft (1999) and Blunden and Curry (1990)

180 **'The Lake District area...'**: Hobhouse Report, Cmd. 7121, July 1947, p. 10

181 **'The Dovedale maps...'**: there is a copy of the Dovedale proposed area map in *Out O' Doors*, July 1933, p. 38

181 **'fireworks from Dovedale'**: EBH to Miss Revel, CPRE, 15 October 1942; reply 16 October 1942; University of Reading, Special Collections SR CPRE C/I/78/6

181 **'the most needed of all...'**: *The Hope Valley Disaster*, CPRE Sheffield publication, 1949, University of Reading, Special Collections SR SHPK/C/III/3

181 **'This song was recorded...'**: Hobhouse Report, Cmd. 7121, July 1947, p. 91

183 Cave Dale Rally, 24 June 1951. Report in *Manchester Guardian*, 25 June 1951, p. 3

184 **'sleepless guardian'**: 30 June 1951 – Degree citation, University of Reading, Special Collections SR CPRE C/1/78/6

184 **'motoring accident in Ireland'**: letter from Ethel to Herbert Griffin, 5 March 1948, University of Reading, Special Collections SR CPRE C/1/78/6

184 **'whether the recreational needs of the many...'**: Dower (1945), p. 32

184 **'one of the most spectacular flops...'**: 'The Kinder Scout Trespass', *Guardian*, 17 April 2012

184 Structure of the Peak Park Joint Planning Board in Blunden and Curry (1990), pp. 96–103

185 **'a cause of bewilderment'**: Jones (2001), p. 108

185 **'long and manful fight'**: Jones (2001), p. 90

Notes to chapter 10

186 **'Dorothy Pilley broke her hip...'**: she puts the date of the motor accident as 9 November 1958 in Pilley (1959), p. 14

186 **'the stuff of North American legend'**: see for example Pratt (1993), pp. 11–19; Merrick (1933)

186 **'As the government of Daniel arap Moi...'**: details of the Moi regime in Branch (2011)

186 **'It's the silence that hurts'**: quoted in Branch (2011), p. 189

187 **'She was winning grants...'**: Michaelson (1994), p. 551

187 **'dilapidated prefab office building...'**: history of the early years of the GBM in Muchiri (2011), Michaelson (1994) and Ndegwa (1996)

187 **'Since reforestation...'**: Michaelson (1994), p. 546

187 **'the headwaters of the mighty...'**: Greene (2005), pp. 41–43

189   **'their one millionth tree...'**: details of the GBM's planting records in Ndegwa (1996); see pp. 89–90: by 1986, just over 1million trees had been planted, with 850,000 surviving

189   **'she abandoned early trials...'**: interview with Mia Macdonald, 16 August 2023

189   **'it takes four years to grow...'**: interview with Professor Karanja Njoroge, Director of Friends of Karura Forest, and former CEO of the Green Belt Movement, 15 August 2023; Ndegwa (1996)

189   **'First the women collect the seeds'**: Ndegwa (1996)

190   **'Often these meetings would start with singing...'**: interview with Vert Mbaya, 9 November 2023

190   Men of the Trees details in St Barbe Baker (1932)

191   **'He gave it to us...'**: Sweeney (1986)

191   **'They work[ed] quietly...'**: Maathai (2004)

191   **'She took seedlings...'**: in Maathai (2006), p. 132; also Maathai (1988) and Muchiri (2011)

191   **'The chief official at the Kenyan Forestry Service...'**: Maathai (1988), pp. 7–8

191   Details of the Kenyan Forestry Department since 1982 in Ofcansky (1984)

192   **'kept scrupulous records'**: Ndegwa (1996), p. 87; Michaelson (1994), p. 551

192   **'often she would join...'**: Maathai (2008), p. 137

192   **'disobedient woman'**: Maathai (2006), p. 159

192   **'The Moi government was also increasingly concerned...'**: Worthington (2003), p. 147

192   **'I often asked her if she was scared...'**: voice notes interview with Wanjira Mathai via WhatsApp, 4 October 2023

193   **'Mia Macdonald...'**: interview with Mia Macdonald, 16 August 2023

194   Details of how she lost her job in Maathai (2008), pp. 162–163

194   Unrest at the University in Ogot (1995), pp. 192–200

194   **'Her fellow academic Vert Mbaya'**: interview with Vert Mbaya, 9 November 2023

195   **'an unassuming clutter ...'**: Ndegwa (1996), p. 86

195   Louise Sweeney: Sweeney (1986), p. 23

195   **'I was a very decent...'**: Graydon (2005)

196   **'MPs in Parliament publicly cursed her...'**: various reports in the *Daily Nation*, for example 'MPs Condemn Prof Maathai', 9 November 1989, p. 1; 'MPs want Maathai Movement Banned', 24 November 1989, p. 1

196   Letters in the *Daily Nation* – virtually daily throughout November

196   **'round the world collecting money'**: Mwai (1989), p. 4

197   Maathai's response to the MPs: 'Prof Maathai Replies to MPs', *Daily Nation*, 10 November 1989, p. 1

197   **'She had no hard words...'**: interview with Professor Njoroge, 15 August 2023

197   **'shows no respect...'**: 'Maathai Loses', *Weekly Review*, December 1989, p. 9; Worthington (2003), p. 157

198   **'Maathai feted at reception'**: *Daily Nation*, 1 December 1989, p. 3

198   **'But we still had fun...'**: interview with Vert Mbaya, 9 November 2023

198   **'the most unpopular NGO in Kenya'**: Ndegwa (1996), p. 95

199 **'The police would claim…'**: Tami Hultman, 'I am Woman', *Africa News Service*, 8 June 1992

199 **'Wangari was, yet again, due in court…'**: Maathai (2008), p. 227

199 Wangari's speech to the UN Earth Summit can be found here: www.youtube.com/watch?v=azWQzersZgo

199 **'George Bush senior…'**: report of the Earth Summit in Vidal (2012)

200 **'Journalists investigating'**: see for example 'Loggers Invade Forest' and 'Logs Hidden in Forests', *Daily Nation*, 9 and 15 October 1998

200 **'land-grabbing mania'**: Branch (2011), p. 205; see also Presbey (2013) and Cesar (2010)

200 **'According to one estimate…'**: Ngigi and Tateishi (2004)

200 Karura Forest details in Croze and Boy (2019)

200 **'like the doomed Dodo…'**: Hengst (2009)

201 **'People began to…'**: interview with Professor Njoroge, 15 August 2023

201 **'The citizens of Kenya wrote letters…'**: see for example 'Forest Destruction Appalling', *Daily Nation*, 7 October 1998, p. 7; 'Karura Forest Must be Saved', *Daily Nation*, 3 October 1998, p. 7

201 **'campaign of guerilla tree planting'**: Cesar (2010)

Notes to chapter 11

207 **'the outdoors is a contested space…'**: see Hewitt (2023)

208 **'Planted deep in most women's psyches…'**: Thomas (1980), p. 105

208 **'Outdoor woman … will…'**: Nichols (1978), p. ix

208 **'Modern US studies…'**: McNeil et al. (2012); Virden and Walker (1999)

208 **'Even in the remotest region…'**: Nash et al. (2019)

208 **'still taking notes…'**: interview with Anthony Pilley, 25 November 2023

208 Evelyn's last expeditions to Tarifa in 1958 are recorded in Cheesman (1960)

209 **'Her divorce settlement…'**: Hart (2005), p. 398

209 **'her friend Helen Bridgman…'**: Bridgman (1920), p. 81

209 **'In a letter to her publisher…'**: John Murray Archives, National Library of Scotland MS. 40377

210 **'In some of the modern…'**: see for example Berton (1978)

210 **'New England *primness*'**: McKibben (2000), p. xi

213 Cheesman's Line in Hamilton et al. (2010)

214 **'I am quite overwhelmed…'**: letter to Captain Riley, 15 February 1955, Papers of Evelyn Cheesman, Natural History Museum

215 **'her lack of means [was] somewhat eased'**: 'Miss Evelyn Cheesman', *Times*, 17 April 1969, p. 11

215 **'the 'urge…'**: Cheesman (1960), pp. 10; 78–79

215 **'this noisy, bustling world of ours…'**: Cheesman (1960), p. 79

216 **'1,000 insects'**: from 'Account of Trip to Tarifa', Papers of Evelyn Cheesman, Natural History Museum, Box C:1

216 **'more than 200 species…'**: Touzel and Garner (2018)

216 **'A drunken driver…'**: Pilley (1959), p. 14

216 **'There is a limit to what a ruined hip…'**: Pilley (1959), p. 14

217 **'And that stiff-frozen Dawn'**: Richards (1960), p. 76

217   **'Once despised wire...'**: Pilley (1962), p. 250
217   **'*Climbing Days* is going...'**: DEP diary, 2 June 1935
218   **'mockery and waggery'**: Pilley (1971), p. 5
218   **'learn[ing] to live with the void...'**: DEP letter to Mr Templeman, 17 December 1981 (Alpine Club Archives)
219   **'playing "the great lady"'**: telephone interview with Anthony Pilley, 25 November 2023
219   **'It was a magical...'**: email exchange with Anthony Pilley, 5 September 2023
219   **'caged bird'**: Richards (2016), p. 147
219   **'As always when...'**: letter from Anthony Pilley to Muriel Files, 19 January 1987
220   **'on a drizzly autumn morning...'**: Zoom interview with Chris Pilley, 14 December 2023
220   **'We have them in our bones...'**: Resign! Resign! Richards (1978), pp. 49–50

Notes to chapter 12

221   Wanjira Mathai's experience: WhatsApp voice notes to author, 4 October 2023
221   2002 Election result, Maathai (2006), p. 288. Many parties got together under the National Rainbow Coalition for this election, and it wasn't that unusual that some of the candidates for MP won by very large margins, like Wangari. In addition, many parts of Kenya are dominated by distinct ethnic groups, like the Kikuyus, and Wangari's seat was in a heavily Kikuyu district
221   For illegal forest clearing see for example 'Government Plans to Seal Off Mt Kenya Forest', *East African Standard*, 11 February 2003
221   **'nearly 1,000 forestry officers...'**: 'Forests: Were Leakey's Men the Targets?' *East African Standard*, 3 November 2003
222   Mia in the van with Wangari: interview, 16 August 2023
223   **'put my hands...'**: Maathai (2008), p. 292
223   **'I rode along...'**: Macdonald (2004)
223   **'I had been at the University....'**: interview with Vert Mbaya, 9 November 2023
223   **'A joke...'**: 'Wangari Maathai's Final Journey', *The Nation*, 8 October 2011
224   **'The award of the Nobel...'**: Kabaji (2014)
224   **'In December 2005 she declined...'**: 'Kenya's Nobel Laureate still Unwilling to Accept Post', Xinhua General News Service, 25 December 2005; 'Maathai Told Off for Criticising New Act', *African Standard*, 28 November 2005
224   Details of the development grants work in Mathai (2009)
225   **'She wrote all her letters with pen and ink'**: interview with Jean Smart, 26 May 2022
225   **'At the public inquiry...'**: and other CPRE activities in the 1950s and 1960s: CPRE Archives, Reading (SR SHPK C II 9) 'Account of Fifty-Five Years' Work 1924–1978', pp. 9–14
226   **'In the course of our many...'**: booklet titled *CPRE Sheffield and Peak District Branch. Account Of Fifty-Five Years' Work 1924–1955*, p. 14. CPRE Archives, Reading SR SHPK C II 9
226   Access agreements across the Peak District 1953 and 1954 in *Manchester Guardian*, 11 March 1953

226   'Access to Land in the Peak District', p. 12, and 14 July 1954, 'Extending Public Access Areas in the Peak District', p. 5

226   **'In September 1982...'**: 'Trust Buys Kinder', *Guardian*, 11 September 1982, p. 2; 'Peak Park Gloom over £1.5 Million 'Target' Set for Land Sale', *Guardian*, 20 July 1982, p. 4

227   **'inherited aristocracy...'**: Shrubsole (2019)

227   Access agreements judged a failure by 1970: Hoyle (2010), p. 195

228   **'birch, beech, oller and larch ...'**: Gallimore (1926), p. 94

228   **'Now, nearly 60 per cent are...'**: details of the impact of the Forests Act (2005) are discussed in Waruingi et al. (2023)

228   **'There's a story in Kenya...'**: *Daily Nation*, 15 October 2013, 'The Quiet Force Behind Wangari Maathai', 25 April 2014

228   Karura Forest details in Croze and Boy (2019).

229   **'Kenya holds...'**: see for example www.kws.go.ke/content/kws-marks-national-tree-planting-day-over-5000-trees-planted-nairobi-national-park (accessed 4 February 2024)

229   **'When I think of my mother...'**: voice notes interview with Wanjira Mathai via WhatsApp, 4 October 2023

Bibliography

Archives consulted

Alpine Club Library (Dorothy Pilley files)
Binfield, Clyde (2018). 'Lecture Notes' (Private Collection)
British Library Newspaper Collection
British Library Sound Archive
CPRE General Archives, University of Reading, Special Collections (Museum of English Rural Life, Reading)
CPRE Sheffield and Peak Minutes, Sheffield City Archives
Ethel Mary Bassett Ward 'Impressions of a Fortnight in France' April–June 1913 (private collection)
Glacier National Park Archives
John Murray (publishers), National Library of Scotland
Mina Hubbard Collection (Coll-241), Archives and Special Collections, Memorial University of Newfoundland
National Trust Archives (Mrs Ethel Haythornthwaite)
Papers of Evelyn Cheesman, Natural History Museum
Papers of Evelyn Cheesman, Royal Entomological Society
Papers of G H B Ward, Sheffield City Archives
Papers of Mrs I A Richards (Dorothy Pilley), Pepys Library, Magdalene College, Cambridge
Royal Geographical Society Archives
The Mount, Saint Scholastica, Atchison, Kansas
Sheffield Clarion Ramblers Minute books and Handbooks, Sheffield City Archives
Sheffield Educational Settlement Archives, Sheffield University Library Special Collections
Westfield College Archives (including issues of *Hermes* magazine), Queen Mary University London Special Collections
Women's Library, LSE, London (British Women's Patriotic League Archives; Papers of Alice Stopford Green)
Zoological Society of London Library and Archives

Published primary and secondary works

Abusch, Tevi (2015). *Male and Female in the Epic of Gilgamesh: Encounters, literary history, and interpretation*. Winona Lake: Eisenbrauns.
Aitken, Bill (1994). *The Nanda Devi Affair*. Gurgaon: Penguin.

Arner, Lynn (2006). 'The Ends of Enchantment: Colonialism and Sir Gawain and the Green Knight.' *Texas Studies in Literature and Language* 48/2, pp. 79–101.

Atieno-Odhiambo, E. S. (1995). 'The Formative Years 1945–55.' In Ogot, B. A. and Ochieng, W. R. (eds), *Decolonization and Independence in Kenya 1940–93*. London: James Currey.

Baker, Richard St. Barbe (1932). *Men of the Trees*. London: George Allen and Unwin.

Barnes, Philip (1934). *Trespassers Will be Prosecuted*. Sheffield: P. A. Barnes.

Beedham, Ann (2011). *Days of Sunshine and Rain: Rambling in the 1920s*. Sheffield: Pickard Communication.

Bekler, Ecevit (2023). 'Under the Shade of Colonialism: Mary Kingsley and her travels in West Africa.' *RumeliDE Journal of Language and Literature Studies* 13, pp. 1335–1346.

Bell, Morag and McEwan, Cheryl (1996). 'The Admission of Women Fellows to the Royal Geographical Society, 1892–1914: The controversy and the outcome.' *The Geographical Journal* 162/3, pp. 295–312.

Berton, Pierre (1978). *The Wild Frontier: More tales from the remarkable past*. Toronto: McClelland and Stewart.

Bird, Rebecca (1999). 'Cooperation and Conflict: The behavioural ecology of the sexual division of labor.' *Evolutionary Anthropology* 8, pp. 65–75.

Blunden, John and Curry, Nigel (1990). *A People's Charter? Forty years of the National Parks and Access to the Countryside Act*. London: HMSO.

Branch, Daniel (2011). *Kenya: Between hope and despair 1963–2011*. New Haven: Yale University Press.

Braunholtz, Herman (1931). 'Spear with carved wooden head and a long bamboo shaft. Fibre cord lashing'. *British Museum Collections Index*.

Bridgman, Helen (1920). *Within My Horizon*. Boston: Small, Maynard and Co.

Brinkman, Inge (1996). *Kikuyu Gender Norms and Narratives*. Leiden: Research School CNWS.

Brown, Alfred (1938). *Striding Through Yorkshire*. London: Country Life.

Bryher (1963). *The Heart to Artemis: A writer's memoirs*. London: Collins.

Burton, Eric (2020). 'Decolonization, the Cold War, and Africans' Routes to Higher Education Overseas 1957–65.' *Journal of Global History* 15/1, pp. 169–191.

Burton, Richard (1961 [1860]). *The Lake Regions of Central Africa: A picture of exploration*. New York: Horizon Press.

Cabot, William Brooks (1912). *In Northern Labrador*. Boston: Gorham Press.

Cariou, Warren (2016). 'Indigenous Rights and the Undoomed Indian.' *European Romantic Review* 27/3, pp. 309–318.

Caroli, Rosa (2022). 'Donne e Spazi Sacri in Giappone: Culto en minature el Fuji a Edo.' *Storie delle Donne* 17, pp. 27–58.

Cesar, Dana (2010). 'Jane Addams and Wangari Maathai: Nobel Laureates on educating and organising women for local food security.' *Vitae Scholasticae* 27/2, pp. 123–141.

Chare, Nicholas (2020). 'In Her Hands: Affect, encounter and gestures of witnessing in Shanawdithit's drawings.' *Parallax* 20/3, pp. 286–382.

Cheesman, Edith (1922). *Mesopotamia*. London: A. and C. Black.

Cheesman, Evelyn (1923). 'Notes on the Pairing of the Land Crab *Cardisoma armatum*.' *Proceedings of the Zoological Society of London 1923*, p. 173.

Cheesman, Evelyn (1924). *Everyday Doings of Insects*. London: George Harrap and Co.

Cheesman, Evelyn (1926). 'A New Genus and Species of Miridae (Hemiptera) from the Society Islands.' *The Entomologist* 59/760 (September), pp. 266–267.

Cheesman, Evelyn (1927). *Islands Near the Sun: Off the beaten track in the far, fair Society Islands*. London: H. F. & G. Witherby.

Cheesman, Evelyn (1929). 'Hymenoptera Collected on the St George Expedition in Central America and the West Indies.' *Transactions of the Entomological Society of London* 77/2, pp. 141–154.

Cheesman, Evelyn (1932). *Hunting Insects in the South Seas.* London: Philip Allan and Co.

Cheesman, Evelyn (1933a). *Backwaters of the Savage South Seas.* London: Jarrolds.

Cheesman, Evelyn (1933b). 'The Island of Malekula, New Hebrides.' *The Geographical Journal* 81/3 (March), pp. 193–207.

Cheesman, Evelyn (1940). 'Two Unexplored Islands off Dutch New Guinea: Waigeu and Japen.' *The Geographical Journal* 95/3 (March), pp. 208–217.

Cheesman, Evelyn (1941). 'The Mountainous Country at the Boundary, North New Guinea.' *The Geographical Journal* 98/4 (October), pp. 169–188.

Cheesman, Evelyn (1943). 'The Island of New Guinea.' *Nature* (10 July), pp. 41–43.

Cheesman, Evelyn (1949). *Six-Legged Snakes in New Guinea.* London: Harrap.

Cheesman, Evelyn (1950). 'Naturalists' Expeditions in the Pacific.' In Barrett, Charles (ed.), *The Pacific: Ocean of islands.* Melbourne: N. H. Seward, pp. 55–65.

Cheesman, Evelyn (1951). 'Old Mountains of New Guinea.' *Nature* 168 (6 October), p. 597.

Cheesman, Evelyn (1957). 'Biogeographical Significance of Aneityum Island, New Hebrides.' *Nature* 180 (2 November), pp. 903–904.

Cheesman, Evelyn (1958 [1957]). *Things Worth While.* London: Readers Union.

Cheesman, Evelyn (1960). *Time Well Spent.* London: Hutchinson.

Cheesman, Percy (1933). *Around the Map on a Cable Ship.* London: Golden Eagle Publishing Company.

Cheesman, Robert (1926). *In Unknown Arabia.* London: Macmillan.

Ching Saeturn, Muey (2017). 'A Beacon of Hope for the Community: The role of Chavakali Secondary School in late colonial and early independent Kenya.' *Journal of African History* 58/2, pp. 311–329.

Cole, Daniel and Hart, Richard (2021). 'The Importance of Indigenous Cartography and Toponymy to Historical Lane Tenure and Contributions to Euro/American/Canadian Cartography.' *International Journal of Geo-information* 10/397, pp. 1–14.

Cole, Susan Guettel (2004). *Landscapes, Gender and Ritual Space: The ancient Greek experience.* Oakland: University of California Press.

Collenette, Cyril (1926). *Sea-girt Jungles: The expedition of a naturalist with the St George Expedition.* London: Hutchinson and Co.

Cooper, F. (2002). *Africa Since 1940: The past of the present.* Cambridge: Cambridge University Press.

Craig, Doug (2006). 'Lucy Evelyn Cheesman and the Scourge of the South Pacific.' *British Simuliid Group Bulletin* no. 26 (July), pp. 16–25.

Cresswell, Tim (1993). 'Mobility as Resistance: A geographical reading of Kerouac's "On the Road".' *Transactions of the Institute of British Geographers* 18/2, pp. 249–262.

Crook, J. Mordaunt (ed.) (2001). *Bedford College: Memories of 150 years.* London: Royal Holloway and Bedford New College.

Croze, Harvey and Boy, Gordon (2019). 'The Story of Karura.' In Friends of Karura Forest Association (ed.), *Karura Forest: A visitor's guide.* Nairobi: Friends of Karura Forest Association, pp. 14–33.

Daniell, E. H. (2009). 'Reminiscences.' In Clennett, Margaret (ed.), *Presumptuous Pinnacle Ladies.* Disley: Millrace pp. 27–34.

Davison, Charles (1928). 'The Tango (Japan) Earthquake of 7 March 1927.' *The Geographical Journal* 72/5 (November), pp. 456–461.

Day, John (1964). *Railways of Northern Africa.* London: Arthur Baker Ltd.

Deb Roy, Rohan (2020). 'White Ants, Empire and Entomo-politics in South Asia'. *Historical Journal* 63/2, pp. 411–436.

DeCesare, Lisa (2005). 'A Myxomycete Correspondence Between Arthur and Gulielma Lister and William Gilson Farlow.' *Field Mycology* 6/3 (July), pp. 94–97.

Desbarats, Peter (ed.) (1969). *What They Used to Tell About: Indian legends from Labrador.* Montreal: McLelland and Stewart Ltd.

Dick, Trevor (1982). 'Canadian Newsprint 1913–1930: National policies and the North American economy.' *Journal of Economic History* 42/3, pp. 659–687.

Douglas, A. and Johnson, P. (1926). *The South Seas of Today: Being an account of the cruise of the yacht St George to the South Pacific.* London: Cassell and Co.

Dower, John (1945). *National Parks in England and Wales.* London: HMSO.

Ebesson, Jonas (2022). 'Getting it Right: Advances of human rights and the environment from Stockholm 1972 to Stockholm 2022.' *Environmental Policy and Law* 52/2, pp. 79–92.

Echevarria, Evelio (2014). 'Summit Archaeology: Prehistoric ascents in the world's highest mountains,' *The Alpine Journal* 2014, pp. 190–198.

Epp, Michael (2014). ' "Good, Bad Stuff": Editing, advertising and the transformation of genteel literary production in the 1890s.' *American Periodicals* 24/2, pp. 186–205.

Fan, Xinyu and Wu, Lingwei (2020). 'The Economic Motives for Foot-Binding.' Discussion Paper Series, Collaborative Research Center Transregio 224.

Fara, Patricia (2004). *Pandora's Breeches: Women, science and power in the Enlightenment.* London: Pimlico.

Fitzhugh, William (1977). 'Indian and Eskimo/Inuit Settlement History in Labrador: An archaeological view.' In Brice-Bennett, Carol (ed.), *Our Footprints are Everywhere: Inuit land use and occupancy in Labrador.* Labrador Inuit Association.

Friberg, Eino (trans.) (2021). *Kalevala: The epic of the Finnish people.* London: Penguin Classics.

Gallimore, Ethel Bassett (1926). *The Pride of the Peak.* London: Jonathan Cape.

Gallimore, Ethel Bassett (1932). 'Preface: The scenery of the Peak District.' In *The Threat to the Peak.* Sheffield: CPRE.

Gates, Barbara (1998). *Kindred Nature: Victorian and Edwardian women embrace the living world.* Chicago: University of Chicago Press.

Gaze, John (1988). *Figures in a Landscape: A history of the National Trust.* London: Barrie and Jenkins.

Glotfelty, Cheryll (1996). 'Femininity in the Wilderness: Reading gender in women's guides to backpacking.' *Women's Studies* 25/5, pp. 439–456. DOI: 10.1080/00497878.1996.9979129.

Goodwin, Grainne (2013). 'An Adamless Eden: Counterpublics and women writers' sociability at the fin de siècle through the experiences of Flora Annie Steele.' *Women's History Review* 22/3, pp. 440–459.

Grace, Sherill (2004). 'Introduction.' In Hubbard, Mina, *A Woman's Way Through Unknown Labrador.* Montreal: McGill-Queen's University Press.

Gray, Marion (2000). *Productive Men, Reproductive Women: The agrarian household and the emergence of separate spheres during the German Enlightenment.* New York: Berghahn Books.

Graydon, Nicola (2005). 'Wangari Maathai: Fighting for Kenya's environment.' *The Ecologist,* March. https://theecologist.org/2005/mar/01/wangari-maathai-fighting-kenyas-environment (accessed 23 June 2023).

Green, Alice Stopford (1901). 'Mary Kingsley.' *African Affairs* 1/1 (October), pp. 1–16.

Greene, Bryan (2005). 'Introduction.' In Buchanan, Roberta, Hart, Anne and Greene, Bryan (eds), *The Woman who Mapped Labrador: The life and expedition diary of Mina Hubbard.* Montreal: McGill-Queen's University Press.

Gribble, Francis Henry (1899). *The Early Mountaineers*. London: T. F. Unwin.

Grund, Brigid (2017). 'Behavioural Ecology, Technology and the Organisation of Labor: How a shift from spear thrower to self bow exacerbates social disparities.' *American Anthropologist* 119/1, pp. 104–119.

Haas, Randall et al. (2020). 'Female Hunters of the Early Americas.' *Science Advances* 6, pp. 1–10.

Halliday, Thomas (2022). *Otherlands: A world in the making*. London: Penguin.

Hamilton, Alison et al. (2010). 'Biogeographic Breaks in Vanuatu, a Nascent Archipelago.' *Pacific Science* 64/2, pp. 149–159.

Hansen, Peter (2013). *The Summits of Modern Man: Mountaineering after the Enlightenment*. Cambridge, MA: Harvard University Press.

Harper, Jim (2017). 'Tom Mboya and the African Student Airlifts: Inclusion, equity and higher education among Kenyan women and men.' *Africology: The Journal of Pan African Studies* 10/9, pp. 82–105.

Hart, Anne (2005). 'Finding her Way.' In Buchanan, Roberta, Hart, Anne and Greene, Bryan (eds), *The Woman who Mapped Labrador: The life and expedition diary of Mina Hubbard*. Montreal: McGill-Queen's University Press.

Hawke, E. and Champion, P. (1952). 'Report on the Snow Survey of Great Britain for the Season 1950–51.' *Journal of Glaciology* 2/11, pp. 25–38.

Haythornthwaite, Ethel (1944). *The Peak District: A National Park*. Sheffield: Joint Committee for the Peak District National Park.

Heddon, Deirdre and Turner, Cathy (2012). 'Walking Women: Shifting the tales and scales of mobility.' *Contemporary Theatre Review* 22/2, pp. 224–236.

Hengst, Han den (2009). 'The Dodo and Scientific Fantasies: Durable myths of a tough bird.' *Archives of Natural History* 36/1, pp. 136–145.

Hewitt, Rachel (2023). *In Her Nature: How women break boundaries in the great outdoors*. London: Chatto and Windus.

Hey, David (2011). 'Kinder Scout and the Legend of the Mass Trespass.' *The Agricultural Review* 59/2, pp. 199–216.

Hinojosa-Diaz, Ismael and Brosi, Berry (2013). 'First Records and Description of Metallic Red Females Euglossa (Alloglossura) gorgonesnsis Cheesman with Notes on Colour Variation within the Species.' *ZooKeys* 335 (September), pp. 113–119.

Hipperson, Julie (2017). 'Professional Entrepreneurs: Women veterinary surgeons as small business owners in interwar Britain.' *Social History of Medicine* 31/1, pp. 122–139.

Hollis, Dawn and Konig, Jason (eds) (2021). *Mountain Dialogues from Antiquity to Modernity*. London: Bloomsbury Academic.

Howley, James (1915). *The Beothuks or Red Indians*. Cambridge: Cambridge University Press.

Hoyle, Richard (2010). 'Securing Access to England's Uplands, or, How the 1945 Revolution Petered Out.' In Congost, Rosa and Santos, Rui (eds), *Contexts of Property in Europe: The social embeddedness of property rights in land in historical perspective*. Turnhout: Brepols.

Hubbard, Leonidas (1903a). 'Off Days on Superior's North Shore.' *Outing* 42/6 (September), pp. 716–723.

Hubbard, Leonidas (1903b). 'Diary.' Contained in Hubbard, Mina, 'A Woman's Way Through Unknown Labrador.' *Manchester Geographical Society* 23/4, pp. 205–254.

Hubbard, Mina (1906a). 'My Explorations in Unknown Labrador.' *Harper's Monthly Magazine* (May), pp. 813–823.

Hubbard, Mina (1906b). 'Labrador, from Lake Melville to Ungava Bay.' *Bulletin of the American Geographical Society* 38/9, pp. 529–539.

Hubbard, Mina (1907). 'A Woman's Way Through Unknown Labrador.' *Manchester Geographical Society* 23/4, pp. 169–182.

Hubbard, Mina (1908a). *A Woman's Way Through Unknown Labrador: An account of the exploration of the Nascaupee and George Rivers.* London: John Murray.

Hubbard, Mina (1908b). 'Through Lonely Labrador.' *Englishwoman's Review* 15 April, pp. 82–88.

Hubbard, Mina (1908c). 'Exploring Inner Labrador.' *Windsor Magazine* 27, pp. 554–561.

Hubbard, Mina (2005 [1905]). 'Expedition Diary.' In Buchanan, Roberta, Hart, Anne and Greene, Bryan (eds), *The Woman who Mapped Labrador: The life and expedition diary of Mina Hubbard.* Montreal: McGill-Queen's University Press.

Hubbard, Phil and Wilkinson, Eleanor (2019). 'Walking a Lonely Path: Gender, landscape and "new nature writing".' *Cultural Geographies in Practice* 26/2, pp. 253–261.

Hunt, Doug (2007). 'Hunting the Blackbirder: Ross Lewin and the Royal Navy.' *Journal of Pacific History* 42/1, pp. 37–53.

Huxley, Anthony (1962). *Standard Encyclopaedia of World Mountains.* New York: Putnam.

Ireton, Sean and Schaumann, Caroline (2020). 'The Meaning of Mountains: Geology, history and culture.' In Ireton, Sean and Schaumann, Caroline (eds), *Mountains and the German Mind: Translations from Gessner to Messner.* Rochester: Camden House.

Jacobs, Sally (2011). *The Other Barack: The bold and reckless life of President Obama's father.* New York: Public Affairs.

Jamie, Kathleen (2008). 'A Lone Enraptured Male.' *London Review of Books* 30, pp. 25–27.

Jones, Melvyn (2001). *Protecting the Beautiful Frame.* Sheffield: Hallamshire Press.

Kabaji, Egara (2014). 'Conference Honours Wanjala's Role in Kenyan Literature.' *Daily Nation*, 25 April, https://nation.africa/kenya/life-and-style/weekend/conference-honours-wanjala-s-role-in-kenyan-literature–976654 (accessed 2 September 2024).

Kaua, Caxton Gitonga and Gitonga, Teresa Muthoni (2023). 'Gender Analysis of Access and Control of Resources and Livelihoods in Pastoral Livelihood Systems: The case of Kurikuri Community land in Laikipia County, Kenya.' *SN Social Sciences* 3/167, pp. 166–206.

Kenyatta, Jomo (1965 [1938]). *Facing Mount Kenya.* New York: Vintage Books.

Kingsley, Mary (1982 [1897]). *Travels in West Africa.* London: Virago Press.

Knight, W. J. (1980). 'Obituary, William Edward China, CBE, MA, Dip. Agric. (Cantab.), Sc. D, F. I. Biol, F. R. E. S.' *Entomologist's Monthly Magazine* 115, pp. 164–175

Lang, Andrew (1889). *The Blue Fairy Book.* London: Longmans, Green and Co.

LaFramboise, Lisa (2001). '"Just a Little Like an Explorer": Mina Hubbard and the making of *A Woman's Way*.' *Papers of the Bibliographical Society of Canada* 39/1 (Spring), pp. 7–44.

Laracy, Hugh (2013). *Watriama and Co: Further Pacific Islands portraits.* Canberra: ANU Press.

Le Houerou, H. N. (1997). 'Climate, Flora and Fauna Changes in the Sahra Over the Past 500 Million Years.' *Journal of Arid Environments* 37/4, pp. 619–647.

Lerner, Gerda (1986). *The Creation of Patriarchy.* Oxford: Oxford University Press.

Lipman, Andrew (2015). *The Saltwater Frontier: Indians and the contest for the American coast.* New Haven: Yale University Press.

Littrell, Frederick and Bertsch, Andy (2013). 'Traditional and Contemporary Status of Women in the Patriarchal Belt.' *Equality, Diversity and Inclusion: An International Journal* 23/3, pp. 310–324. DOI 10.1108/EDI-12-2012-0122.

Lomas, Janice (2000). '"Delicate Duties": Issues of class and respectability in government policy towards the wives and widows of British soldiers in the era of the Great War.' *Women's History Review* 9/1, pp. 123–147.

Lonsdale, Sarah (2020). *Rebel Women Between the Wars: Fearless writers and adventurers*. Manchester: Manchester University Press.

Lowerson, John (1980). 'Battles for the Countryside.' In Gloversmith, Frank (ed.), *Class, Culture and Social Change: A new view of the 1930s*. Sussex: Harvester Press.

Luckett, Richard (1990). 'Introduction.' In Constable, John (ed.), *Selected Letters of I. A. Richards*. Oxford: Clarendon.

Lujan, Leonardo Lopex (trans. Ortiz de Montellano, Bernard R. and Ortiz de Montellano, Thelma) (1994). *The Offerings of the Templo Mayor of Tenochtitlan*. Albuquerque: University of New Mexico Press.

Lunn, Arnold (1957). *A Century of Mountaineering 1857–1957*. London: Allen and Unwin.

Maathai, Wangari (1962). 'Mountie Citizens of British Colony View Progress, Independence of African Home.' *Mount Mirror* 19 January, p. 3.

Maathai, Wangari (1988). *The Green Belt Movement: Sharing the approach and the experience*. Nairobi: Environment Liaison Centre International.

Maathai, Wangari (2004). 'The Challenge is to Restore the Home of the Tadpoles and Give Back to our Children a World of Beauty and Wonder.' 2004 Nobel Peace Prize Speech, Oslo, www.youtube.com/watch?v=1kfQoZgsTCk.

Maathai, Wangari (2008 [2006]). *Unbowed: One woman's story*. London: Arrow Books.

Maathai, Wangari (2009). *The Challenge for Africa*. London: Heinemann.

Maathai, Wangari (2010). *Replenishing the Earth: Spiritual values for healing ourselves and the world*. New York: Doubleday.

Macdonald, Mia (2004). 'An "Oh, Wow, Great, Yea" Moment.' *Los Angeles Times*, 17 October, www.latimes.com/archives/la-xpm-2004-oct-17-op-macdonald17-story.html.

Marshall, Ingeborg (1996). *A History and Ethnography of the Beothuk*. Montreal and Kingston: McGill-Queen's University Press.

Matless, David (2016). *Landscape and Englishness*. London: Reaktion.

Maxon, Robert (1995). 'Social and Cultural Changes.' In Ogot, B. A. and Ochieng, W. R. (eds), *Decolonization and Independence in Kenya 1940–93*. London: James Currey.

McClanahan, T. R. and Young, Y. P. (1996). *East African Ecosystems and their Conservation*. Oxford: Oxford University Press.

McDowell, R. B. (1967). *Alice Stopford Green: A passionate historian*. Dublin: Figgis and Co.

McKibben, Bill (2000). 'Introduction' to Davidson, James West and Rugge, John, *Great Heart: The history of a Labrador adventure*. Montreal: McGill-Queen's University Press.

McNeil, Jamie, Harris, Deborah and Fondren, Kristi (2012). 'Women and the Wild: Gender socialisation in wilderness recreation advertising.' *Gender Issues* 29, pp. 39–55.

Meadowcroft, Leslie (1994). '100 – Not Out.' In *A Century of Footpath Preservation*. Stockport: Peak and Northern Footpaths Society.

Mennen, Kristian Martinus (2023). 'One Movement, Three Clusters: The National Parks movement in England and Wales 1929–1948.' *Contemporary British History* 37/2, pp. 266–300.

Mernissi, Fatima (1994). *Dreams of Trespass: Tales of a harem girlhood*. New York: Basic Books.

Merrick, Elliott (1933). *True North*. New York: Scribner's.

Michaelson, Marc (1994). 'Wangari Maathai and Kenya's Green Belt Movement: Exploring the evolution and potentialities of consensus movement mobilisation.' *Social Problems* 41/4, pp. 540–561.

Mills, Sara (1993). *Discourses of Difference: An analysis of women's travel writing and colonialism*. London: Routledge.

Milne, Catherine and McGillis, Donna (1990). 'Bewdley', www.cobourg.ca/en/recreation-and-culture/resources/Library/Bewdley.pdf (accessed 17 June 2022).

Moore, Ben (2021). '"Of Pride and Joy No Common Rate": From the surplus women problem to surplus Jouissance.' *Journal of Victorian Culture* 26/1, pp. 119–133.

Moraldo, Delphine (2013). 'Gender Relations in French and British Mountaineering: The lens of autobiographies of female mountaineers, from d'Angeville (1794–1871) to Destivelle (1960–).' *Revue de Géographie Alpine* 101/1, pp. 1–13.

Morris, Joseph (1914). *The Peak Country*. London: A & C Black.

Moss, John (1998). 'Gender Notes: Wilderness unfinished.' *Revue d'etudes Canadienees* 33/2, pp. 168–176.

Muchiri, Margaret (2011). 'One Woman's Struggle: A reflection of servant-leadership.' *International Journal of Servant-Leadership* 7/1, pp. 91–104.

Muiruri, Veronica et al. (2022). 'Late Holocene Environmental Change and Anthropogenic: Ecosystem interaction on the Laikipia Plateau, Kenya.' *Ambio* 51, pp. 785–798.

Murunga, Godwin and Shadrack, Nasong'o (2007). *Kenya: The struggle for democracy*. Dakar: Codesria Books.

Mwai, Muthui (1989). 'MPs Condemn Prof Maathai.' *Daily Nation*, 9 November, pp. 1 and 4.

Namulundah Florence (2013). 'Bukusu (Kenyan) Folktales: How women perpetuate patriarchy.' *International Feminist Journal of Politics* 15/3, pp. 370–390.

Nash, Meredith et al. (2019). '"Antarctica Just Has This Hero Factor…": Gendered barriers to Australian Antarctic research and fieldwork.' *PLoS ONE* 14/1, pp. 1–22.

Navickas, K. (2019). 'Conflicts of Power, Landscape and Amenity in Debates over the British Super-Grid in the 1950s.' *Rural History* 30/1, pp. 88–103.

Ndegwa, Stephen (1996). *NGOs and Politics in Africa: The two faces of civil society*. West Hartford: Kumarian Press.

Ngigi, Thomas G. and Tateishi, Ryutaro (2004). 'Monitoring Deforestation in Kenya.' *International Journal of Environmental Studies* 61/3, pp. 281–291.

Nicholls, Brendon (2010). *Ngugi wa Thiong'o: Gender and the ethics of postcolonial reading*. London: Routledge.

Nichols, Maggie (1978). *Wild, Wild Woman: A complete woman's guide to enjoying the great outdoors*. New York: Berkeley.

Ochieng, William (1995). 'Structural and Political Changes.' In Ogot, B. A. and Ochieng, W. R. (eds), *Decolonization and Independence in Kenya 1940–93*. London: James Currey.

Oddy, Derek (2003). *From Plain Fare to Fusion Food: British diet from the 1890s to the 1990s*. Woodbridge: Boydell and Brewer.

Ofcansky, Thomas (1984). 'Kenya Forestry Under British Colonial Administration, 1895–1963.' *Journal of Forest History* 28/3, pp. 136–143.

Ogot, B. A. (1995). 'Politics of Populism.' In Ogot, B. A. and Ochieng, W. R. (eds), *Decolonization and Independence in Kenya 1940–93*. London: James Currey.

Optiz, Donald (2013). 'A Triumph of Brains over Brute: Women and science at the Horticultural College, Swanley 1890 – 1910.' *Isis* 104/1, pp. 30–62.

Pardoe, Heather and Lazarus, Maureen (2018). 'Images of Botany: Celebrating the contribution of women to the history of botanical illustration.' *Collections* 14/4, pp. 547–567.

Park, Claudia Mi Young and Maffii, Margherita (2017). '"We Are Not Afraid to Die": Gender dynamics and agrarian change in Ratanakiri Province, Cambodia.' *Journal of Peasant Studies* 44/6, pp. 1235–1254.

Parker, Gavin and Ravenscroft, Neil (1999). 'Benevolence, Nationalism and Hegemony: Fifty years of the National Parks and Access to the Countryside Act 1949.' *Leisure Studies* 18/4, pp. 297–313.

Paseta, S. (2004). 'Alice Stopford Green (1874–1929).' *Oxford Dictionary of National Biography*. DOI: 10.1093/ref:odnb/33531.

Pennock, Caroline Dodds (2011). '"A Remarkably Patterned Life": Domestic and public in the Aztec household city.' *Gender and History* 23/3, pp. 528–546.

Pennock, Caroline Dodds (2018). 'Women of Discord: Female power in Aztec thought.' *Historical Journal* 61/2, pp. 275–299.

Pennock, Caroline Dodds (2020). 'Aztecs Abroad? Uncovering the early indigenous Atlantic.' *American Historical Review* (June), pp. 787–814.

Pilley, Dorothy (1931). 'Woman Alpinist Tells of Storm on Mount Fuji.' *Japan Advertiser*, 17 July.

Pilley, Dorothy (1932). 'The Diamond Mountains.' *Journal of the Fell and Rock Climbing Club* 9-2/26, pp. 144–152.

Pilley, Dorothy (1959). '40 Years and Back.' *Pinnacle Club Journal* 9, pp. 9–14.

Pilley, Dorothy (1962). 'Agua.' *Journal of the Fell and Rock Climbing Club* 19-3/56, pp. 250–254

Pilley, Dorothy (1965 [1935]). *Climbing Days*. London: Secker and Warburg.

Pilley, Dorothy (1971). 'Our Fiftieth Birthday.' *Pinnacle Club Journal* 14, pp. 5–7.

Pilley, D. and Richards, I. A. (1931). 'The North Ridge of the Dent Blanche.' *Alpine Journal* 43/242, pp. 276–283.

Polack, Fiona (ed.) (2018). *Tracing Ochre: Changing perspectives on the Beothuk*. Toronto: University of Toronto Press.

Pratt, Alexandra (1993). *Lost Lands, Forgotten Stories: A woman's journey into the heart of Labrador*. Toronto: Harper Flamingo.

Pratt, Mary Louise (1992). *Imperial Eyes: Travel writing and transculturation*. London: Routledge.

Presbey, Gail (2013). 'Women's Empowerment: The insights of Wangari Maathai.' *Journal of Global Ethics* 9/3, pp. 277–292.

Ramaer, R. (1974). *Steam Locomotives of the East African Railways*. Newton Abbott: David and Charles.

Report of the National Park Committee, 1931 (Cmd. 3851). London: HMSO.

Report of the National Parks Committee (England and Wales), 1947 (Cmd. 7121). London: HMSO.

Richards, Dan (2016). *Climbing Days*. London: Faber.

Richards, I. A. (1960). *The Screens and Other Poems*. New York: Harcourt Brace.

Richards, I. A. (1978). *New and Selected Poems*. London: Faber.

Richards, I. A. (1990). *Selected Letters of I. A. Richards*, edited by John Constable. Oxford: Clarendon.

Ridanpää, Juha (2010). 'A Masculinist Northern Wilderness and the Emancipatory Potential of Literary Irony.' *Gender, Place and Culture* 17/3, pp. 319–335. DOI: 10.1080/09663691003737595.

Riria Ouko, Jennifer (1985). 'Women Organisations in Kenya.' *Journal of Eastern African Research and Development* 15, pp. 188–197.

Roche, Clare (2013). 'Women Climbers 1850–1900: A challenge to male hegemony?' *Sport in History* 33/3, pp. 236–259.

Rodman, Margaret (2001). *Houses Far from Home: British colonial spaces in the New Hebrides*. Honolulu: University of Hawaii Press.

Ross, W. Gillies (2004). 'The Arctic Council of 1851: Fact or fancy?' *Polar Record* 40/213, pp. 135–141.

Routledge, W. Scoresby and Routledge, Katherine (1968). *With a Prehistoric People: The Akikuyu of British East Africa*. London: Frank Cass and Co.

R. P. H. (1926). 'Miss Gertrude Lowthian Bell 1868–1926.' *Alpine Journal* 28/233 (November), pp. 296–298.

Russo, John Paul (1989). *I. A. Richards: His life and work.* Baltimore: Johns Hopkins University Press.

Salisbury, Eve (2014). '"Lybeaus Disconsus": Transformation, adaptation and the monstrous-feminine.' *Arthuriana* 24/1, pp. 66–85.

Savard, Bemi (1969). 'Commentary.' In Desbarats, Peter (ed.), *What They Used to Tell About: Indian legends from Labrador.* Montreal: McClelland and Stewart.

Schaumann, Caroline (2020). *Peak Pursuits: The emergence of mountaineering in the nineteenth century.* New Haven and London: Yale University Press.

Schuiteman, André (2013). 'A New, Blue-Flowered *Dendroboim* from Waigeo Island, Indonesia.' *Malesian Orchid Journal* 12, pp. 19–21.

Scott, Sara (2015). 'Indian Forts and Religious Icons: The Buffalo Road (Qoq'aalx 'Iskit) trail before and after the Lewis and Clark expedition.' *International Journal of Historical Archaeology* 19/2, pp. 384–415.

Shanguhiya, Martin (2015). *Population, Tradition and Environmental Control in Colonial Kenya.* Rochester: University of Rochester Press.

Sheldrake, Merlin (2020). *Entangled Life: How fungi make our worlds, change our minds and shape our futures.* London: Vintage.

Shepherd, Nan (2014 [1934]). *In the Cairngorms.* Cambridge: Galileo.

Shrubsole, Guy (2019). *Who Owns England?* London: William Collins.

Smith, K. G. V. (1969). 'Lucy Evelyn Cheesman 1881–1969.' *Entomologist's Monthly Magazine* 105 (October–December), pp. 217–219.

Smith, Roly (2020). *Walking Class Heroes: Pioneers of the right to roam.* Oxford: Signal Books.

Sondheimer, Janet (1983). *Castle Adamant in Hampstead: A history of Westfield College 1882–1982.* London: Westfield College.

Sonik, Karen (2021). 'Minor and Marginal(ized)? Rethinking women as minor characters in the Epic of Gilgamesh.' *Journal of the American Oriental Society* 141/4, pp. 779–801.

Sparke, Matthew (1995). 'Between Demythologizing and Deconstructing the Map: Shanawdithit's New-Found-Land and the alienation of Canada.' *Cartographica* 32/1, pp. 1–21.

St. Barbe Baker, Richard (1932). *Men of the Trees.* London: George Allen and Unwin.

Stephens, Robert (2013). *Kenyan Students to America 1959–1960: An educational odyssey.* Kampala: East African Educational Publishers.

Stratton-Porter, Gene (1909). *A Girl of the Limberlost.* New York: Grosset and Dunlap.

Sweeney, Louise (1986). 'The Greening of Kenya.' *Christian Science Monitor*, 7 October, p. 23.

Tan, Delfin, Haththotuwa, Rohana and Fraser, Ian (2017). 'Cultural Aspects and Mythologies Surrounding Menstruation and Abnormal Uterine Bleeding.' *Best Practice and Research Clinical Obstetrics and Gynaecology* 40, pp. 121–133.

Thomas, Lynn (1980). *The Backpacking Woman.* New York: Anchor Books.

Thomas, Natalie and Nigam, Sumant (2018). 'Twentieth Century Climate Change over Africa: Seasonal hydroclimate trends and Sahara Desert expansion.' *Journal of Climate* 31/9, pp. 3349–3370.

Thoreau, Henry David (1951). 'Walking.' In Browne, Waldo R. (ed.), *Joys of the Road: A little anthology in praise of walking.* Chicago: Browne's Bookstore, pp. 56–75 (originally published in *Atlantic Monthly*, June 1862).

Touzel, Grace and Garner, Beulah (2018). '"The Person Herself is not Interesting": Lucy Evelyn Cheesman's life dedicated to the faunistic exploration of the Southwest Pacific.' *Collections: A Journal for Museum and Archives Professionals* 14/4, pp. 495–530.

Turner, David (2018). '"Delectable North Wales" and Stakeholders: The London and North Western Railway's marketing of North Wales c. 1904–1914.' *Enterprise and Society* 19/4, pp. 864–902.

Van Dyke, Henry (1903). *Little Rivers.* London: David Nutt.

Vidal, John (2012). 'Rio+20: Earth Summit dawns with stormier clouds than in 1992.' *Guardian*, 19 June.

Virden, Randy and Walker, Gordon (1999). 'Ethnic/Racial and Gender Variations Among Meanings Given to, and Preferences for, the Natural Environment.' *Leisure Sciences* 21/3, pp. 219–239.

Wadden, Marie (1991). *Nitassinan: The Innu struggle to reclaim their homeland.* Vancouver: Douglas and McIntyre.

Waguespack, Nicole (2005). 'The Organisation of Male and Female Labor in Foraging Societies: Implications for early Paleoindian archaeology.' *American Anthropologist* 107/4, pp. 666–676.

Wallace, Dillon (1905). *The Lure of the Labrador Wild: The story of the exploring expedition conducted by Leonidas Hubbard, Jr.* London: Hodder and Stoughton.

Ward, G. H. B. (ed.) (1927). 'Commentary' on Ethel Gallimore's poem in Sheffield Clarion Rambler Handbook 1926–1927. Sheffield: Sheffield Clarion Ramblers, p. 33.

Ward, G. H. B. (ed.) (1928). 'Commentary' on Ethel Gallimore's poem in Sheffield Clarion Rambler Handbook 1927–1928. Sheffield: Sheffield Clarion Ramblers, p. 18

Ward, G. H. B. (ed.) (1939). 'Longshaw Estate' Sheffield Clarion Ramblers Handbook 1939–1940. Sheffield: Sheffield Clarion Ramblers, p. 146.

Waruingi, Esther et al. (2023). 'Understanding the Nexus between Forest Dependence and Willingness to Pay for Forest Conservation: Case of forest dependent households in Kenya.' *Forestry Economics Review* 5/1, pp. 23–43.

White, Randall (1985). *Ontario, 1610–1985.* Toronto: Dundurn Press.

Whitney, Caspar (1905). 'View Point.' *Outing* 46 (August), pp. 618–620.

Williams, Cicely (1973). *Women on the Rope: The feminine share of mountain adventure.* London: George Allen and Unwin.

Wilson, Frances (2021). *The Ballad of Dorothy Wordsworth.* London: Faber and Faber.

Wood, J. G. (1876a). *Illustrated Natural History; Volume One Mammalia.* New York: The Home Book Company.

Wood, J. G. (1876b). *Illustrated Natural History; Volume Two Birds.* New York: The Home Book Company.

Wood, J. G. (1876c). *Illustrated Natural History; Volume Three Reptiles, Fishes etc.* New York: The Home Book Company.

Worthington, Nancy (2003). 'Shifting Identities in the Kenyan Press: Representations of Wangari Maathai's media complex protest.' *Women's Studies in Communication* 26/2, pp. 143–164.

Wyckoff, William and Dilsaver, Larry (1997). 'Promotional Imagery of Glacier National Park'. *The Geographical Review* 87/1, pp. 1–26.

Zaman, Habiba (1995). 'Resistance Against Seclusion: Women, work, and patriarchy in Bangladesh.' *Canadian Journal of Development Studies* 16/4, pp. 105–122. DOI: 10.1080/02255189.1995.9669630.

Index

EU authorised representative for GPSR:

Easy Access System Europe, Mustamäe tee 50, 10621 Tallinn, Estonia gpsr.
requests@easproject.com